SHOTS

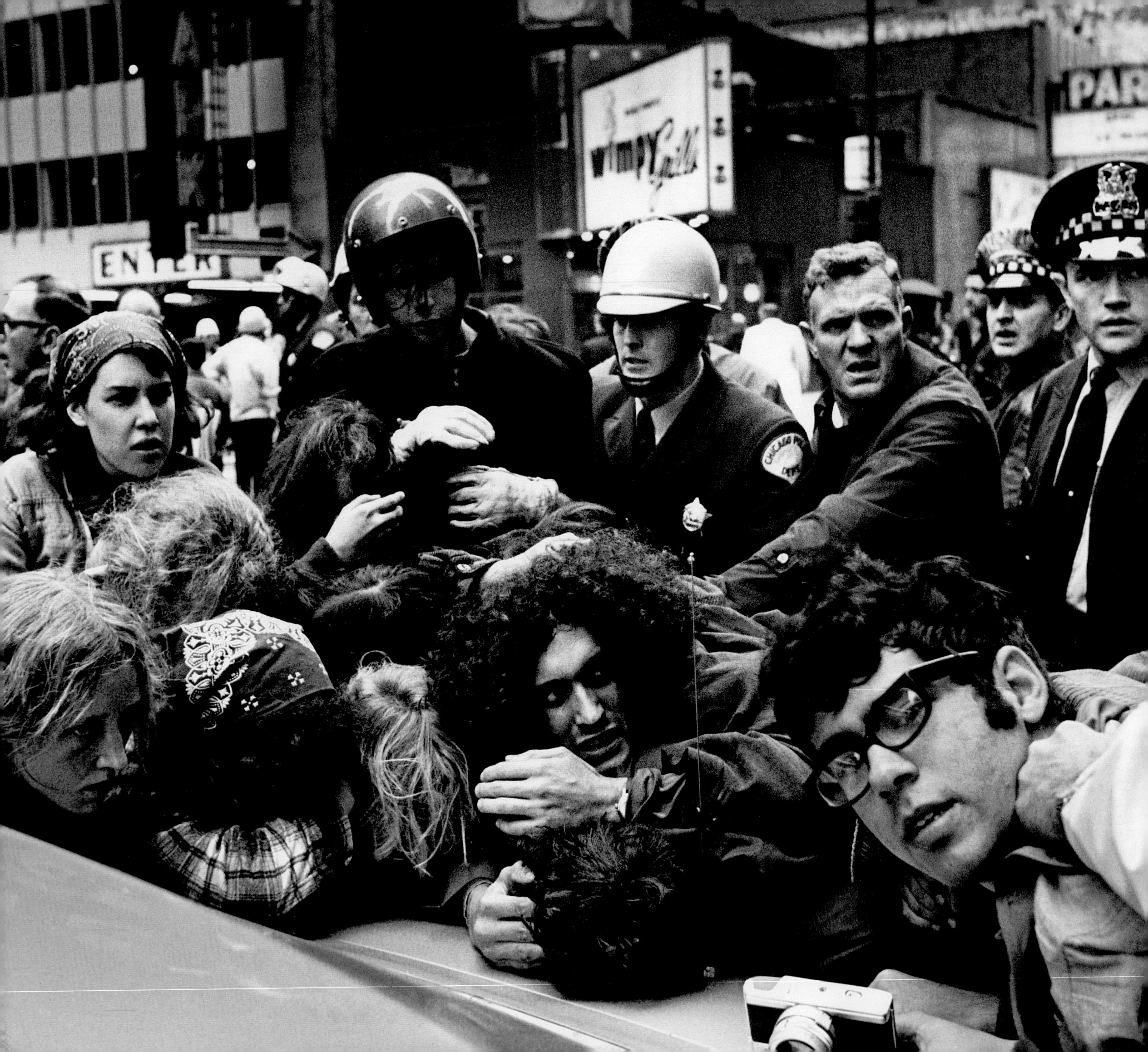
Wimpy Grill

SHOTS

DAVID FENTON

Foreword by **TOM HAYDEN**

Commentary by **NORMAN MAILER**

an american photographer's journal 1967-1972

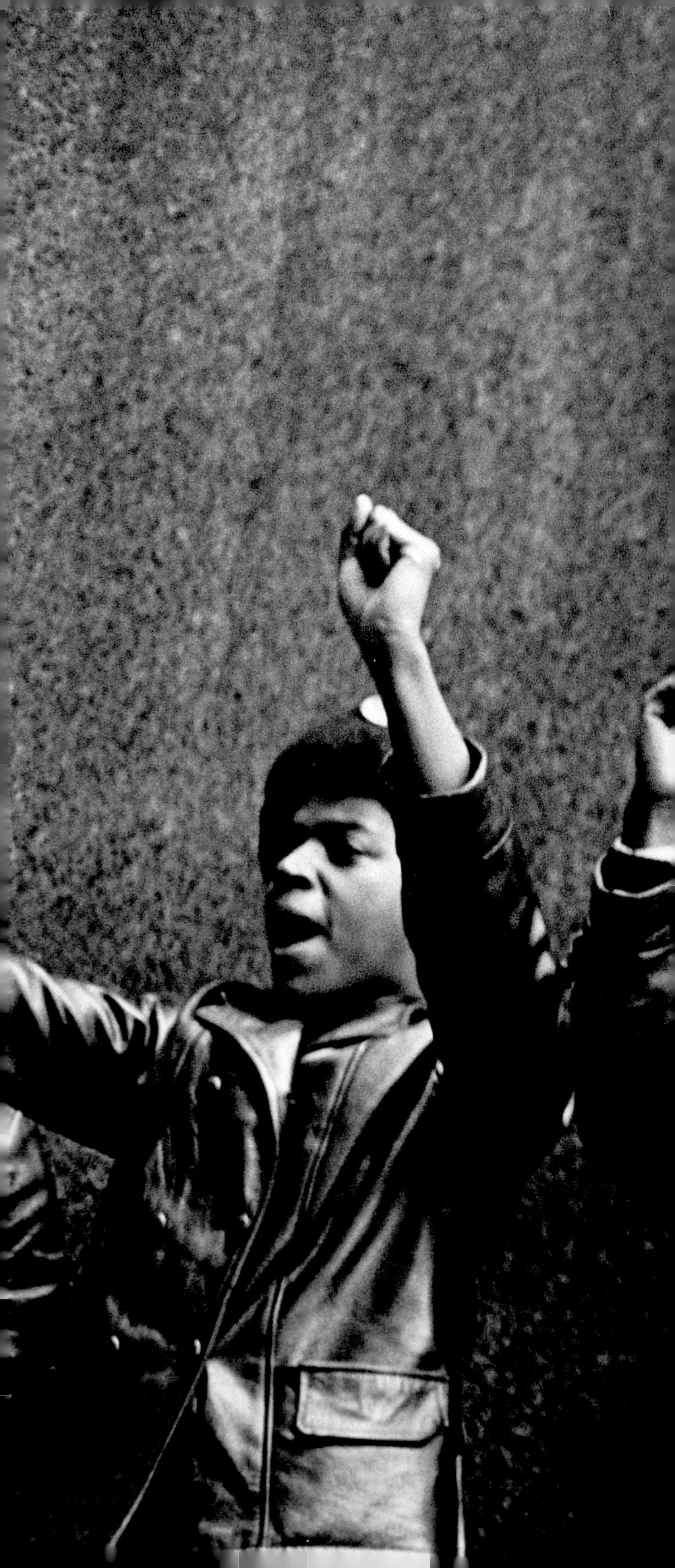

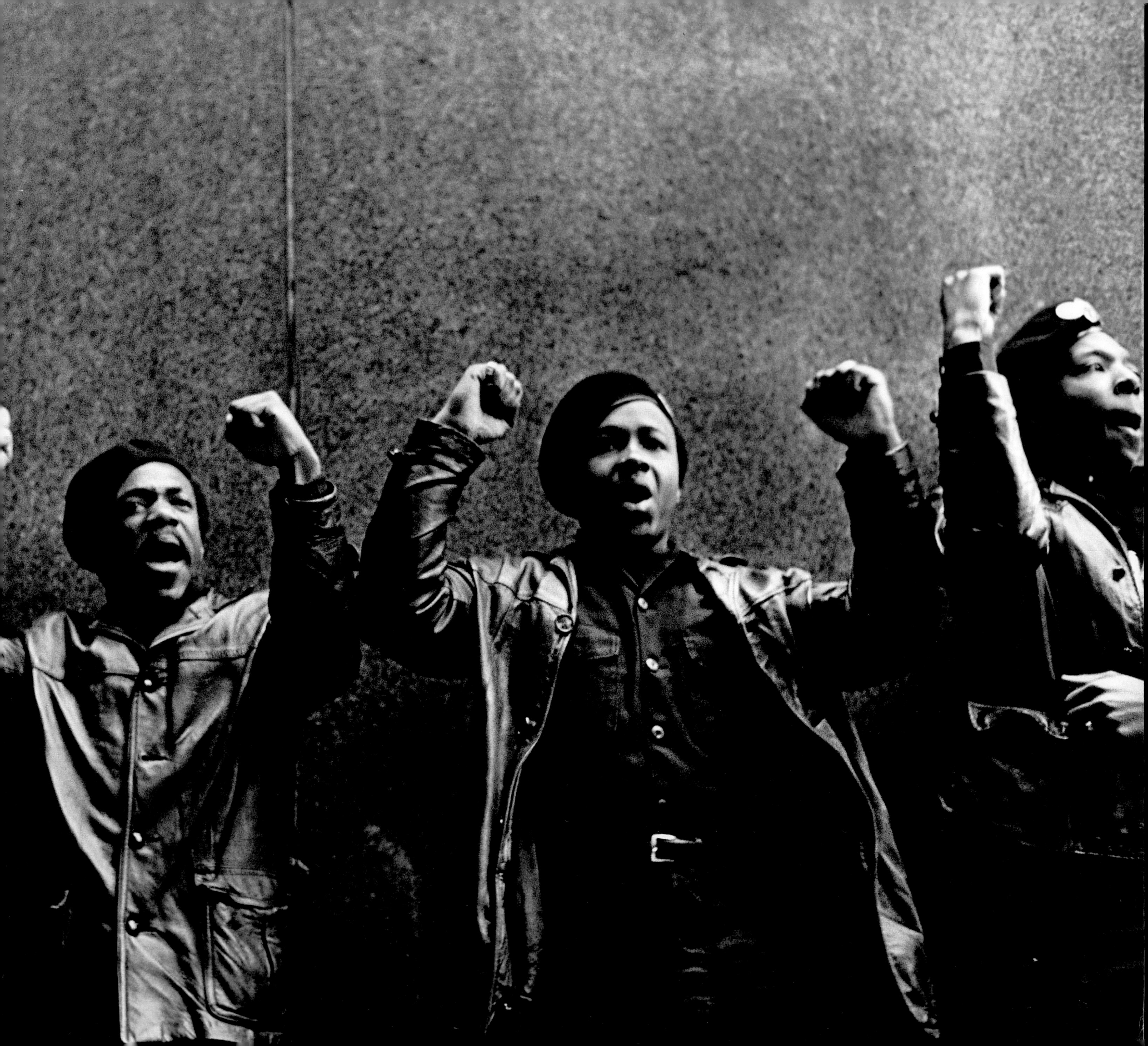

C O N T E N T S

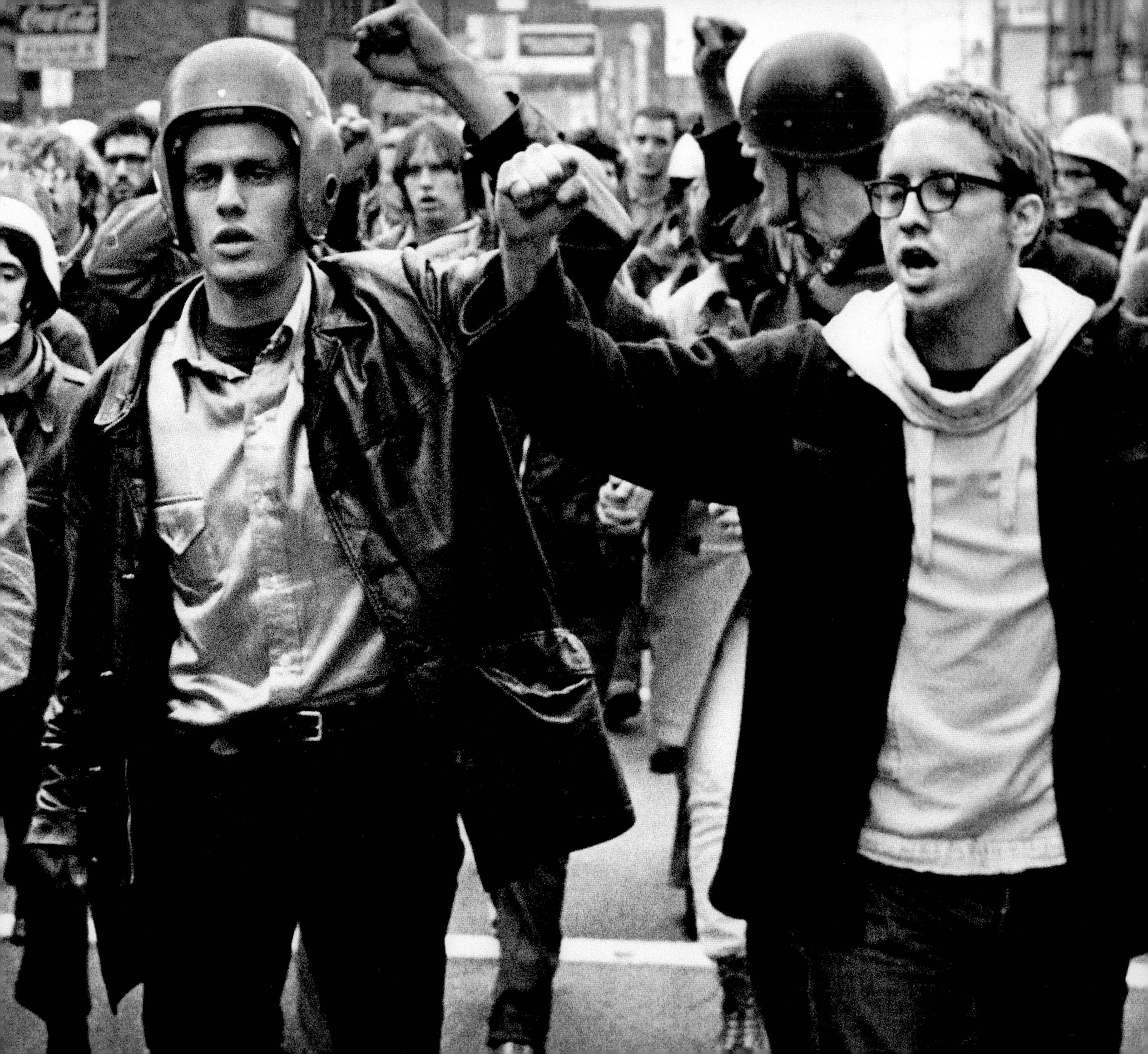

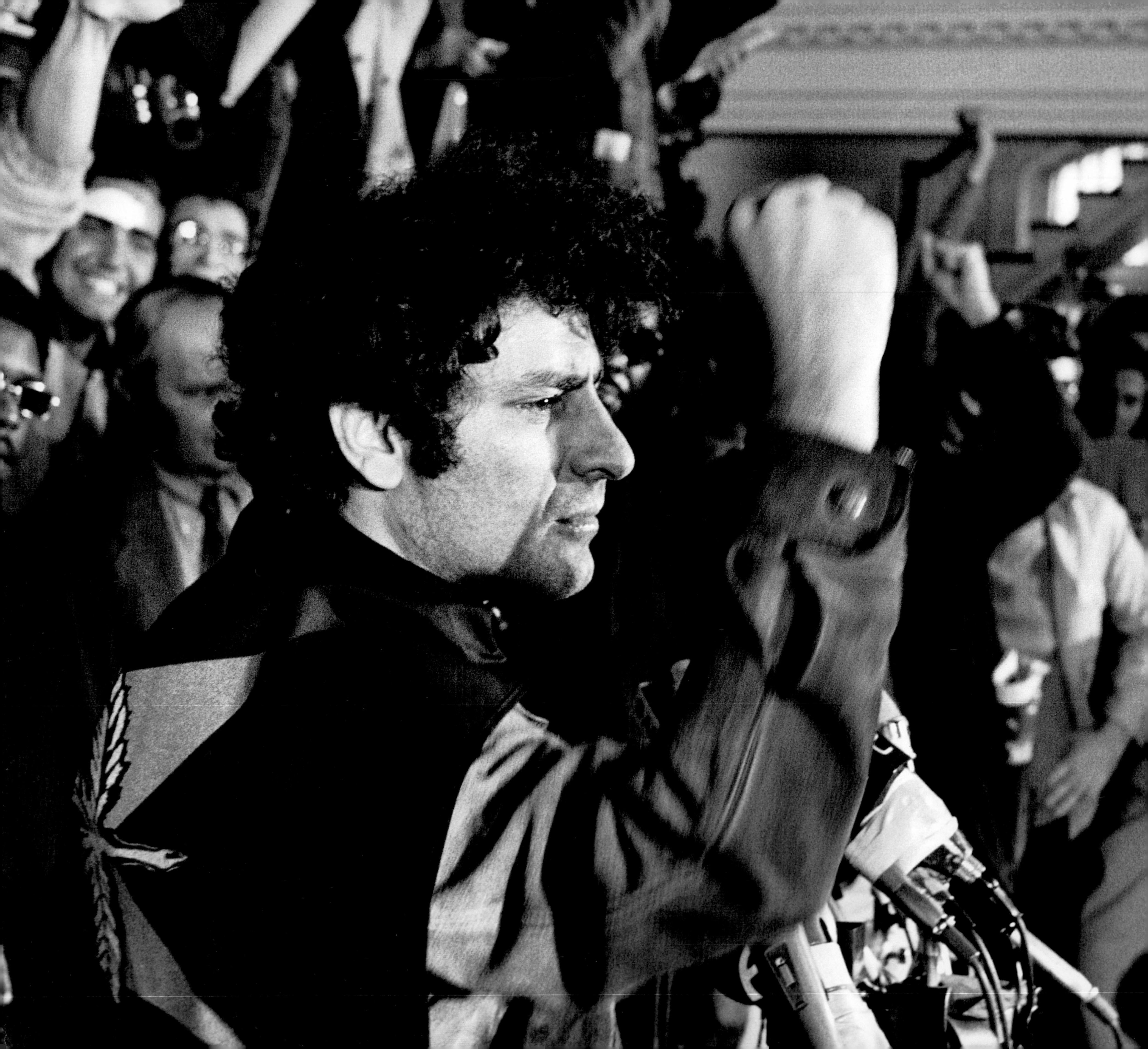

To my sons Alexander, Adrian, Cole and Theo. Never stop protesting.

To the memory of Abbie Hoffman, humorist and activist who named this book.

Special thanks to Lely Constantinople, who chose these photographs
from my collection and without whom this book would not exist.

*Abbie Hoffman attends a press conference during
a rally in support of the Black Panther Party, New
Haven, CT, April 30-May 1, 1970*

Foreword Tom Hayden

One of the founders of Students for a Democratic Society (SDS), Tom Hayden (also a member of the Chicago 7), later served as a California State Senator (D—Santa Monica)

In the beginning of the movement, there were no photographs. I have fewer than five black–and–white pictures from early meetings of the Students for a Democratic Society. (One shows me snoring in front of a chalk marked blackboard proclaiming "Work Harder!") I've never seen a photo of the 62 SDS members drafting the 1962 Port Huron Statement. Was it a lack of technology, or an absence of visual sensibility? There were exceptions in those early days, as when the world suddenly saw images of buses burning on freedom rides through Alabama in 1961, but the visual history of the early Sixties is sparse. Photos of ourselves, by ourselves, are even more uncommon.

Soon came a realization that we had to keep a visual history of our movement to see ourselves in history. We were beginning to understand the value of oral histories as well, including stories such as those of ex–slaves in the Deep South, brought to the nation's attention by Danny Lyons. He came along and began photographing the participants in the 1964 *Freedom Summer*, shaping a memory of a magical time. Danny was an exception.

Then everything seemed to change. Did the media discover us, or did we discover the media? As the second half of the Sixties began, the new realities started playing out in images on–screen, no longer just through our grassroots door–knocking campaigns or low–key meetings. Marshall McLuhan provided the explanation and suddenly media images were becoming more important than the realities they referred to. The images could impact public opinion. Recall the blown–out brains of a Saigon police chief's Vietcong prisoner, the napalmed girl running naked down the road in Vietnam, a weeping survivor of the Kent State murders. Styles of expression became media conscious too—Panther uniforms, dreadlocks and Woodstock bodies, for example, became synonymous with the movement. The system would commodify these images, erasing their authenticity, and yet the "Image" went forth to a fascinated world.

The late Sixties were a time of extreme polarization, unlike anything since the strikes and sit–downs of the 1930s Depression (where are the photos of those times?). Hundreds of Americans and thousands of Vietnamese were dying each and every week. Police on horseback were clubbing young boys in public parks (page 28). Live ammunition was being used to kill and maim bystanders during a march to reclaim a Berkeley park (page 122). A Mexican–American reporter for the *Los Angeles Times*, Ruben Salazar, was shot and killed during the Chicano Moratorium. Black Panthers and Young Lords were crushed for rising up in self–determination (pages 46–47, 59–87). U.S. troops gassed and rounded up thousands of antiwar demonstrators in the shadow of the White House (pages 104–105).

This was not the deadened America of the Fifties or the blessed community of the early Sixties. This was America the Unthinkable, where everything was spiraling downward, where drugs seemed more comforting than parents and education consisted of lies about a cultural melting pot. For David Fenton, this grotesque environment seemed to be the real America, AmeriKKKa, a reality wrenched right out of his boyhood at Bronx Science High School (the alma mater he shares with then radical political leader Stokely Carmichael).

David Fenton came of age at this time, when the camera was becoming more natural than the manifesto and more powerful than the machine gun. Perhaps this is why his present book is entitled SHOTS. These are warning shots, flares, perhaps shots seen 'round the world. Some of these shots are all we have to bring back the dead, not only the bodies of the departed but the memories that are dying from our collective amnesia. These shots are genuine, reflecting the eye of a young man attempting to process the chaos of worlds falling apart and being born. They save the authentic from both co–optation and disappearance.

SHOTS is also a moving reminder of a moment in our history that is frequently glossed, even repressed. The early Sixties—from the first 1960 Greensboro sit–in to the 1965 invasion of Vietnam by 150,000 U.S. troops—is usually recalled with media images of well–dressed Negro youth marching toward the fulfillment of the American promise or with Dr. Martin Luther King Jr., a saint of nonviolence, the Kennedys his benefactors.

But the later period, 1965–1973, was an ugly time, growing malignantly from the failure of America to deliver on the earlier hopes of civil rights, jobs and peace. The dream was assassinated, the conspirators left the scene. The military draft sucked young black, brown and working class whites into the shock treatment of a losing war. Many came back traumatized, trained to kill, on smack or dishonorably discharged. All these tragedies inflamed the already existing tensions in the inner cities. While the Watts 1965 riot was immortalized as an image of fire, few recall that at least 125 other cities experienced insurrections in those years. While Chicago 1968 is an image of generational meltdown, few know that 60 mainstream reporters were beaten up and gassed there. While the image of a charred New York townhouse recalls the Weather Underground, who blew themselves up, little is remembered of the Weatherman's bombings of the U.S. Congress, military contractors and draft boards.

This superpower was pushed toward collapse, and in large part withdrew from Vietnam to avoid deeper polarization at home. When it was all falling apart, when madness was loosed, the establishment retreated. The "wise men" counseled President Johnson to quit the presidency and abandon Vietnam. The Democratic Party was reformed, and the 18–year–old vote was offered to the disaffected young (who hadn't demanded it). When Richard Nixon tried to "push the country so far to the right you won't even recognize it" (the words were those of his Attorney General, John Mitchell), he self–destructed in the Watergate scandal. America began to stabilize by bringing its alienated young people in from the cold, offering the opportunity to "make it" in the new mainstream.

David Fenton is one who has succeeded in surviving honorably on the edge of the mainstream. He has contracted, counseled and trained with countless grass–roots groups and campaigns struggling to be seen and taken seriously in recent decades. He has experienced the underground press of his youth evolve in many directions, from investigative reporting to the explosive rise of Indymedia. He's been there, from a time when no one carried cameras to their protests, to an era in which the video camera is a ubiquitous eyewitness to everything that goes down.

Fenton is still taking shots.

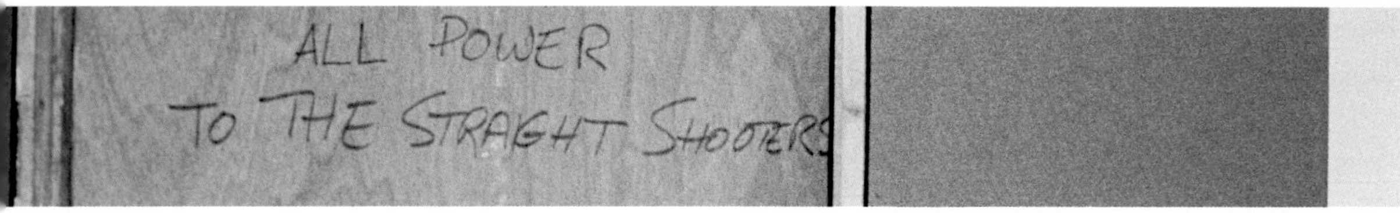
ALL POWER
TO THE STRAIGHT SHOOTERS

Introduction David Fenton

Abbie Hoffman named this book.

In 1970, I was assembling a book of photographs from underground antiwar newspapers and called him up. "Call it Shots of War," he said. I was a bit more mainstream, so I said, "Too strong, let's call it Shots." *Shots: Photographs from the Underground Press* was published in 1971.

As the saying goes, if you can remember the 60s, you weren't there. Luckily, I have these photographs. In 1969 I was a teenage high school dropout turned full–time photojournalist. I worked for Liberation News Service (LNS), the Associated Press of the antiwar movement. LNS provided independent critical news coverage of the Vietnam war when it was largely missing from the mainstream press. My photographs were published in hundreds of underground antiwar and counterculture newspapers throughout the United States and the world, as well as in the *New York Times, Life, Look, Newsweek* and the *Saturday Review.*

I made $25 a week plus free "collective" dinners and had a modest expense account that I used to fly around the country photographing riots, demonstrations and rock stars. My standard equipment, besides two Leicas and a Nikon, included a helmet, gas mask and my lawyer's phone number written on my hand in case of arrest.

I turned 16 in 1968. The years 1967–1972 were my most active photographically. Those years were intense beyond what one can even imagine now. After the assassinations of Martin Luther King, Jr. and the Kennedy brothers, we thought the apocalypse had arrived. Knowing that Richard Nixon was a crook, we were convinced he would cancel the 1972 elections. The FBI assassinated numerous Black Panther leaders including Fred Hampton, who at 21 was the youngest leader of a Panther chapter, while other Panthers were often jailed on false charges under the personal direction of J. Edgar Hoover. The police rioted at the 1968 Democratic Convention but the protestors were arrested and put on trial instead. And 50,000 Americans were dying in Vietnam for a lie.

Because I was part of the counterculture movement (LNS was a chapter of Students for a Democratic Society, or SDS) and not part of the establishment media, I had access to people and places that other photographers didn't. I got to know Abbie Hoffman, Jerry Rubin, Rennie Davis, Dave Dellinger and Tom Hayden of the Chicago 7, Huey P. Newton, Eldridge Cleaver, Bobby Seale and many other Black Panthers, activist lawyer William Kunstler, Allen Ginsberg, who taught me meditation, the entire leadership of the infamous Weather Underground, who tried to recruit me to join their anarchist exploits, and many other central figures of the time.

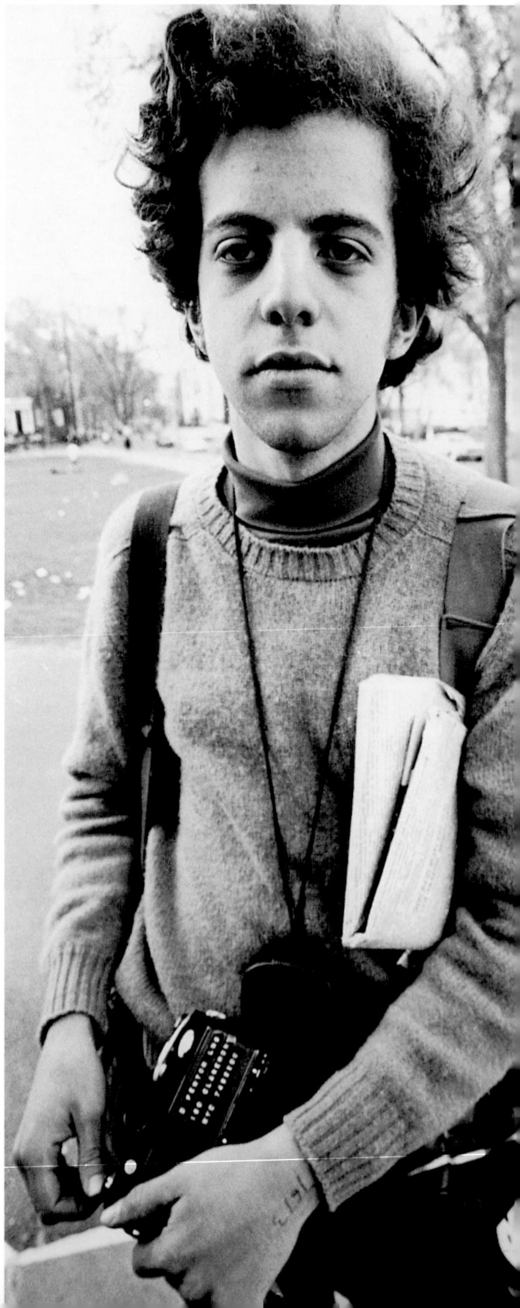

The author in 1969, age 17
Photo courtesy of Stephen Shames

I was present for most of the large antiwar demonstrations in Washington and New York. I went to post–demonstration parties that had to be abandoned when tear gas–soaked clothing made conversation impossible. I watched an Underground Press convention surrounded by state troopers with shotguns who proceeded to search everyone for drugs without a warrant. I went to "Be–Ins" at Central Park in New York City where I watched hippies throwing hundreds of flowers at police cars, and police on horseback chasing and beating a kid who had burned an American flag. I watched people strip naked in the Reflecting Pool of the Washington Monument while protesting the war.

I saw the brilliant but manic Abbie Hoffman drop LSD in the middle of an antiwar march, surrounded by thousands of National Guardsmen with bayonets. I attended strategy meetings of the defendants of the Chicago 7 conspiracy trial, and sat with them as they watched the nightly network news, the equivalent of their daily theatrical review. I saw the Weatherman faction shot at by police as they broke every window in Chicago's shopping district during the "Days of Rage" actions. I watched police beat up antiwar demonstrators beyond all reason, including trampling them on horseback.

I witnessed the birth of the women's and gay liberation movements, with all of their passion and early excess. I saw married couples break apart as women revolted against their subservient status and other marriages break apart as gays came out of the closet. I witnessed the triumphant return of my gay colleagues from the Stonewall rebellion. These high–voltage years criss–crossing the country on assignment became the foundation of my education in activism and American politics. The passion, the unreason, the fury of the times marked me indelibly.

Of course the backdrop for all of this was the war. Americans my age were dying every day in Vietnam, participants in a war based largely on government lies. Innocent Vietnamese were dying every day, victims of our policies and violence. The bombs being dropped in our name were more than we could take. The draft made us literally crazy. I saw people burn their draft cards in public, making them liable to prosecution. I watched otherwise rational protestors become so frustrated that they engaged in behavior so alienating to most Americans that they actually hurt our cause–carrying Viet Cong flags, shouting "Off the pigs!" during demonstrations and most absurdly, going underground to blow up buildings to protest the war.

Of course those years were not only about rebellion. It was also a uniquely hopeful and positive era: the Summer of Love, the "Be–Ins", psychedelic visions of unity and peace, Woodstock. I was privileged to witness fantastic music in the making and photograph it: Janis Joplin, the *Rolling Stones, Jefferson Airplane*, Phil Ochs, Arlo Guthrie, John Lennon and Yoko Ono, the *Grateful Dead*, blues masters Howlin' Wolf, Muddy Waters, BB King, jazz giants Miles Davis, Bobby Blue Bland, Archie Shepp and many others. Music was another method of our resistance.

I stopped taking photographs, except of my children, around 1972 when I started publishing an underground newspaper and helped start a third political party, the Human Rights Party. Later, I worked at *Rolling Stone* magazine and co–produced the *No Nukes* concerts in 1979 with Bruce Springsteen, Bonnie Raitt and Jackson Browne.

In 1982, I founded Fenton Communications to lead media campaigns in support of the environment, public health, social justice and human rights. As of December, 2004, there are 45 staff members nationwide, including those in New York, Washington and San Francisco. We are deeply involved with campaigns such as those against George W. Bush in the 2004 presidential election, and developing strategies with MoveOn.org, the 3–million–member online democracy group. Now protest is my business.

And it's all because of Abbie! I was just a kid when I fell under his influence. He was far ahead of his time in understanding the impact of television on politics, and taught me a lot. The photographs in this book are a testament to that passionate and energetic time.

A Look Back at 1968
Commentary by Norman Mailer

No one has better captured the stark contrasts and subtle contradictions of the 1960s like the two–time Pulitzer Prize–winning author Norman Mailer. His extraordinary coverage of both the Republican and Democratic conventions of 1968, *Miami and the Siege of Chicago*, not only illuminates the often hidden life of American politics but provides a brave and honest portrait of how personal our politics really are. From the re–emergence of Richard Nixon in Miami to the violent victory of Hubert Humphrey in Chicago, Norman Mailer holds a large mirror up to the American soul.

The Republicans

"Yet here they were, the economic power of America (so far as economic power was still private, not public) the family power (so far as position in society was still a passion to average and ambitious Americans), the military power (to the extent that important sword–rattlers and/or patriots were among the company, as well as cadres of corporations not unmarried to the Pentagon) yes, even the spiritual power of America (just as far as Puritanism, Calvinism, conservatism and golf still gave the Wasp an American faith more intense than the faith of cosmopolitans, one–worlders, trade–unionists, Black militants, New Leftists', acid–heads, tribunes of the gay, families of the Mafia, political machinists, fixers, swingers, Democratic lobbyists, members of the Grange, and government workers, not to include the Weltanschauung of every partisan in every minority group). No, so far as there was an American faith, a belief, a mystique that America was more than a sum of its constituencies, its trillions of dollars and billions of acres, its constellation of factories, empyrean of communications, mountain transcendent of finance, and heroic of sport, transports of medicine, hygiene, and church, so long as belief persisted that America, finally more than all this, was the world's ultimate reserve of rectitude, final garden of the Lord, so far as this mystique could survive in every American family of Christian substance, so then were the people entering this Gala willy–nilly the leaders of this faith, never articulated by any of them except on the most absurd and taste–curdling jargons of patriotism mixed with religion, but the faith existed in those crossroads between the psyche and the heart where love, hate, the cognition of grace, the all but lost sense of the root, and adoration of America congregate for some.

They believed in America as they believed in

God—they could not really ever expect that America might collapse and God yet survive, no, they had even gone so far as to think that America was the savior of the world, food and medicine by one hand, sword in the other, highest of high faith in a nation which would bow the knee before no problem since God's own strength was in the dye. It was a faith which flared so high in San Francisco in 1964 that staid old Republicans had come near to frothing while they danced in the aisle, there to nominate Barry, there to nominate Barry. But their hero had gone down to a catastrophe of defeat, blind in politics, impolite in tactics, a sorehead, a fool, a disaster. And, if his policies had prevailed to some degree, to the degree of escalating the war in Vietnam, so had the policy depressed some part of America's optimism to the bottom of the decade, for the country had learned an almost unendurable lesson—its history in Asia was next to done, and there was not any real desire to hold armies on that land; worse, the country had begun to wear away inside, and the specter of Vietnam in every American city would haunt the suburb, the terror of a dollar cut loose from every standard of economic anchor was in the news,

and some of the best of the youth were mad demented dogs with teeth in the flesh of the deepest Republican faith.

They were a chastened collocation these days. The high fire of hard Republican faith was more modest now, the vision of America had diminished. The claims on Empire had met limits.

Yet he felt himself unaccountably filled with a mild sorrow. He did not detest these people, he did not feel so superior as to pity them, it was rather he felt a sad sorrowful respect. In their immaculate cleanliness, in the somewhat antiseptic odors of their astringent toilet water and perfume, in the abnegation of their walks, in the heavy sturdy moves so many demonstrated of bodies in life's harness, there was the muted tragedy of the Wasp—they were not on earth to enjoy or even perhaps to love so very much, they were here to serve, and serve they had in public functions and public charities (while recipients of their charity might vomit in rage and laugh in scorn), served on opera committees, and served in long hours of duty at the piano, served as the sentinel in

concert halls and the pews on the aisle in church, at the desk in schools, had served for culture, served for finance, served for salvation, served for America—and so much of America did not wish them to serve any longer, and so many of them doubted themselves, doubted that the force of their faith could illumine their path in these new modern horror–head times. On and on they came through the door, the clean, the well–bred, the extraordinarily prosperous, and for the most astonishing part, the almost entirely proper. Yes, in San Francisco in '64 they had been able to be insane for a little while, but now they were subdued, now they were modest, now they were looking for a leader to bring back America to them, their lost America, Jesus–land.

"Nelson Rockefeller is out of his mind if he thinks he can take the nomination away from Richard Nixon," the reporter said suddenly to himself. It was the first certitude the convention had given him. [1]

"There was a modesty among these delegates today, they were the center of the nation, but they were chastened in their pride

15

—these same doctors and small–town lawyers or men not so unlike them, had had their manic dreams of restoring order to America with the injunction and the lash just four years ago. Then the nation had lived in their mind like the sure strong son of their loins, and they had been ready to take the fight anywhere, to Vietnam, to China, into the Black ghettos, they had been all for showing the world and some minorities in America where the real grapes of wrath were stored. But the last four years had exploded a few of their secret policies, and they were bewildered now. No matter what excuse was given that there might have been better ways to wage the war, the Wasp had built his nest with statistics, and the figures on the Vietnam war were badly wrong. How could the nation fail to win when its strength was as five to one, unless God had decided that America was not just? —righteousness had taken a cruel crack on the bridge of its marble brow. Much else was wrong, the youth, the Negro, the dollar, the air pollution and river pollution, the pornography, the streets—the Wasps were now a chastened crew. It was probable the Presidency would soon be theirs again, but the nation was profoundly divided, nightmares loomed—for the first time in their existence, the Wasps were modest about power. They were not certain they would know what to do with it." [2]

The Democrats

On March 31, on a night when the latest Gallup Poll showed L.B.J. to be in favor with only 36% of the American public (while only 23% approved his handling of the war) Johnson announced on national television that he would not seek nor "accept the nomination of my party as your President." On April 2, there was talk that Humphrey would run—McCarthy had taken the Wisconsin primary with 57% of the vote to Johnson's 35% (and it was estimated that if Johnson had not resigned, the vote would have been more like 64% to 28%).

On April 4, Martin Luther King, Jr. was assassinated by a white man, and violence, fire and looting broke out in Memphis, Boston and Newark over the next week. Mayor Daley gave his famous "shoot to kill" instruction to the Chicago police, and National Guard and U.S. troops were sent to some of these cities.

On April 23, Columbia students barricaded the office of a Dean. By another day the campus was disrupted, then closed, and it was never to be comfortably open again for the rest of the semester. On May 10, as if indicative of a spontaneous world–wide movement, the students of the Sorbonne battled the Paris police on barricades and in the streets. On the same day, Maryland was quietly pledging its delegates to Humphrey.

On June 3, Andy Warhol was shot. On June 4, after winning the California primary 45% to 42% for McCarthy, and 12% for Humphrey, R.F.K. was shot in the head and died the next day. The cannibalistic war of the McCarthy and Kennedy peace forces was at an end. McCarthy had been all but finished in Indiana, Nebraska, Iowa and South Dakota.

Meanwhile Humphrey had been picking up delegates in states like Missouri, which did not have primaries, and the delegates in states which did, like Pennsylvania, after it had given 90% of its vote to McCarthy. [3] Hubert Humphrey...was a hawk not a

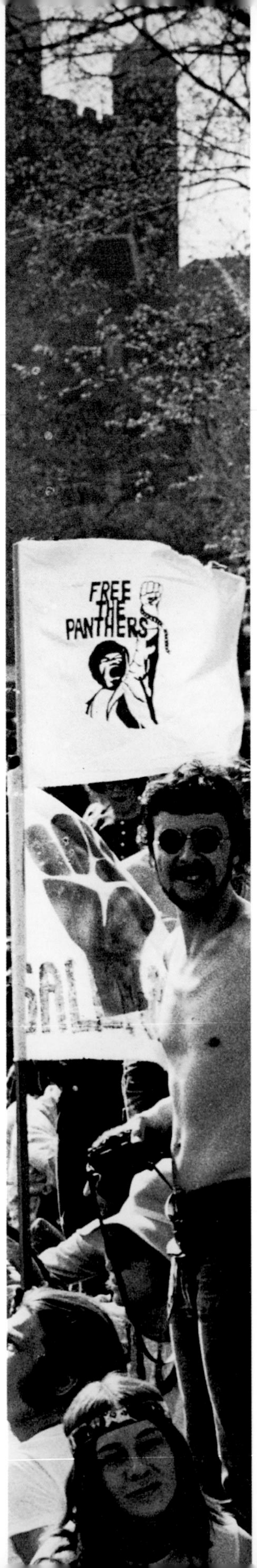
FREE THE PANTHERS

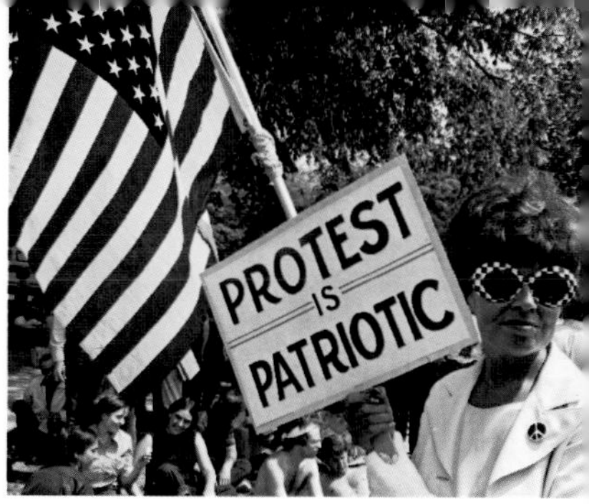
PROTEST
IS
PATRIOTIC

dove for the most visceral of reasons—his viscera were not firm enough to face the collective wrath of that military–industrial establishment he knew so well in Washington, that rifleman's schizophrenia one could see in the eyes of the clerks at the Pentagon, yes, his fear went beyond political common sense and a real chance to win, it went beyond slavery to L.B.J. (because L.B.J. finally had also been afraid of the Pentagon), it came down to the simple fear that he was not ready to tell the generals they were wrong. Peace they might yet accept, but not the recognition that they were somewhat insane—as quickly tell dragons to shift their nest. [4]

So "Democracy in South Vietnam" was established because the use of the word by Lyndon Johnson and himself had established it. The radiance of the sensation of democracy came from the word itself. "Democracy!" Halos in his eyes. "When you look over the world scene, those elections [in South Vietnam] stand up pretty well and the basis of the Government today is a broader–base Government." Earlier he had actually said, "We have not sought to impose a military solution. Regrettably, wars have their built–in escalation." One would have to be a great novelist to dare to put this last remark in the mouth of a character so valuable as Humphrey. "The roadblock to peace, my dear friends, is not in Washington, D.C. It is in Hanoi, and we ought to recognize it as such." [5]

"There were two groups to the army of young people who assembled in Chicago; one could divide them conveniently as socialists and existentialists…

The New Left was interested for the most part in altering society (and being conceivably altered themselves—they were nothing if not Romantic) by the activity of working for a new kind of life out in the ghettoes, the campuses, and the antiwar movement. [6]

…the Yippies were the militant wing of the Hippies, Youth International Party… A tribal unity had passed through the youth of America (and half the nations of the world) a far–out vision of orgiastic revels stripped of violence or even the differentiation of sex. …some went screaming down the alleys of the mad where cockroaches drive like Volkswagens on the oilcloth of the moon, gluttons found vertigo in centrifuges of consciousness, vomitoriums of ingestion; others found love, some manifest of love in light, in shards of Nirvana, sparks of satori—they came back to the world a twentieth–century tribe wearing celebration bells and filthy garments. Used–up livers gave their complexions a sickly pale, and hair grew on their faces like weeds. Yet they had seen some incontestable vision of the goof—the universe was not absurd to them; like pilgrims they looked at society with the eyes of children: society was absurd. Every emperor who went down the path was naked, and they handed flowers to policemen. [7]

Just as he had known for one instant at the Republican Gala in Miami Beach that Nelson Rockefeller had no chance of getting the nomination, so he knew now on this cool gray Sunday afternoon in August, chill in the air like the chill of the pale and the bird of fear beginning to nest in the throat, that trouble was coming, serious trouble. The air of Lincoln Park came into the nose with that tender concern which air seemed always

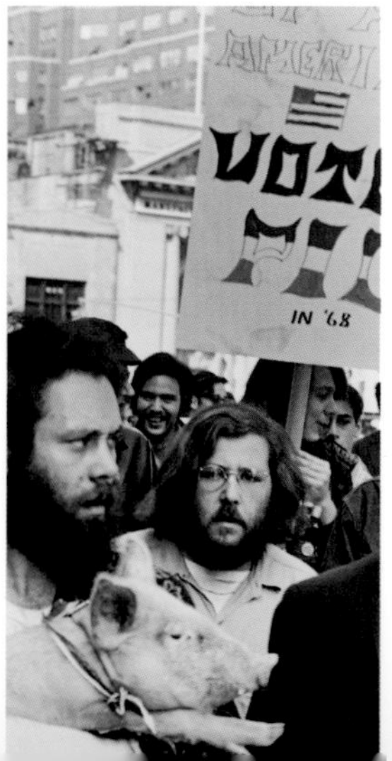
IN '68

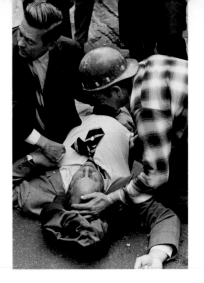

ready to offer when danger announced its presence. The reporter took an unhappy look around, "Were these odd unkempt children the sort of troops with whom one wished to enter battle?" [8]

Michigan Avenue was now suddenly jammed with people in the march, perhaps as many as four or five thousand people, including on-lookers on the sidewalk who jumped in…with dreams of a march on to the Amphitheatre four miles beyond, and in the full pleasure of being led by the wagons of the Poor People's March, the demonstrators shouted to every-one on the sidewalk, "Join us, join us, join us," and the sidewalk kept disgorging more people ready to march.

…just before Michigan Avenue reached the Hilton, the marchers were halted by the police… The mules were allowed to cross Balbo Avenue, then were separated by a line of police from the marchers, who now, several thousand compressed in this one place, filled the intersection of Michigan Avenue and Balbo. There, dammed by po-lice on three sides, and cut off from the wag-ons of the Poor People's March, there, right

beneath the windows of the Hilton which looked down on Grant Park and Michigan Avenue, the stationary march was abruptly attacked. The police attacked with tear gas, with Mace, and with clubs, they attacked like a chain saw cutting into wood, the teeth of the saw the edge of their clubs, they at-tacked like a scythe through grass, lines of twenty and thirty policemen striking out in an arc, their clubs beating, demonstra-tors fleeing. Seen from overhead, from the nineteenth floor, it was like a wind blowing dust, or the edge of waves riding foam on the shore.

The police cut through the crowd one way, then cut through them another. They chased people into the park, ran them down, beat them up; they cut through the intersection at Michigan and Balbo like a razor cutting a channel through the head of hair, and then drove columns of new police into a channel who in turn pushed out, clubs flailing, on each side, to cut new channels, and new ones again. As demonstrators ran, they re-formed in new groups only to be chased by the police again. The action went on for ten minutes, fifteen minutes, with the absolute

ferocity of a tropical storm, and watching it from a window on the nineteenth floor, there was something of the detachment of studying a storm at evening through a glass, the light was a lovely gray–blue, the police had uniforms of sky–blue, even the ferocity had an abstract elemental play of forces of nature at battle with other forces, as if sheets of tropical rain were driving across the street in patterns, in curving pat-terns which curved upon each other again. Police cars rolled up, prisoners were beat-en, shoved into wagons, driven away…but here is a quotation from J. Anthony Lukas in *The New York Times*:

> *Even elderly bystanders were caught in the police onslaught. At one point, the police turned on several dozen persons standing quietly behind police barriers in front of the Conrad Hilton Hotel watching the demonstrators across the street.*

For no reason that could be immediately determined, the blue–helmeted policemen charged the barriers, crushing the specta-tors against the windows of the Haymarket Inn, a restaurant in the hotel. Finally the window gave way, sending screaming middle–aged women and children backward through the broken shards of glass.

The police then ran into the restaurant and beat some of the victims who had fallen through the windows and arrested them.

From time to time, the reporter thought again of matters which did not balance him. He thought of the fear Bobby Kennedy must have known. This was a thought he had been trying to avoid all night—it gave eyes to the darkness of his own fear—that fear which came from knowing some of *them* were implacable. *Them*! All the bad cops, U.S. marshals, generals, corporation executives, high government bureaucrats, rednecks, insane Black militants, half–crazy provocateurs, Right–wing faggots, Right–wing high–strung geniuses, J. Edgar Hoover, and the worst of the rich surrounding every seat of Establishment in America.

Yet his own side—his own side as of last night—made jokes about putting LSD in drinking water. They believed in drugs and he did not. They talked of burning money—he thought money was the last sanity for a Romantic (and part of the game). They believed in taking the pill and going bare–ass in the park—he had decided by now that the best things in life were most difficult to reach, for they protected themselves, so beware of finding your true love in a night. (For it could be true love, or the disaster of your life.) Or perhaps he was too old for orgies on the green. Still, these white children were his troops. (And all the Left–wing Blacks would be his polemical associates—the Lord protect him!) The children were crazy, but they developed honor every year, they had a vision not void of beauty; the other side had no vision, only a nightmare of smashing a brain with a brick. The fear came back again. His own brain would not be reserved necessarily for the last brick. Of course, a lot of people were going to be living with some such fear over the next few years. [9]

1 *Miami and the Siege of Chicago: An Informal History of the Republican and Democratic Conventions of 1968*, Norman Mailer. Donald I. Fine, Inc. New York: 1968. 34–36.

2 Ibid, 61.

3 Ibid, 102–103.

4 Ibid, 112–113.

5 Ibid, 124–125.

6 Ibid, 132–133.

7 Ibid, 139–140.

8 Ibid, 144.

9 Ibid, 214.

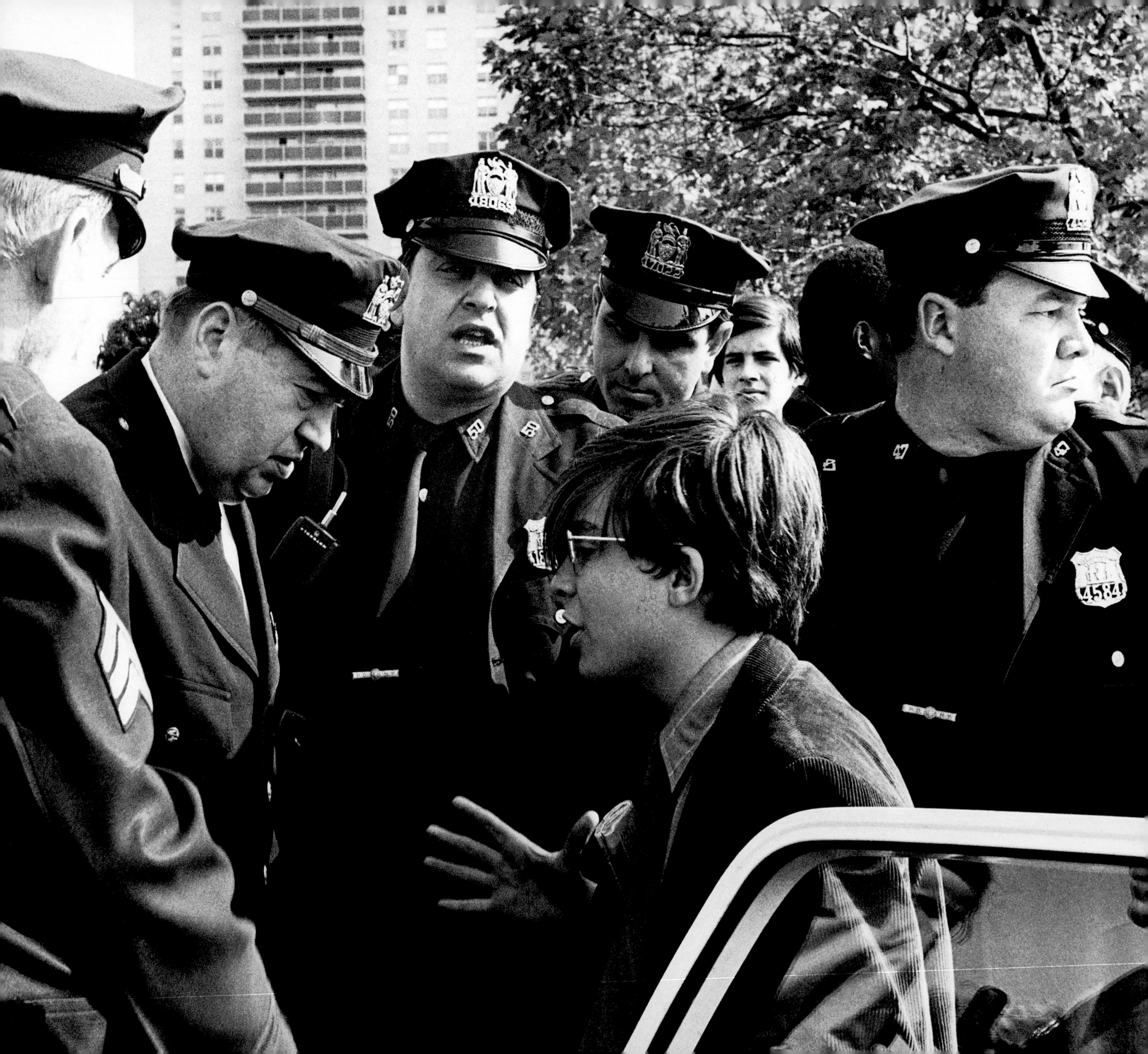
4584

1

Chicago 7

Left to Right: Chicago 7 conspiracy trial defendants Rennie Davis, Abbie Hoffman, Lee Weiner, David Dellinger, John Froines, Jerry Rubin and Tom Hayden with their lawyers Leonard Weinglass (far left) and William Kunstler (far right). Chicago, IL, October 8, 1969

I walked into the courtroom and sat down to watch that day's trial. Black Panther leader Bobby Seale was sitting among the defendants, bound with rope around his hands and legs, his mouth gagged with cloth and tape. He couldn't move and couldn't speak. The judge had ordered Seale forcibly silenced and restrained the day before in response to his repeated pleas to have his own attorney present. After a few minutes, veteran antiwar activist Dave Dellinger stood to protest Seale's treatment, and a group of burly federal marshals pushed him to the floor and attacked. My left eye caught a spectator as he jumped over several rows of benches and landed on the back of one of the marshals, which brought him to the floor. A wild melee ensued. This was my introduction to American jurisprudence.

The Chicago 7 had been charged with crossing state lines as well as conspiracy to incite riots at the 1968 Democratic National Convention. In truth, the only people who rioted were the police, attacking demonstrators wildly on national television while the victims chanted "The whole world is watching."

During the trial, the defendants were inspired to wear judicial robes one day and revolutionary war uniforms the next. I watched lawyers William Kunstler and Leonard Weinglass attempt to plead with their clients to tone it down, to no avail.

When court adjourned I followed the defendants and their lawyers, William Kunstler and Leonard Weinglass, back to their offices. They wouldn't let *The New York Times* in, but I was deemed acceptable. An intense debate began over strategy for the next day until everyone gathered in front of the television at 6:30 pm to watch Uncle Walter (Cronkite). This was routine in their office for months—after a day in court, they all sat down to watch the reviews. (Abbie Hoffman, Jerry Rubin, Tom Hayden, Dellinger and the other defendants were acutely aware that viewers at home were their other, arguably more potent, jury.)

On weekends during this period, I traveled with Abbie, Kunstler and Davis to college campuses around the country where they delivered rousing antiwar speeches, raised funds and held press conferences.

This photo (without Bobby Seale, who was later tried separately) is one of only two that I believe exists. It was exceedingly difficult to get them all together. I had to have three people help just get them into the elevator and onto the street.

Previous Page:
A Bronx Science High School student pleads with police not to arrest him during an antiwar demonstration, New York City, 1968

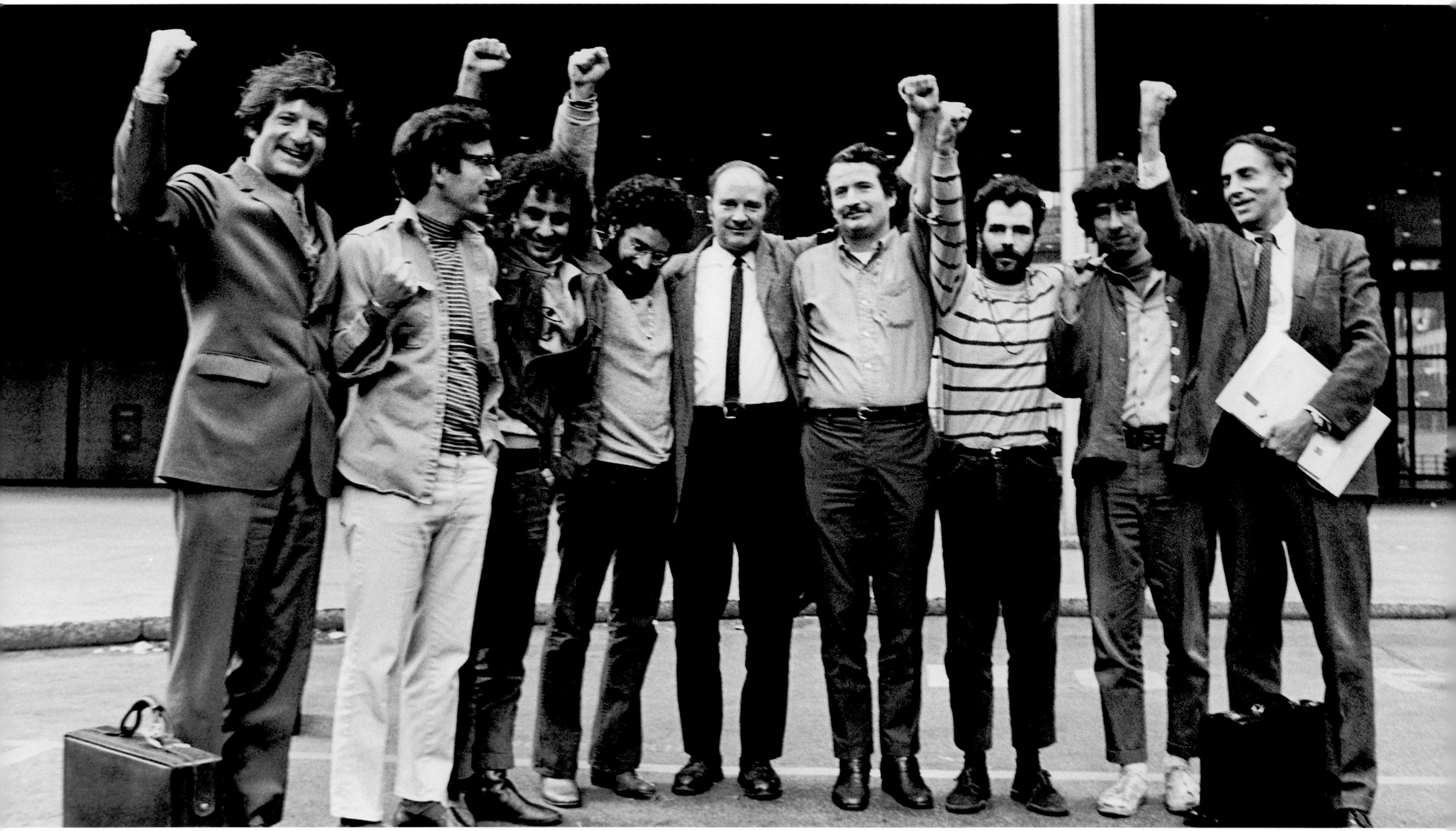

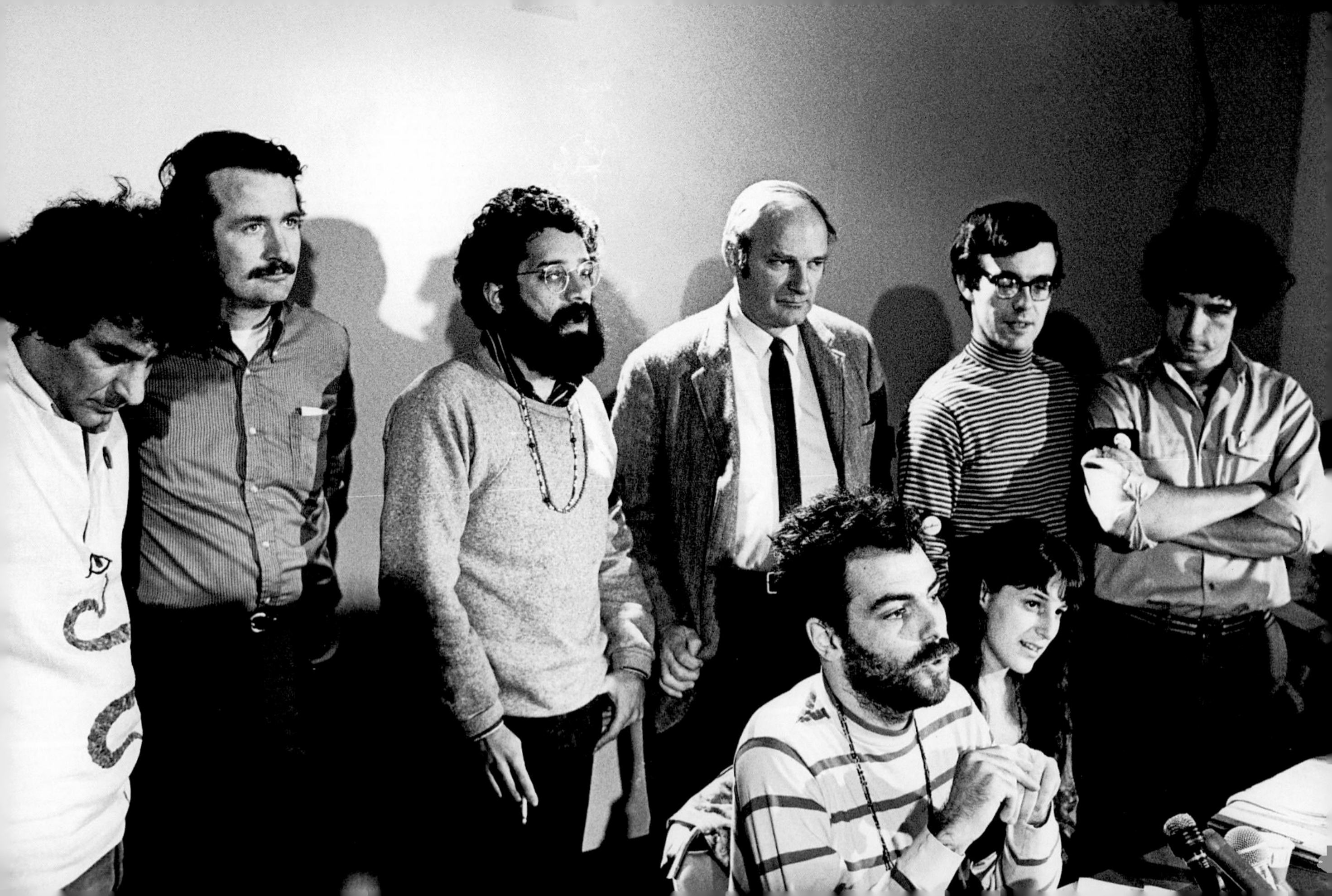

In the end, the jury acquitted all 7 defendants of the conspiracy charges, while convicting 5 of individually crossing state lines to incite violence. Notorious and absurd Judge Julius Hoffman sentenced them to 5 years each, plus another 2 to 4 years for contempt of court—he even sentenced the lawyers to jail. All of these judgments were eventually overturned by higher courts. The government had tied up the antiwar movement in legal battles, while the Chicago 7 used it to broaden the movement. Who do you think won?

Chicago 7 members hold a press conference immediately after being charged with contempt during their conspiracy trial, Chicago, IL, April 8, 1969

Allen Ginsberg

Allen Ginsberg at a rally in support of the Black Panther Party, New Haven, CT, May 1–2, 1970

I first met Allen at the first Central Park "Be–In" in 1967. Here he's pictured sitting meditatively during a rally to free Bobby Seale and Ericka Huggins of the Black Panther Party during their murder trial in New Haven, CT. Typical Allen—calm while all around him is swirling. Sitting next to him are Jerry Rubin's girlfriend Nancy Kurshan and Abbie Hoffman's wife Anita. (Abbie is sitting on the fence). In 1972, Allen taught me how to meditate, using the method of focusing on one's breathing.

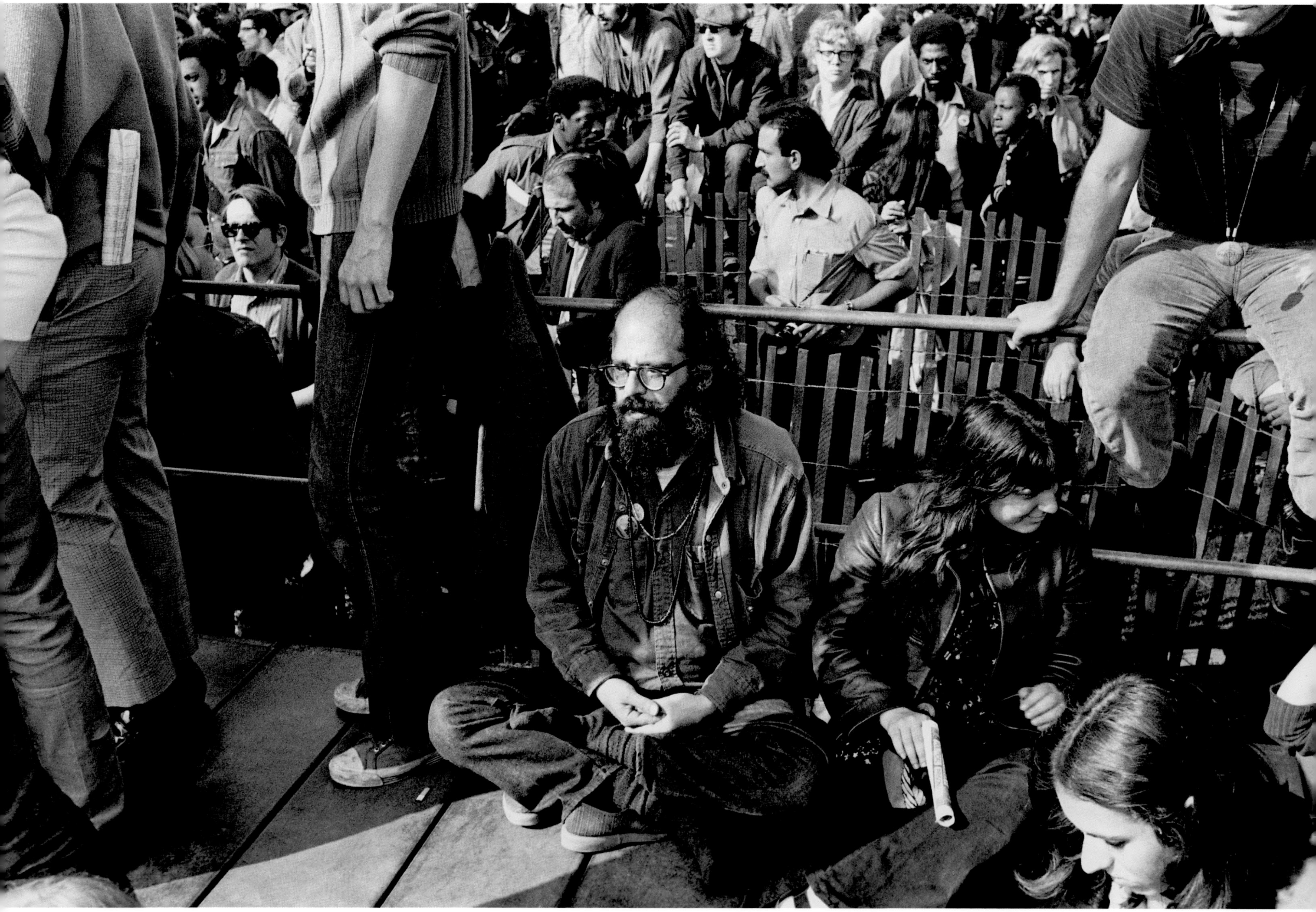

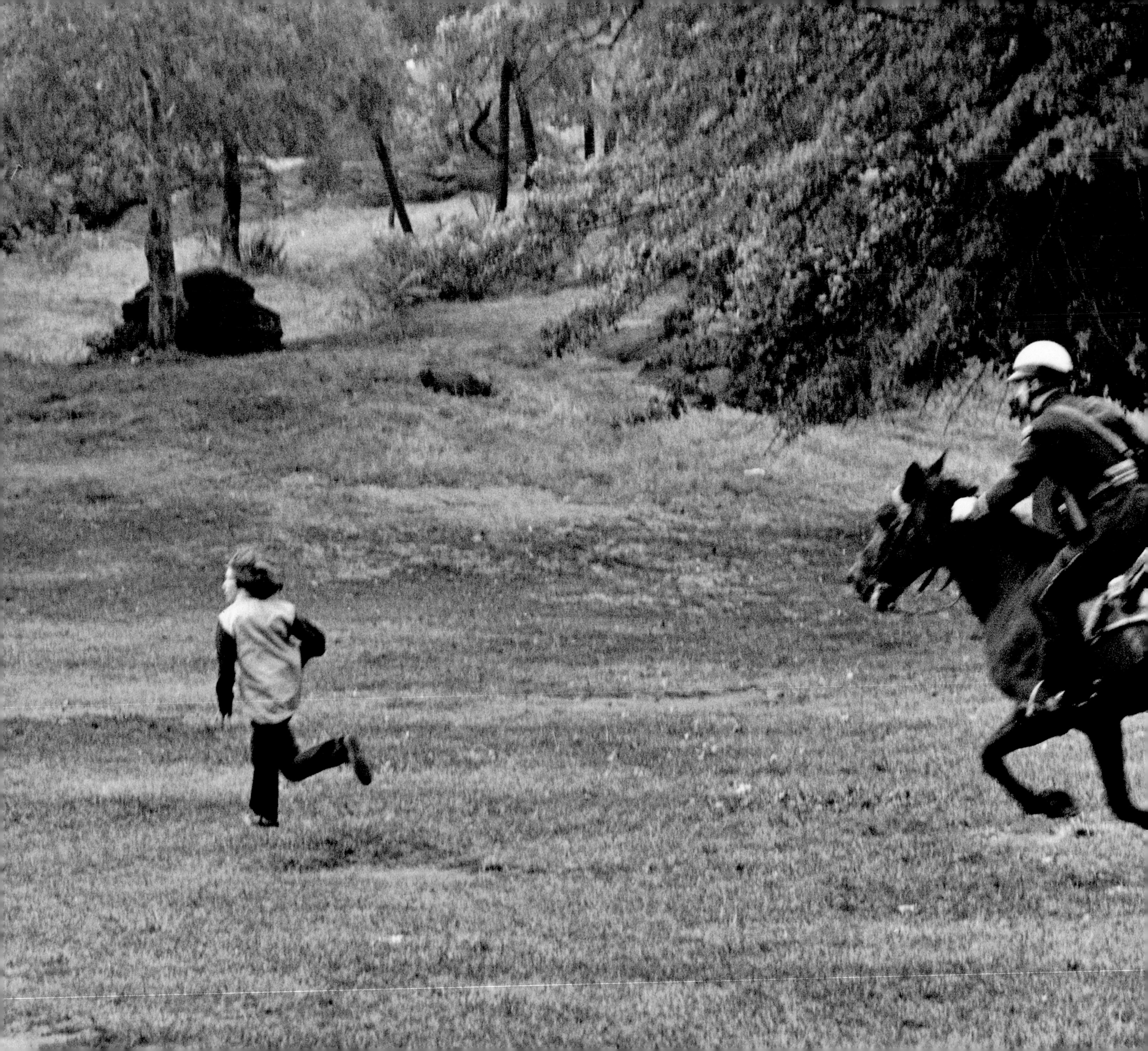

Cops on Horseback

Policemen on horseback chase a boy who burned an American flag during a Central Park "Be–In". The boy was eventually caught, badly beaten and arrested. New York City, October 12, 1968

The boy running had burned an American flag at a Central Park "Be–In" in New York while protesting the war in Vietnam. In those days, even hippie events were politicized by the war. Three mounted cops took off after him, and after a good run, they beat the living daylights out of him. He didn't stand a chance. The police were often violent with the demonstrators, beyond all reason. This photograph was reprinted in hundreds of antiwar and countercultural newspapers all over the world.

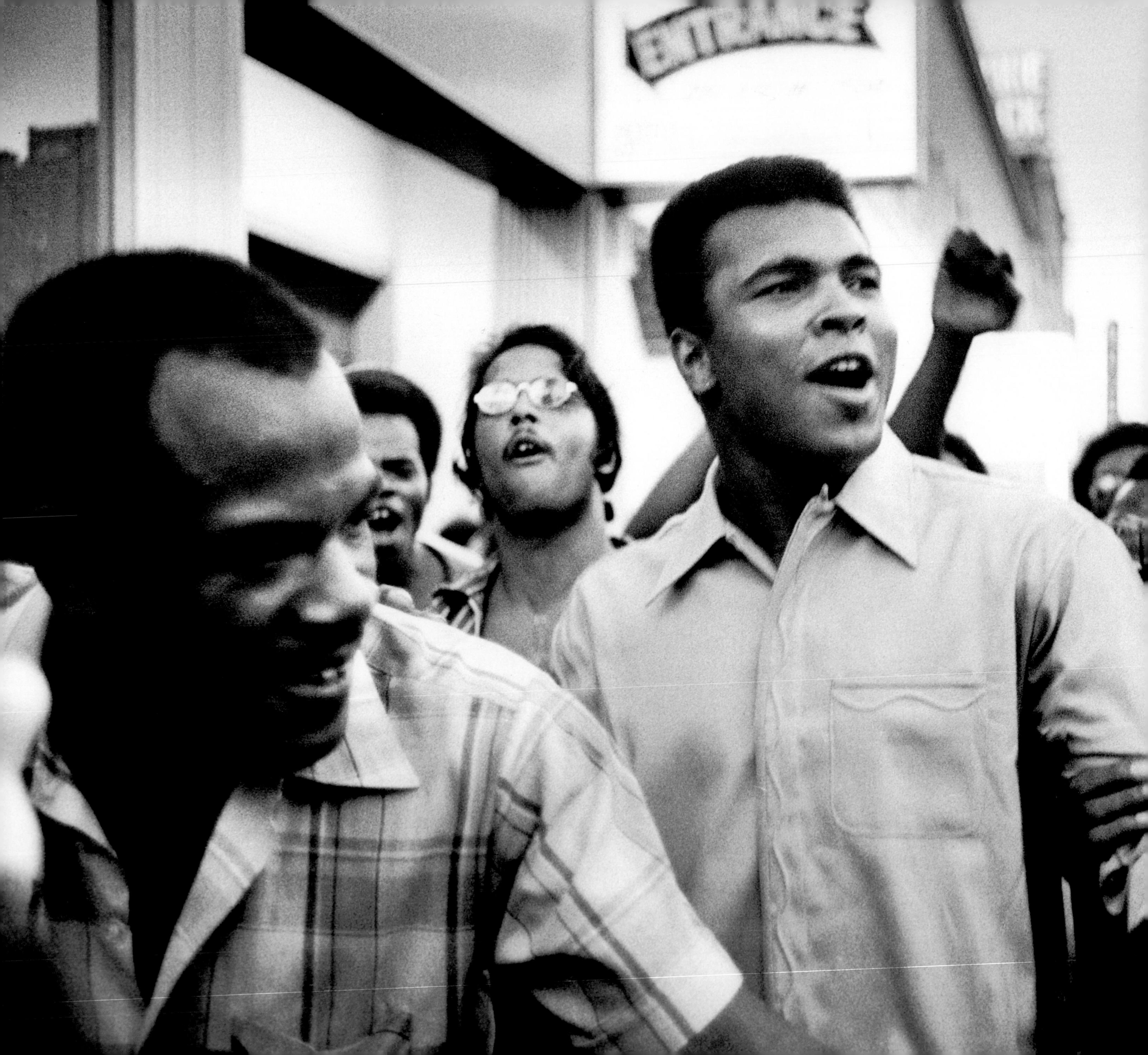
ENTRANCE

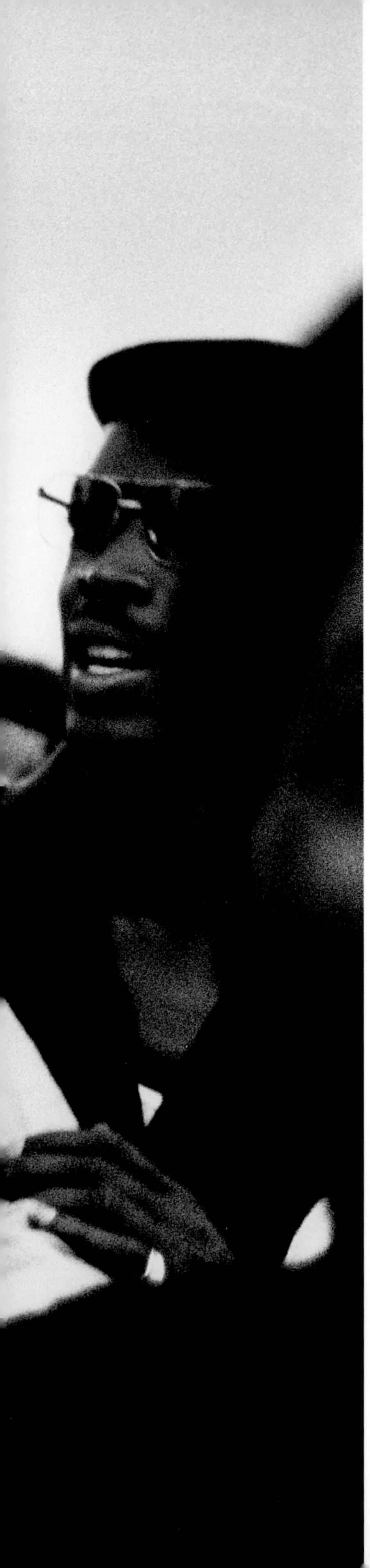

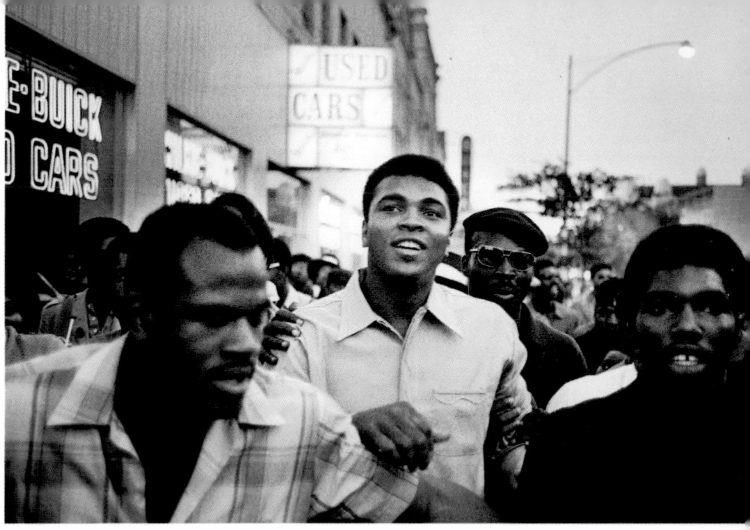

BUICK
CARS
USED
CARS

Muhammad Ali

Left and Above:
Muhammad Ali with members of the Black Panther Party, New York City, September, 1970

For those resisting the draft, Muhammad Ali was a beacon. He was stripped of his World Heavyweight title in 1967 for refusing military service. "I ain't got no quarrel with them Viet Congs," he explained. Convicted of draft evasion in May of that year, he was sentenced to five years in prison, a decision later overturned in 1970. His resistance damaged his fighting career, but made him a hero around the world.

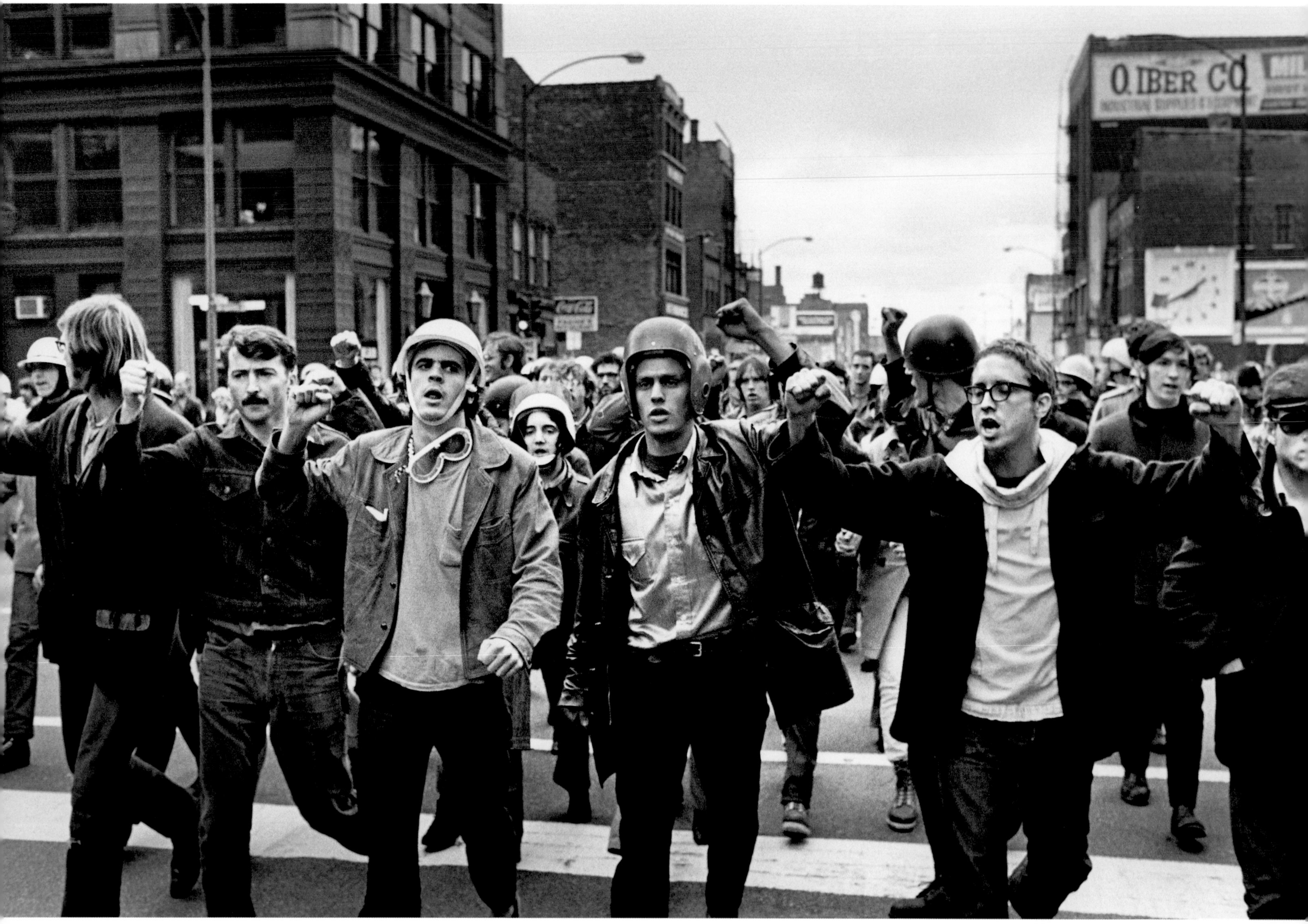
O. IBER CO

Weatherman/Weather Underground

Weatherman members (left to right) Jim Mellen, Peter Clapp, John Jacobs, Bill Ayers and Terry Robbins march during the Days of Rage, Chicago, IL, October 11, 1969

This was the scariest event I ever photographed. These photos were taken at the "Days of Rage" actions in Chicago, October 1969. Led by the Weatherman faction of SDS, the actions were a four–day demonstration targeting the wealthy downtown section of the Loop. What was meant to be a show of force of thousands turned out to be a small riot involving several hundred protestors who were eventually arrested en masse. After demonstrators pulled clubs from under their jackets and started smashing storefront windows and cars, police opened fire on them.

I had met and spent time with many of the Weatherman leaders such as Bernardine Dohrn, Mark Rudd, Terry Robbins, Bill Ayers, John Jacobs and Kathy Boudin. I witnessed their evolution from mild–mannered, upper middle–class college activists into counterproductive anarchists. At one point they tried to recruit me. I was 17 and they were desperate for young people to join. When they split from SDS, they renamed *New Left Notes*, its newspaper, to FIRE! and Mark Rudd kept calling me to move to Chicago and help them edit it. After some indecision, I finally refused, and am glad that I made the decision I did!

There was no excuse for their insanity, but imagine how crazy the Vietnam war made my generation if it led people to risk their lives in this way. News of what we were doing to Vietnamese civilians—dropping napalm and antipersonnel weapons designed to maim villagers—drove people to lose their minds.

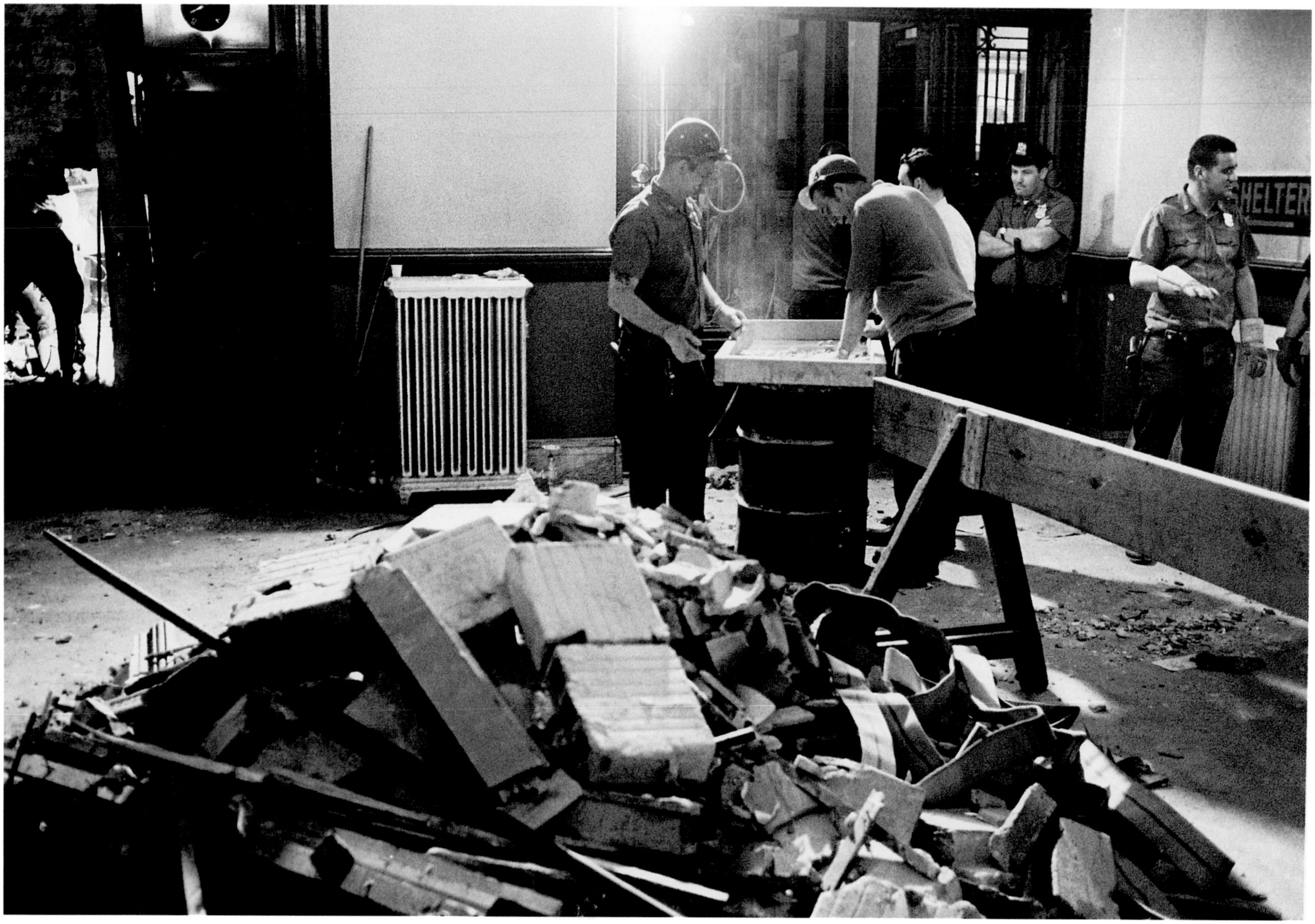
HELTER

After the "Days of Rage" actions, many of the leaders went underground and began attacking symbols of American culture including bombing the New York City police headquarters in June 1970 as well as planting a bomb in the bathroom of the U.S. Capitol in February 1971. Between 1969 and 1975, Weatherman bombed more than twenty locations across the country including local and federal government buildings and several American corporations. Despite their destructive tactics, many radicals at the time followed their every move, including the frequent communiqués from underground after each bombing. At the same time, however, they also alienated potential allies like the Black Panther Party and fed into the divisiveness that eventually toppled the New Left.

The Weatherman faction of SDS bombs police headquarters, New York City, June 9, 1970

Protestors arrested during the Days of Rage, Chicago, IL, October 11, 1969

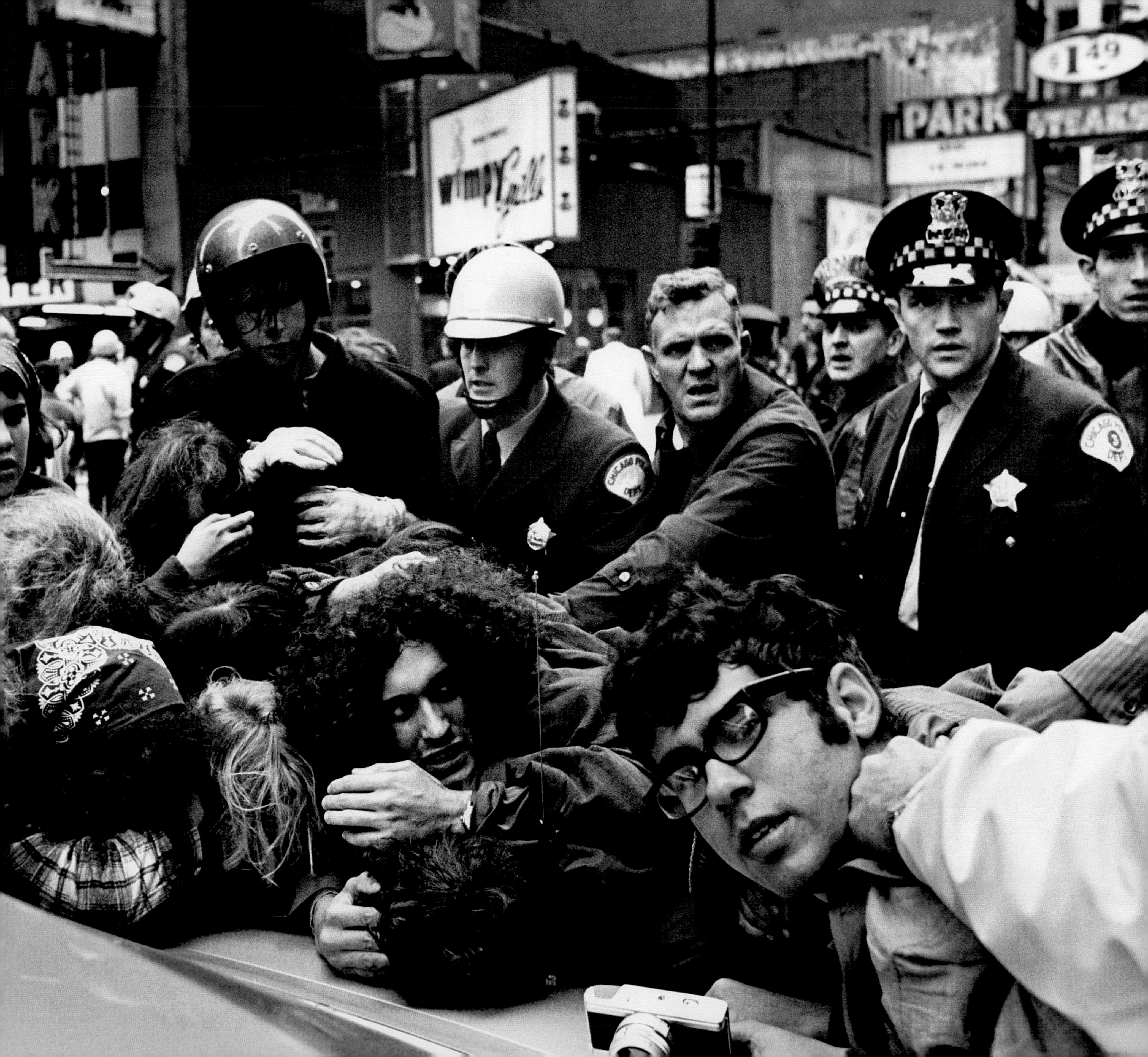
wimpy Grill
PARK

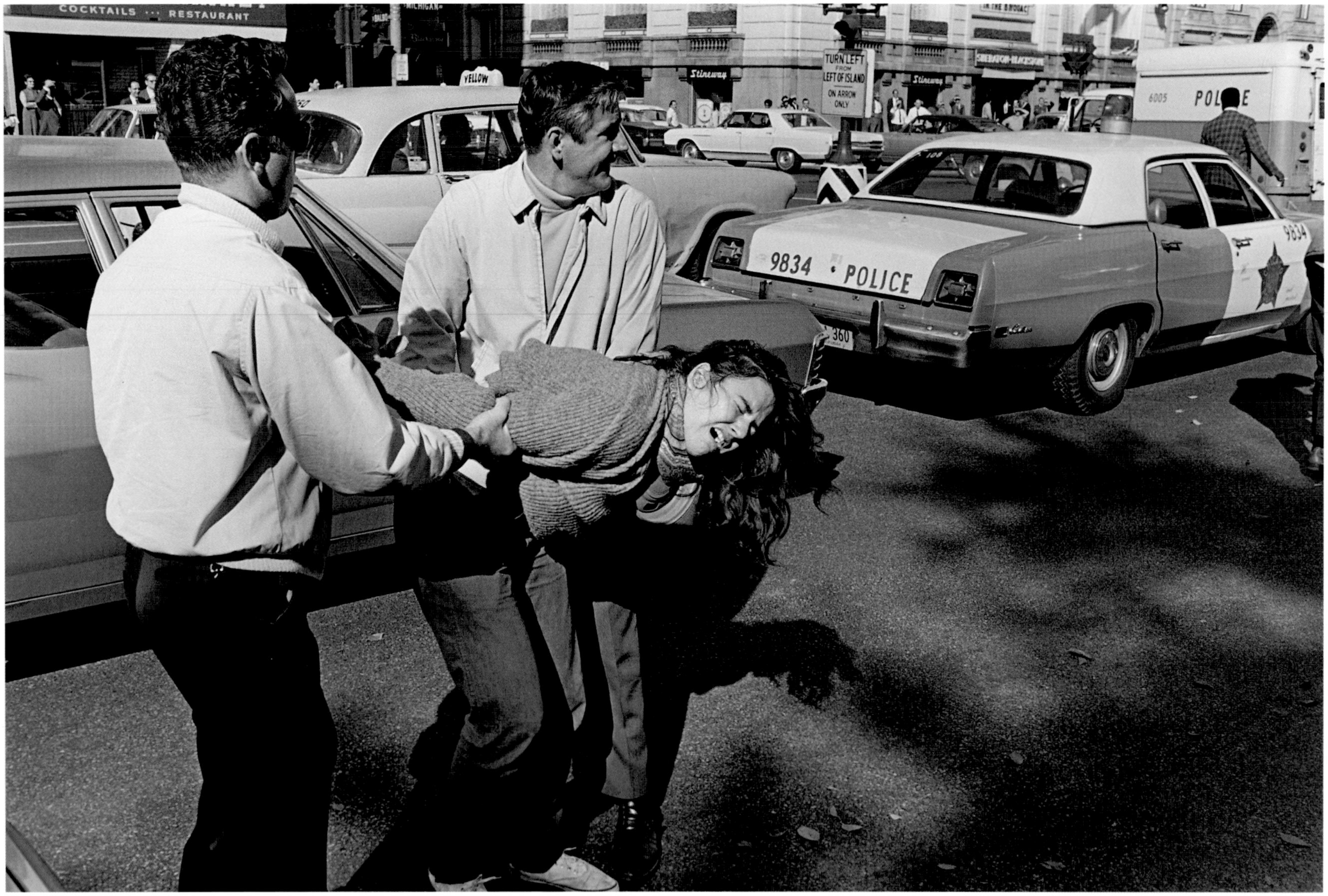
COCKTAILS ··· RESTAURANT
YELLOW
TURN LEFT
FROM
LEFT OF ISLAND
ON ARROW
ONLY
9834 POLICE
9834
6005

A woman is arrested by plainclothed police during the Days of Rage Women's Action, Chicago, IL, October 9, 1969

Richard J. Elrod, an assistant corporation counsel, is tended to after breaking his neck while attempting to stop a protestor being chased by police during the Days of Rage, Chicago, IL, October 11, 1969

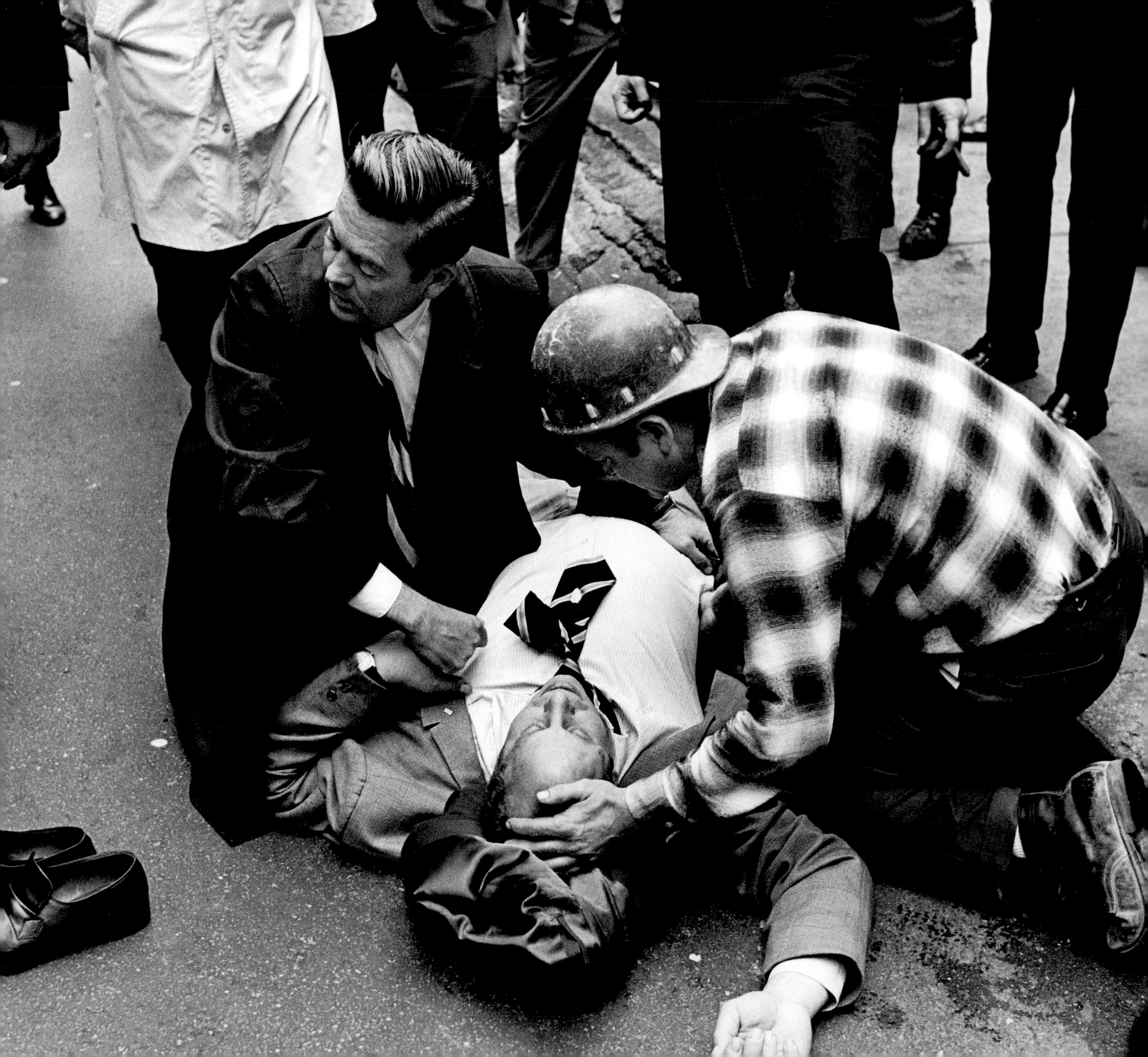

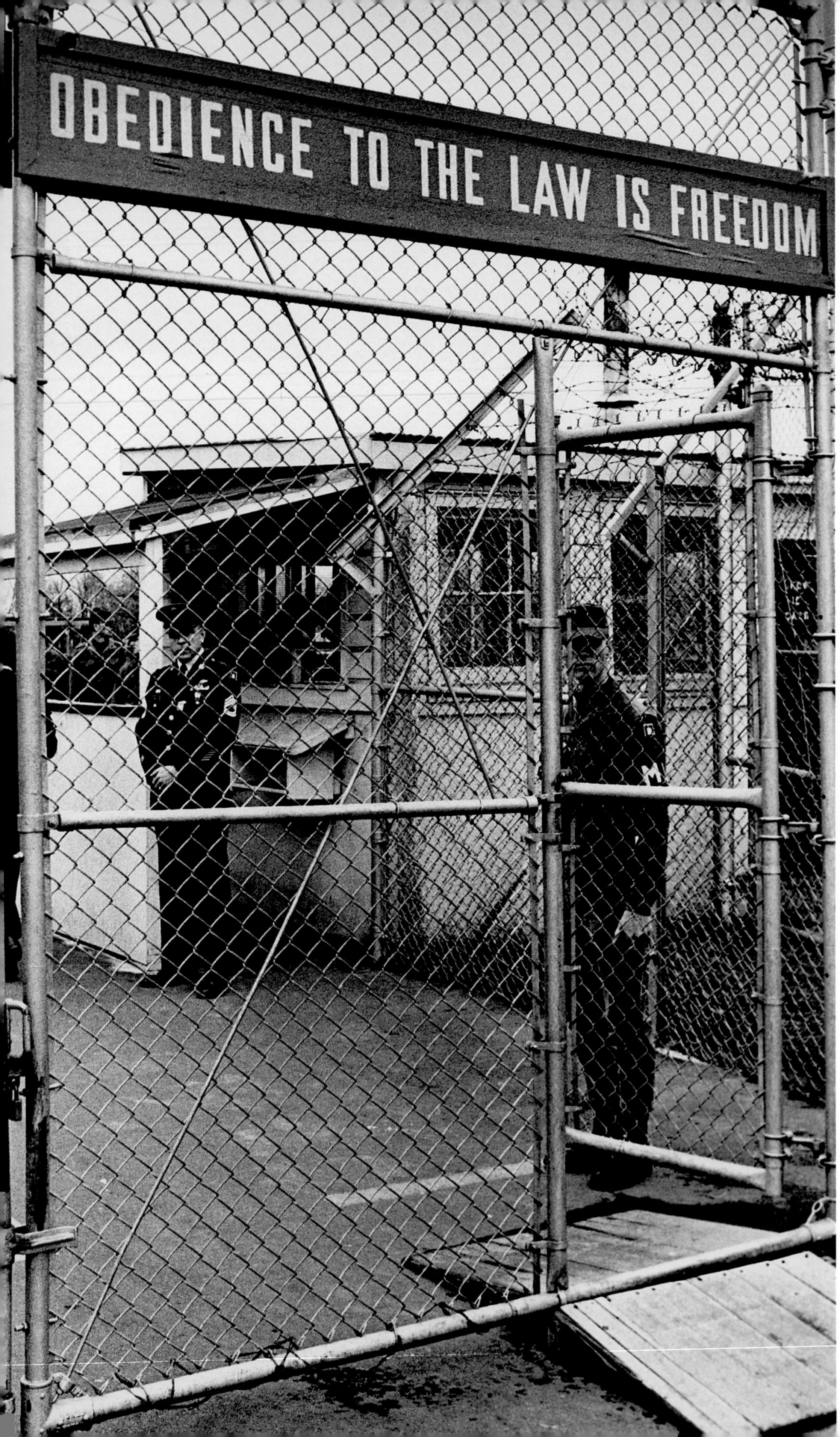
OBEDIENCE TO THE LAW IS FREEDOM

Fort Dix Stockade

Entrance to the Fort Dix stockade, New Jersey, October 12, 1969

Fort Dix, New Jersey served as a major transshipment point for troops going to Vietnam. Soldiers sometimes refused to go, filling the Fort Dix stockade, and the antiwar movement rallied behind these courageous GIs.

On October 12, 1969, demonstrators gathered outside the base. With my police press badge, I was allowed inside. The commanding officer took us on a tour that included the stockade. Above it was this Orwellian slogan, “Obedience to the Law is Freedom.”

This photograph was reprinted all over the world. At the time, there were over one hundred underground antiwar newspapers in the United States alone, and many more abroad. It was reprinted so much that shortly thereafter, the Army took the sign down. I suppose it embarrassed them.

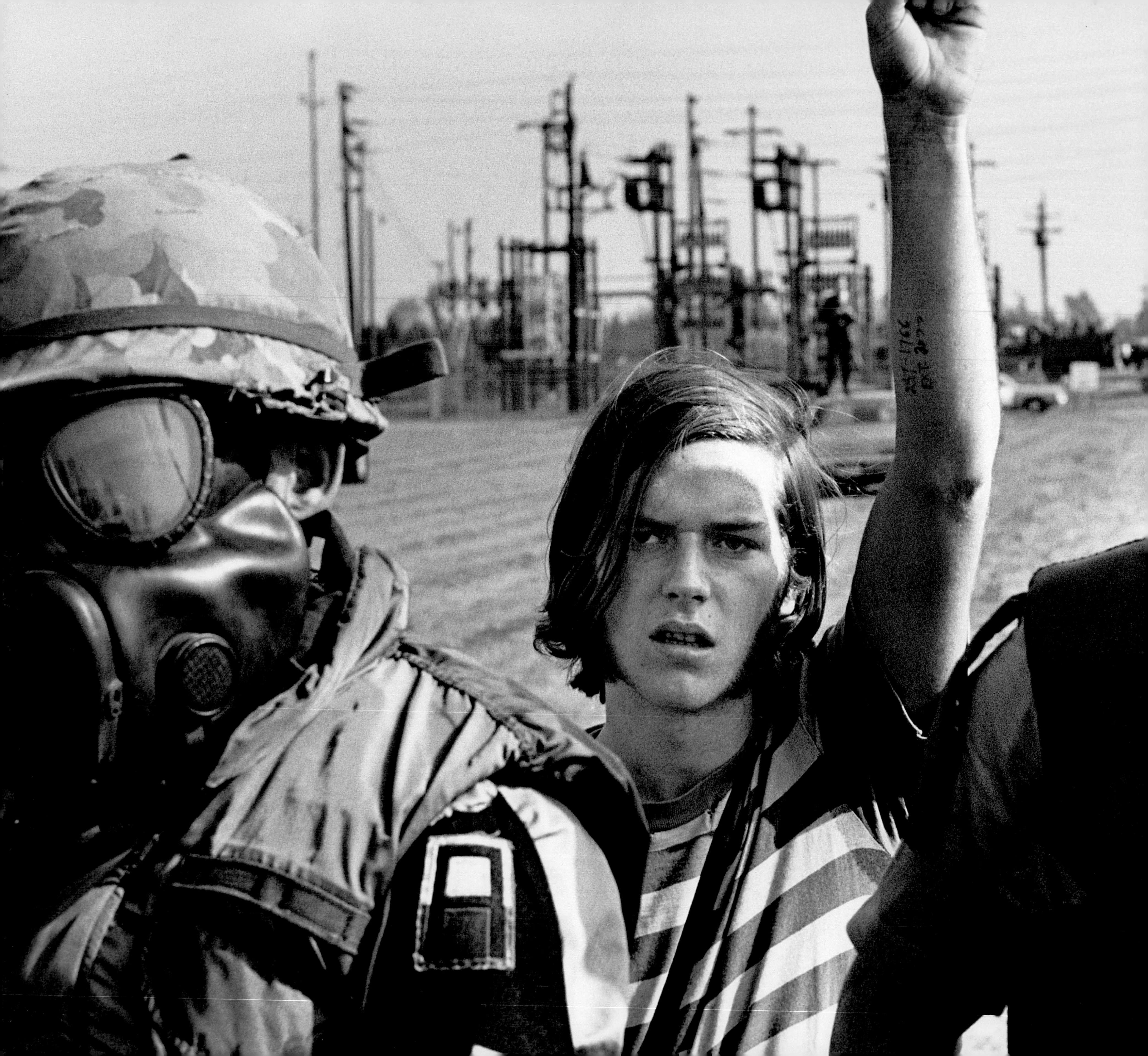

Antiwar protestor, Fort Dix, NJ, October 12, 1969

Left and Right: Women demonstrators outside Fort Dix, a major transshipment port for U.S. Army soldiers leaving for Vietnam, October 12, 1969

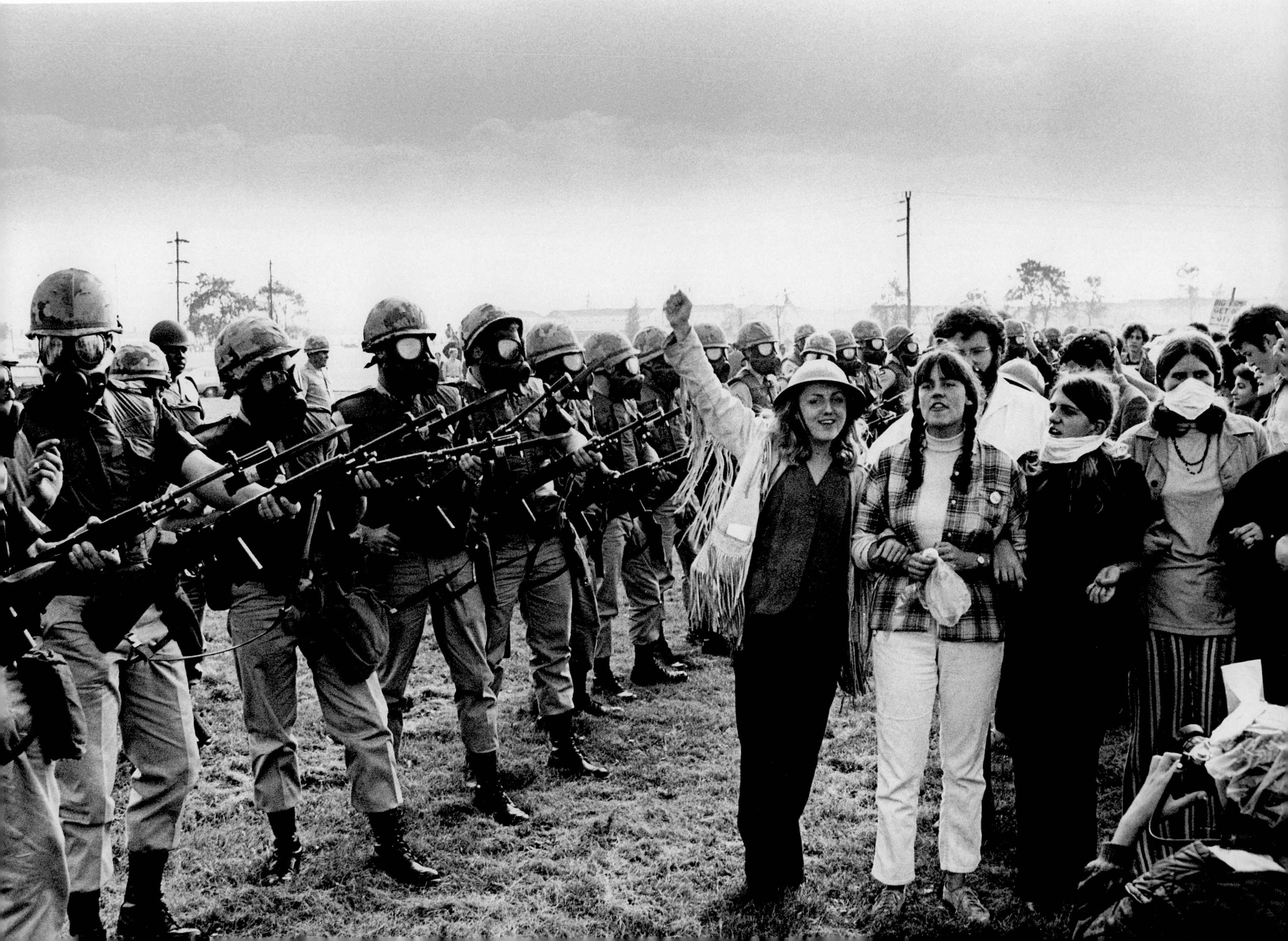

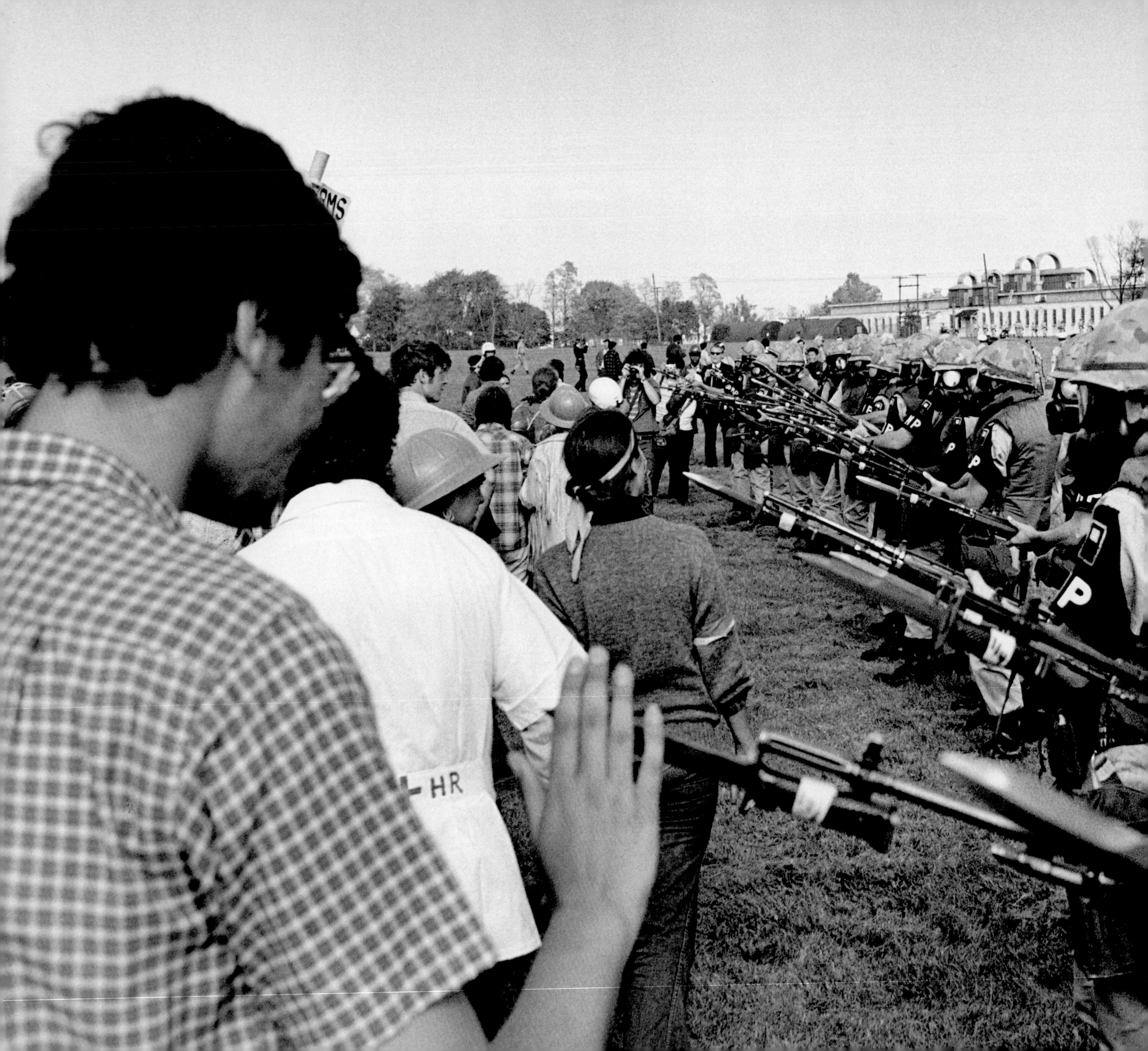
HR

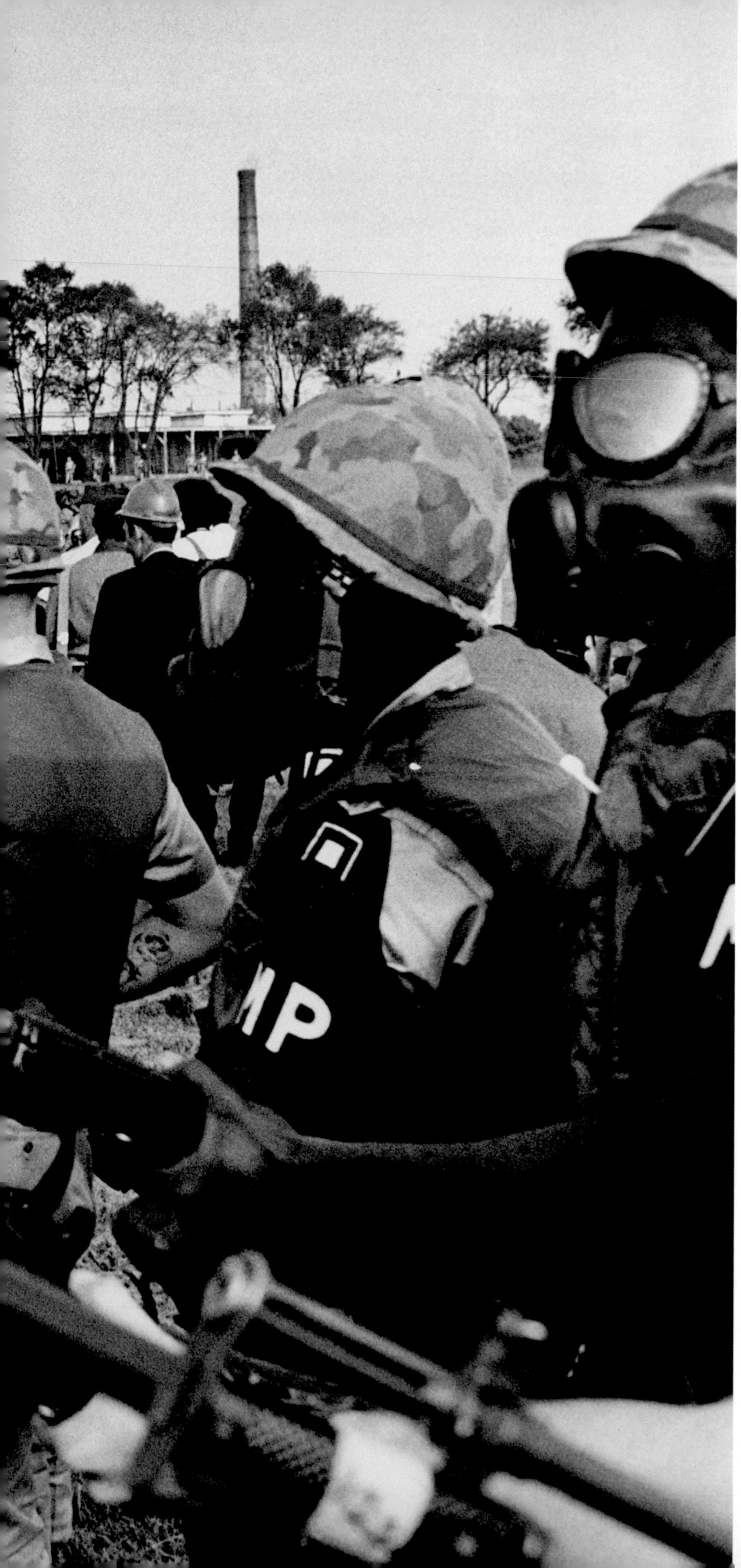
MP

Demonstrators, Fort Dix, NJ, October 12, 1969

Young Lords

Felipe Luciano, co-founder of the Young Lord's Party, Newark, NJ, July 23, 1970

Puerto Rican students already active in the antiwar movement started the Young Lords Party in 1969. Largely inspired by the Black Panther Party and their "serve the people" efforts, the Young Lords provided community–based programs for the poor such as daycare and healthcare, and pushed for better living conditions in poor Latino neighborhoods.

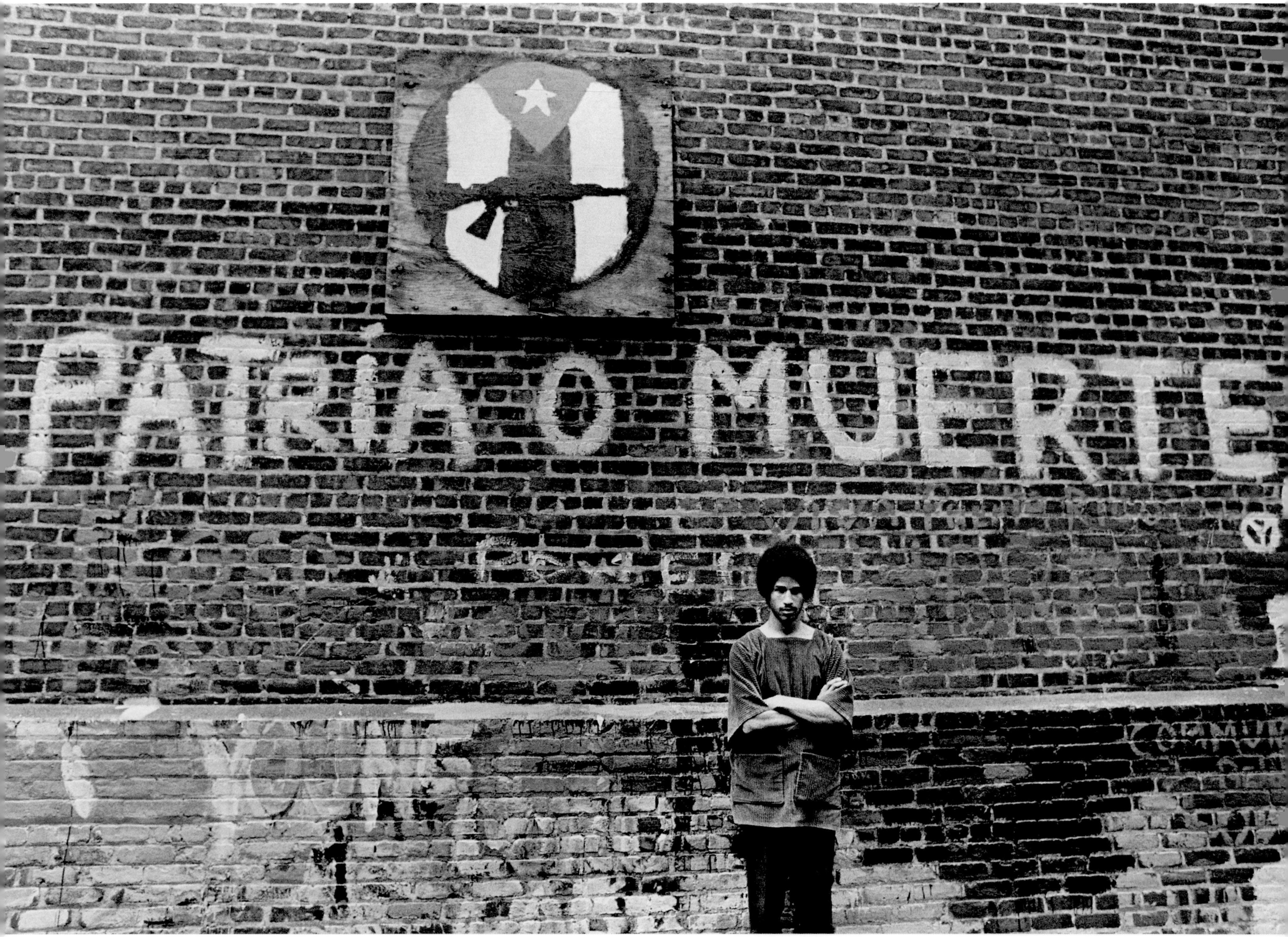
PATRIA O MUERTE

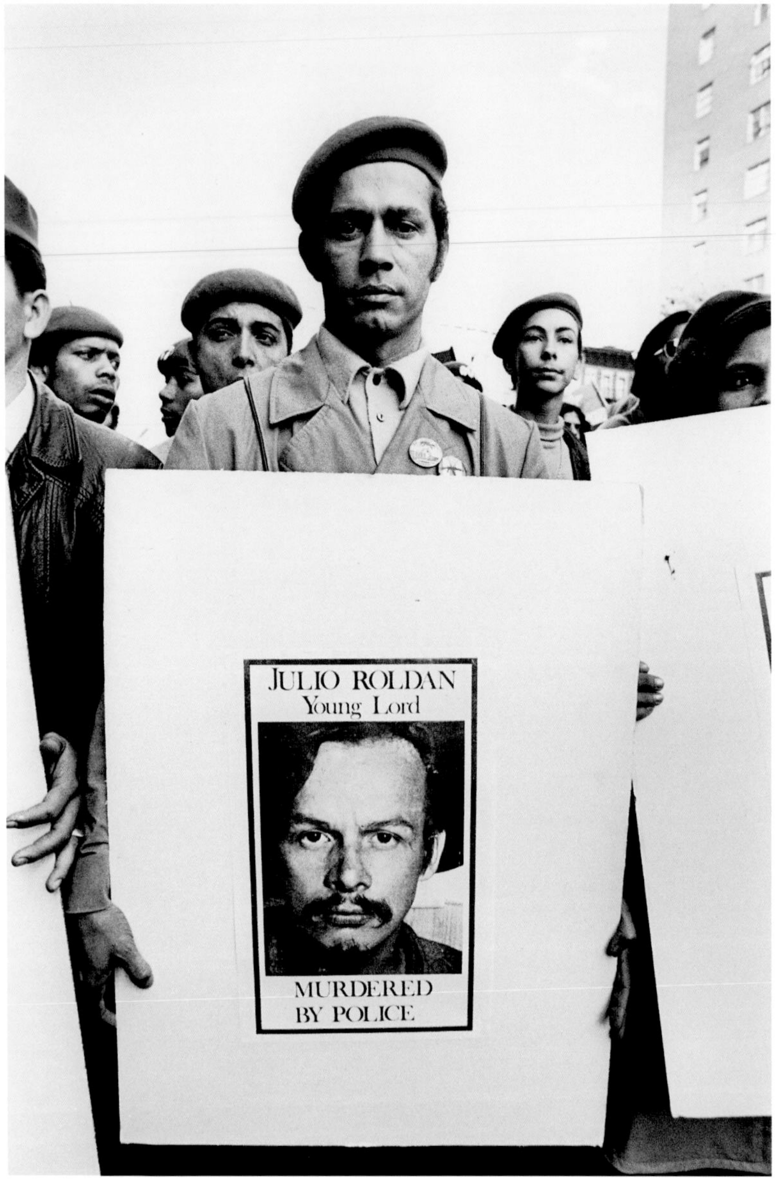
JULIO ROLDAN
Young Lord
MURDERED
BY POLICE

A member of the Young Lords in a funeral procession for Julio Roldan, a murdered comrade, New York City, October 18, 1970

The Young Lords seize the First Spanish Methodist Church, a mostly abandoned church in Harlem on January 7, 1970 and convert it into "La Iglesia de la Gente" or "The Church of the People," a community center. The occupation lasts eleven days. It gains national attention for the Latino rights organization and ends with a police eviction.

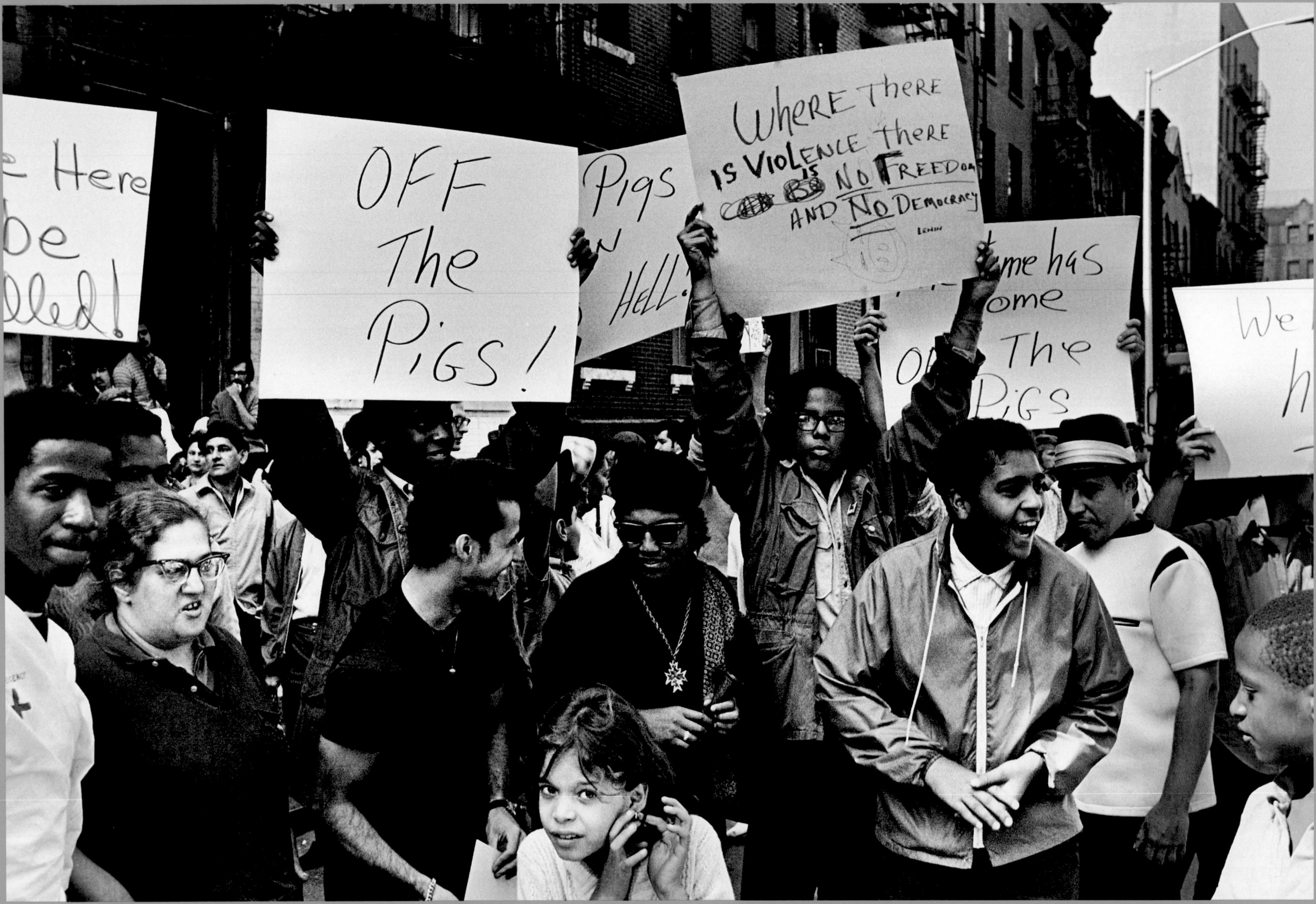
OFF The Pigs!
Where there
IS VIOLENCE there
IS NO FREEDOM
AND NO DEMOCRACY
LENIN

Protestors at a welfare demonstration outside of Public School 15 on the Lower East Side, New York City, September 11, 1969

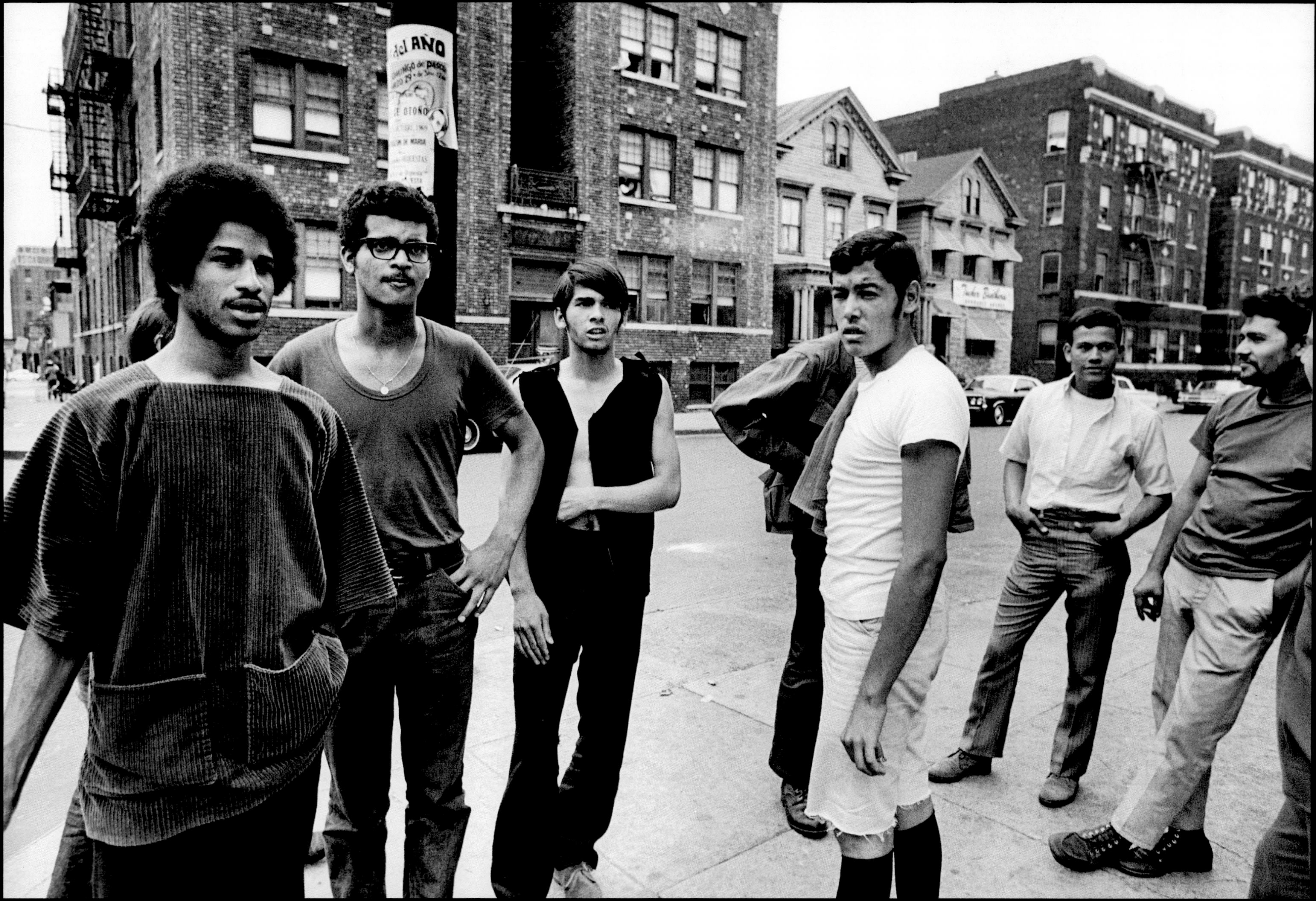
del AÑO

Young Lords Party co-founder Felipe Luciano (left) with other Young Lords, Newark, NJ, July 23, 1970

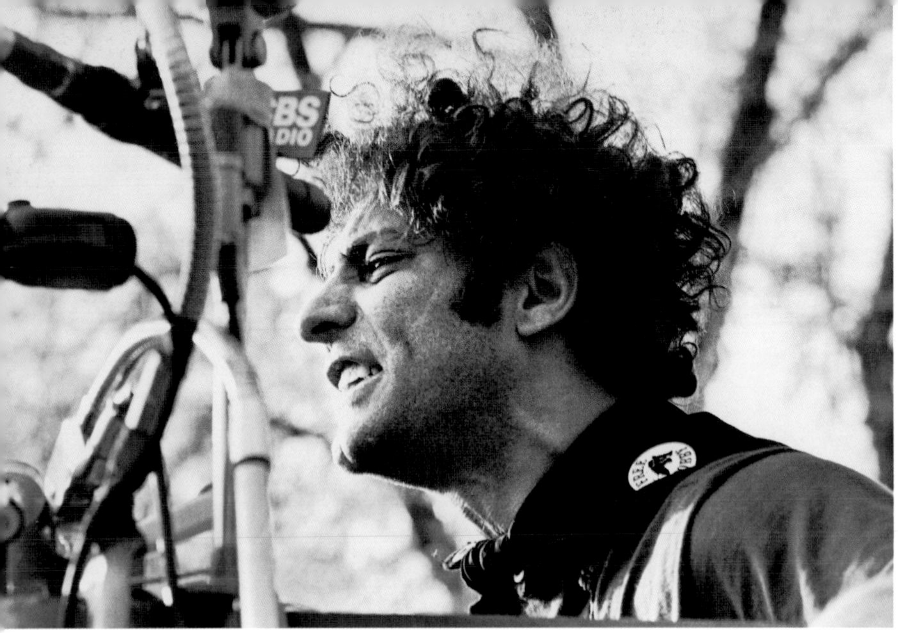
CBS
RADIO

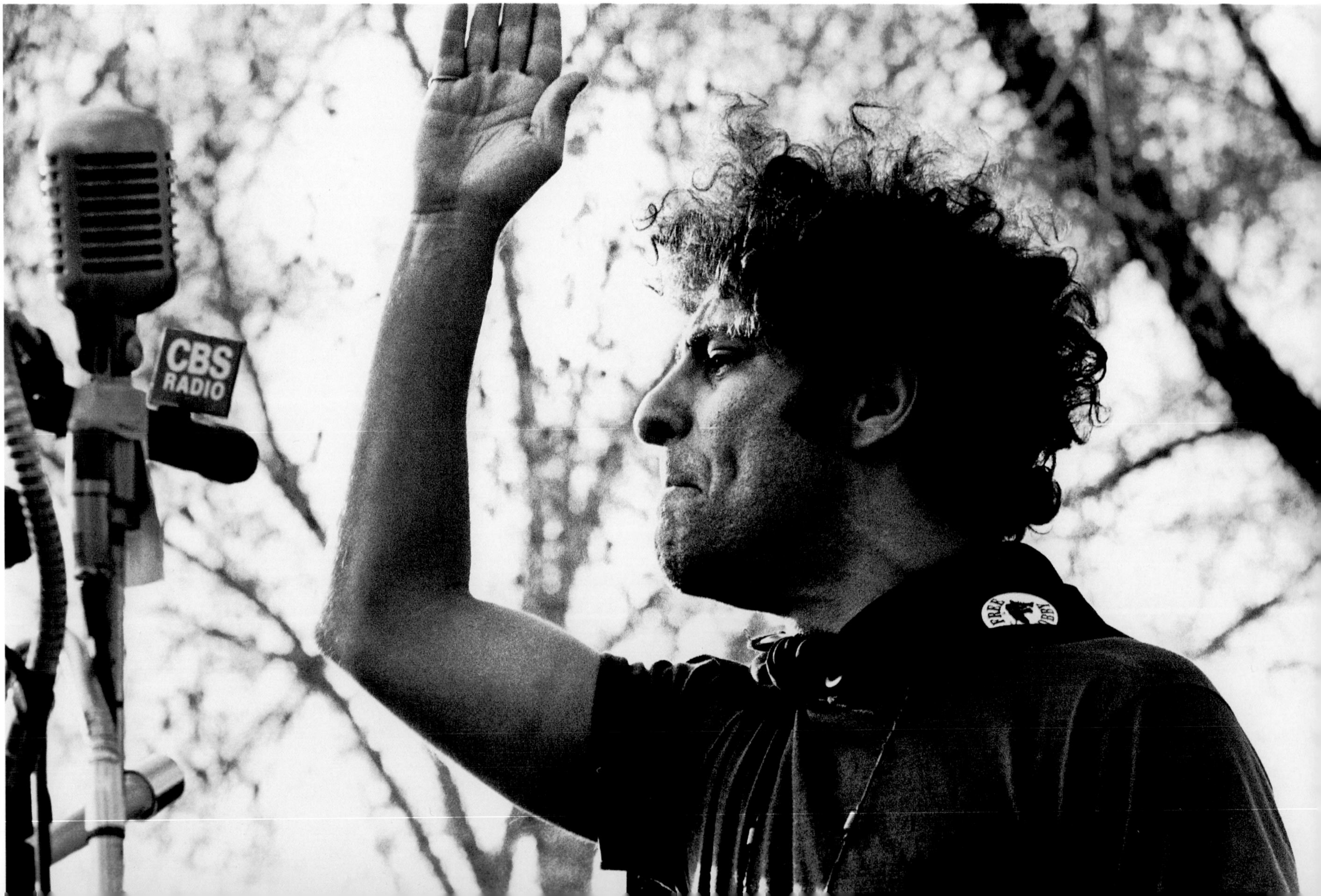
CBS
RADIO

Abbie Hoffman

Abbie Hoffman speaks at a rally in support of Black Panthers, New Haven, CT, May 1, 1970

Abbie Hoffman understood before anyone—except maybe Richard Nixon—the power of television in politics. No one knew how to use the media more effectively—and while having so much fun! Abbie was a scream, the funniest person I have ever known. I owe much of my knowledge of public relations to Abbie and his wild but effective antics. Who else would dream up running a pig for president or ask people to join a demonstration to levitate the Pentagon? Who else would open a store where everything was free? Abbie knew that a small creative band could attract as much attention as a million people in the streets—more, actually. He founded the so-called Yippies, or Youth International Party, as a total media myth. It didn't exist. It was only Jerry Rubin, Ed Sanders, Stu Albert and a few friends. But the *New York Times* and CBS reported their every move as if it was a party of thousands.

Abbie was fearless, having been beaten and arrested scores of times at protests during the Civil Rights movement. He was brilliant, dedicated and also crazy, so much so that he later killed himself during a horrible bout with manic depression.

As a kid growing up in New York, Abbie influenced me before we met. He'd go on the radio and call for people to demonstrate against the war at Grand Central Station, and we did—the police beat people to a pulp, throwing some through plate glass windows. On a lighter note, he asked people to come to the Lower East Side and literally clean up at a "sweep–in," providing brooms and mops. We scrubbed the streets.

My favorite time with Abbie was visiting him while he did his WBAI radio show. No ordinary program, the show consisted of Abbie offering live commentary about the *CBS Evening News* with Walter Cronkite while it aired on television. To Abbie, Walter ran the nation, and Abbie's goal was to insert antiwar politics into Walter's news.

But Abbie also had a dark side, driven by his mania. Once, he pulled out a knife at a press conference and stuck it into the table, while threatening retribution if a buddy wasn't released from prison. I watched him march up and down yelling "Off the Pig," which was not very smart. He was busted on a cocaine charge in 1973 in New York City, for selling to an undercover officer, and swore he was doing research about the drug world.

Abbie skipped bail and skipped town in February of '74 and went underground. One day many years later, I was having dinner at Jerry Rubin's apartment and was introduced to one Barry Freed and his wife Johanna. After about an hour, I figured out it was Abbie. His voice gave him away, despite the plastic surgery. His story was incredible—while underground he had worked to save the St. Lawrence River from environmentally destructive dredging by the Army Corps of Engineers. He had actually been photographed with New York senator Daniel P. Moynihan in his new identity, without being recognized.

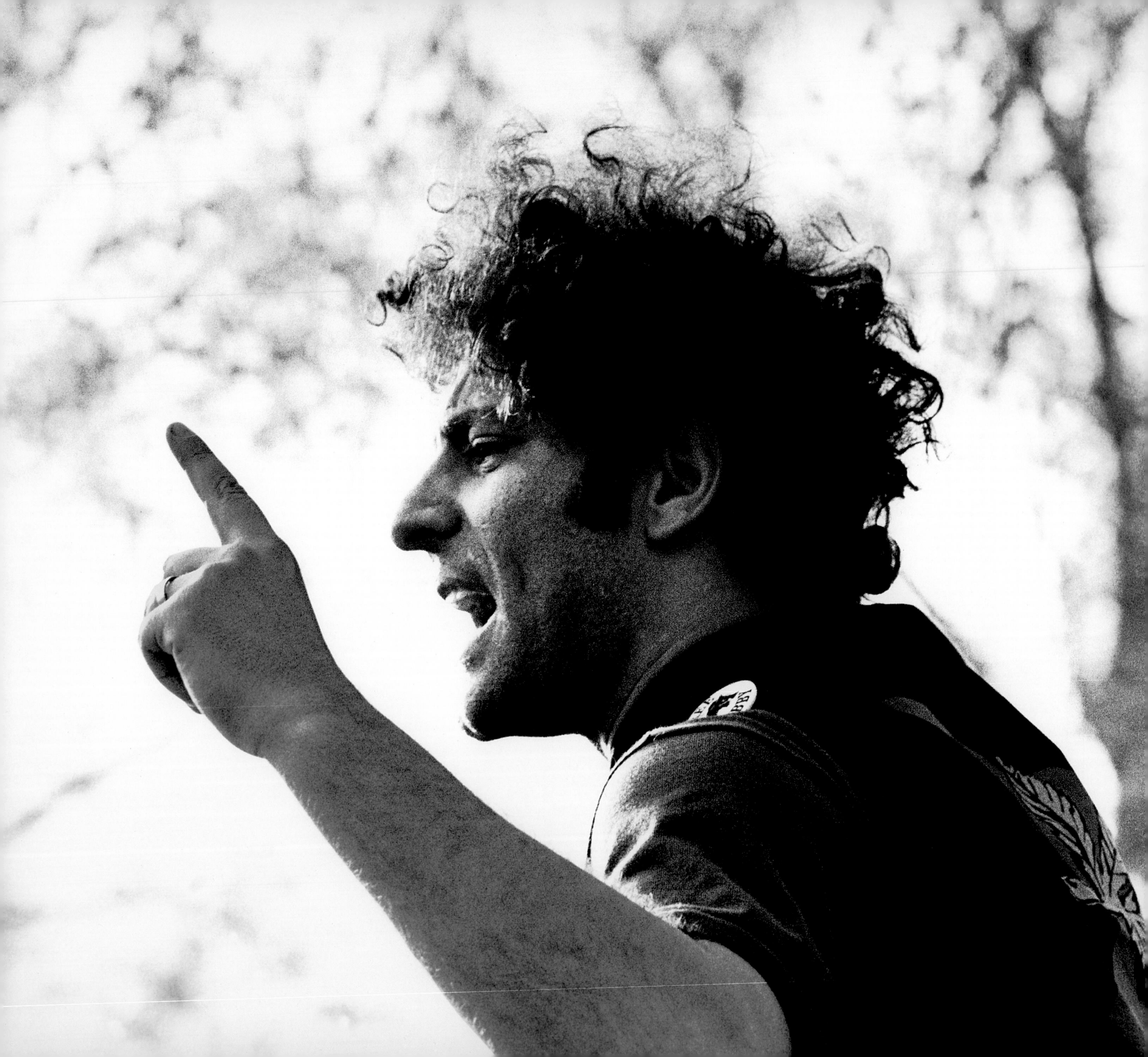

He told me he wanted to turn himself in and get back to activism. I agreed to help. One day I picked up Barbara Walters at her apartment and drove her to the airport. She didn't know where we were taking her or what Abbie had been doing. At the last minute, before boarding the Lear jet, she refused to come with us unless we told her where we were taking her. Who could blame her? But we couldn't tell her until the plane was off the ground, without risking her crew calling the FBI and revealing Abbie's whereabouts. Had he been caught, instead of turning himself in voluntarily, Abbie would have served a long term in prison. I held fast, and Barbara decided to come along anyway and take the risk. She got a great story and Abbie got a light sentence. I miss him to this day.

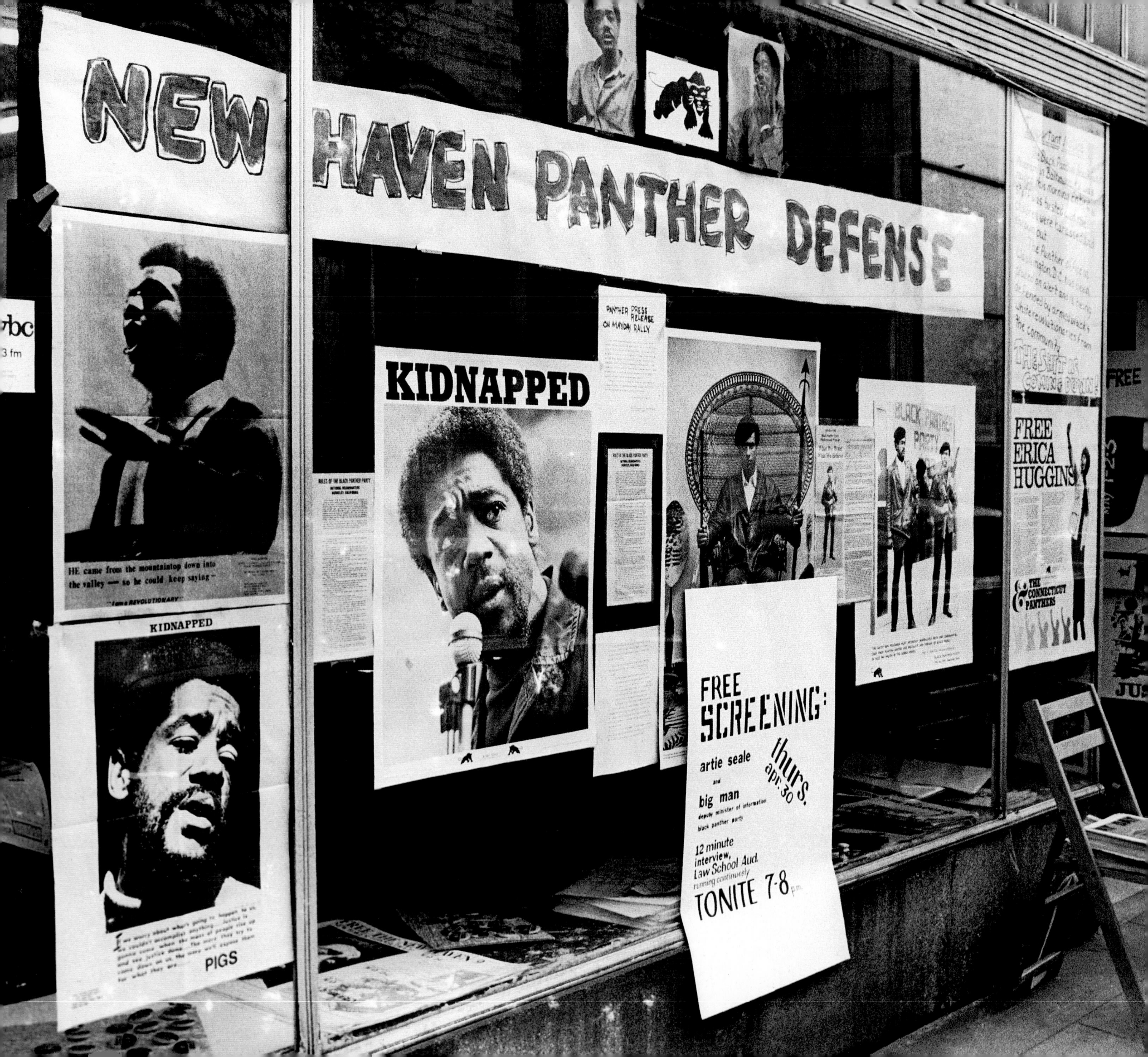
NEW HAVEN PANTHER DEFENSE
KIDNAPPED
HE came from the mountaintop down into the valley — so he could keep saying —
KIDNAPPED
PIGS
PANTHER PRESS RELEASE ON MAYDAY RALLY
BLACK PANTHER PARTY
FREE ERICA HUGGINS
& THE CONNECTICUT PANTHERS
FREE SCREENING:
artie seale
and
big man
deputy minister of information
black panther party
thurs. apr. 30
12 minute interview, Law School Aud.
running continuously
TONITE 7-8 p.m.

2

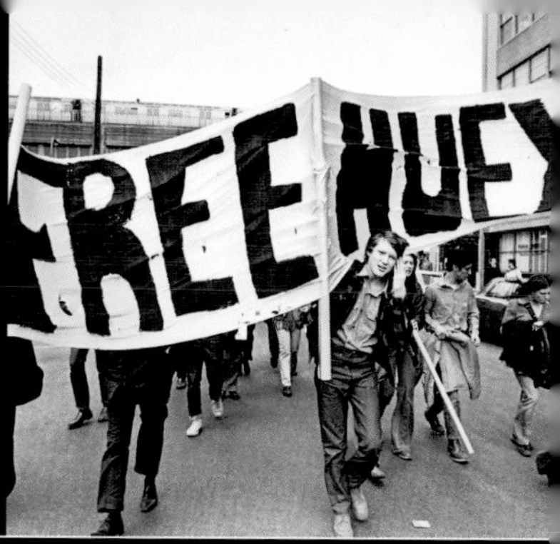

BLACK PANTHERS

Ultimate Justice

Black Panther demonstration at the New York City courthouse in support of the "Panther 21" defendants, April 11, 1969

This photo of a Black Panther Party demonstration in 1969, outside the New York City courthouse, was widely published at the time. The protest, during the trial of the so–called "Panther 21," was in support of 21 Black Panthers arrested and charged with conspiracy to blow up the New York Botanical Gardens and various New York department stores, subways and police stations—156 counts in all. After a lengthy trial but only 45 minutes of jury deliberation, everyone was acquitted on all counts.

The inscription on the courthouse wall, "The Ultimate Justice of the People," crystallized the ideas and images of the Panthers that many, including myself, held at the time. Excerpted from Lincoln's first Inaugural Address in 1860, the full quotation reads: "Why should there be no patient confidence in the ultimate justice of the people? Is there any better, or equal, hope in the world?" In some ways, the Panthers picked up that thread of Lincoln's and made it part of their culture and ideology.

I met some of the leaders and members of the Black Panther Party through Elbert "Big Man" Howard, the editor of *The Black Panther* newspaper. Soon I was spending time with Huey P. Newton, Bobby Seale, David Hilliard, and other leaders of the Party, with access to photograph them in unusually relaxed and informal situations.

The Panthers were disciplined, organized, and provided true social services to the poor, including the famous "Free Breakfast" program for children. They first came to prominence in Berkeley, California, where they walked the streets with rifles to protect the Black community from police brutality. The image of black men holding guns in self–defense became a media sensation and the police and FBI set out to destroy them using subversive tactics such as the infamous COINTELPRO, or Counter–Intelligence Program. The government systematically undermined the effectiveness of the Black Panther Party, at times through actual assassination, as has been well documented, but also through false charges, the use of agent provocateurs, planting of phony evidence, creating splits within the leadership and many other means.

Despite this gross government abuse, the Panthers also had inherent flaws—there were thugs among them and women were treated horribly. (Elaine Brown, a former Panther leader, has written extensively about the darker side of the Party.) Huey P. Newton was eventually convicted of murder and many left the Party disillusioned. Many of their admirers romanticized their platform and behaviors as well as the images they projected.

The Panthers put up with the stress of the U.S. government trying to kill and destroy them, so how many of their problems were due to Hoover's murderous and relentless attacks may never be known.

What is known is that the Panthers left their imprint on American culture with the enduring images of Black Power and individual dignity confronting intimidation and institutional racism.

Previous Page: Office of the New Haven chapter of the Black Panther Party, New Haven, CT, April 30, 1970

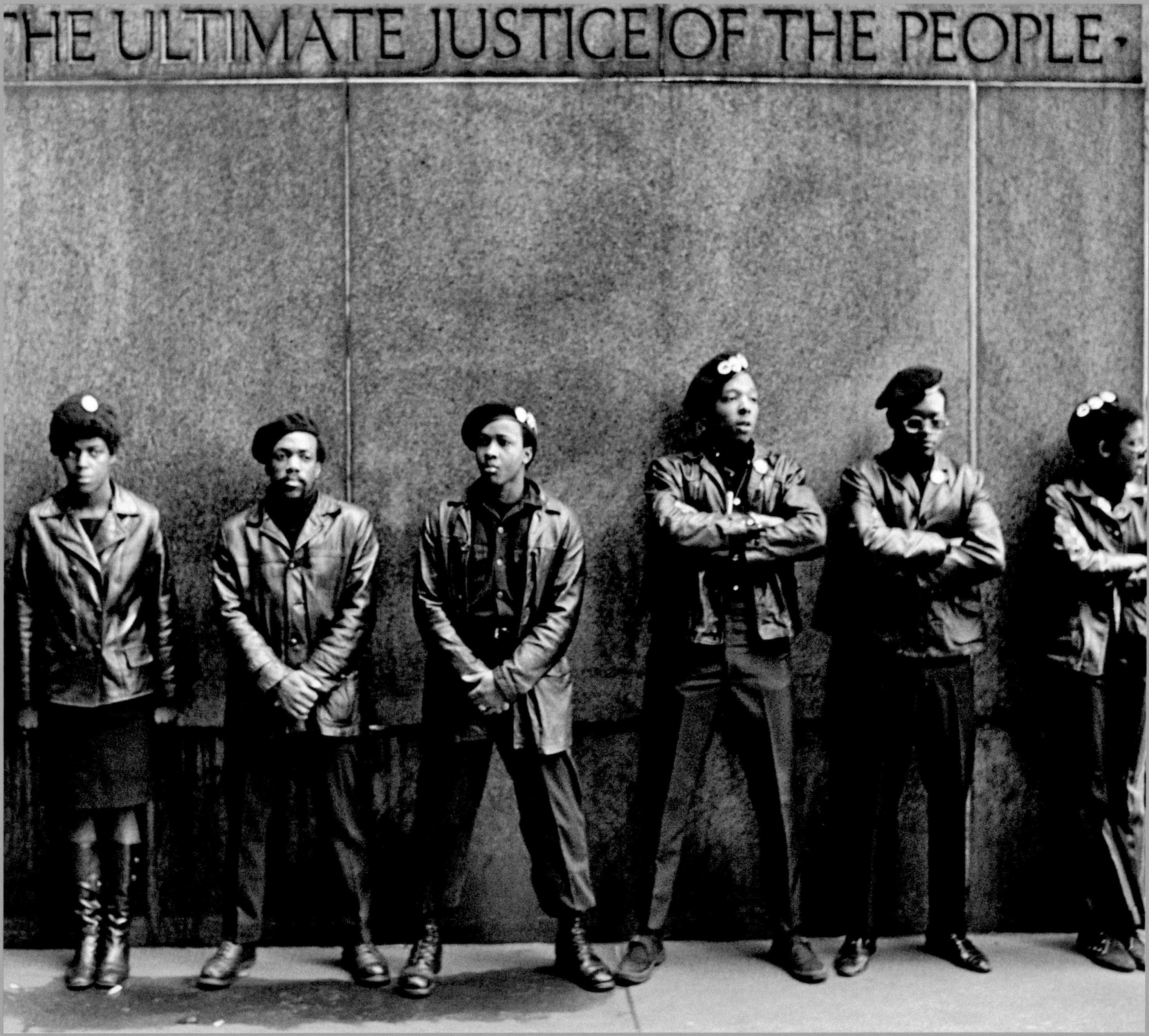
THE ULTIMATE JUSTICE OF THE PEOPLE

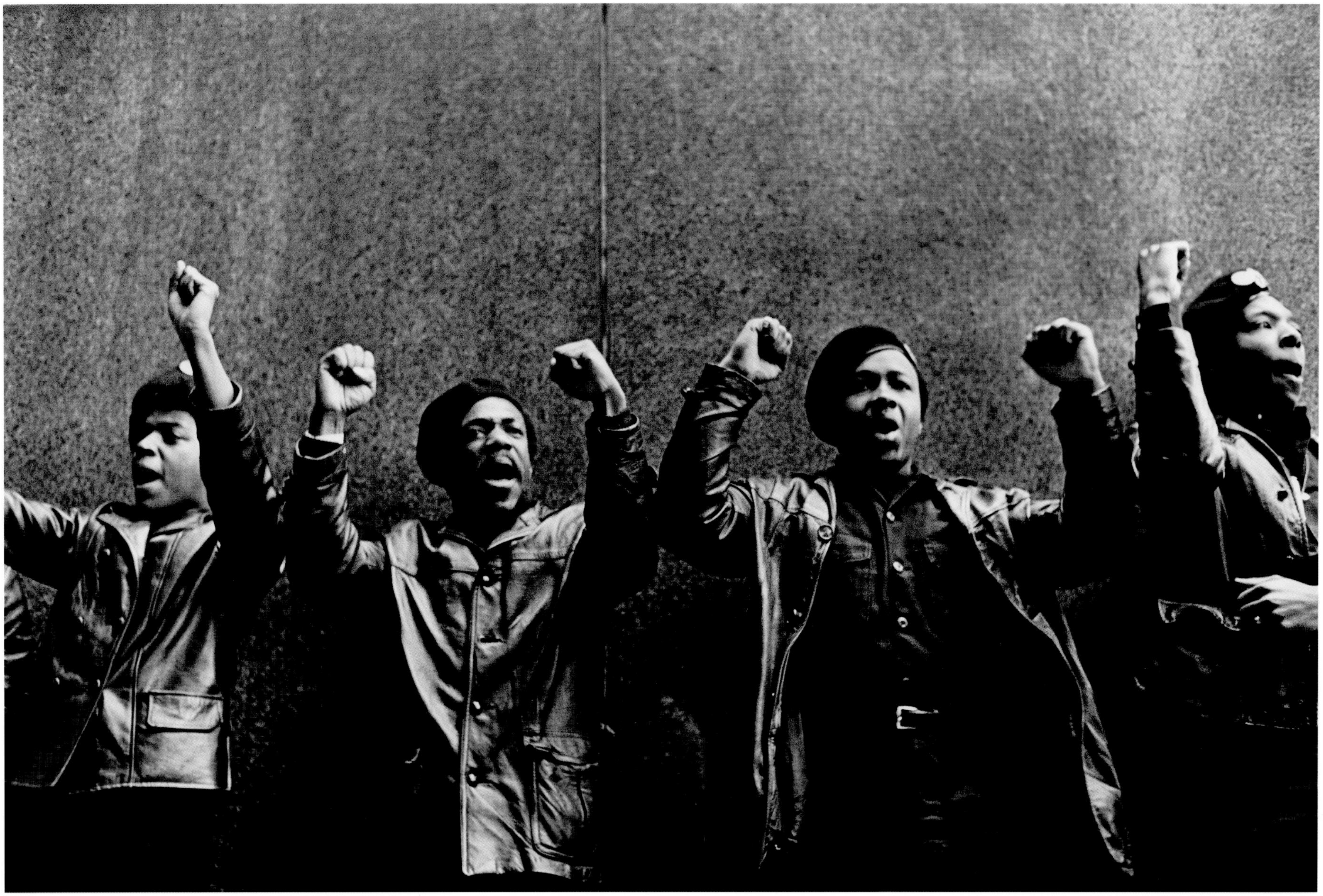

Black Panther Demonstration, New York City, April 11, 1969

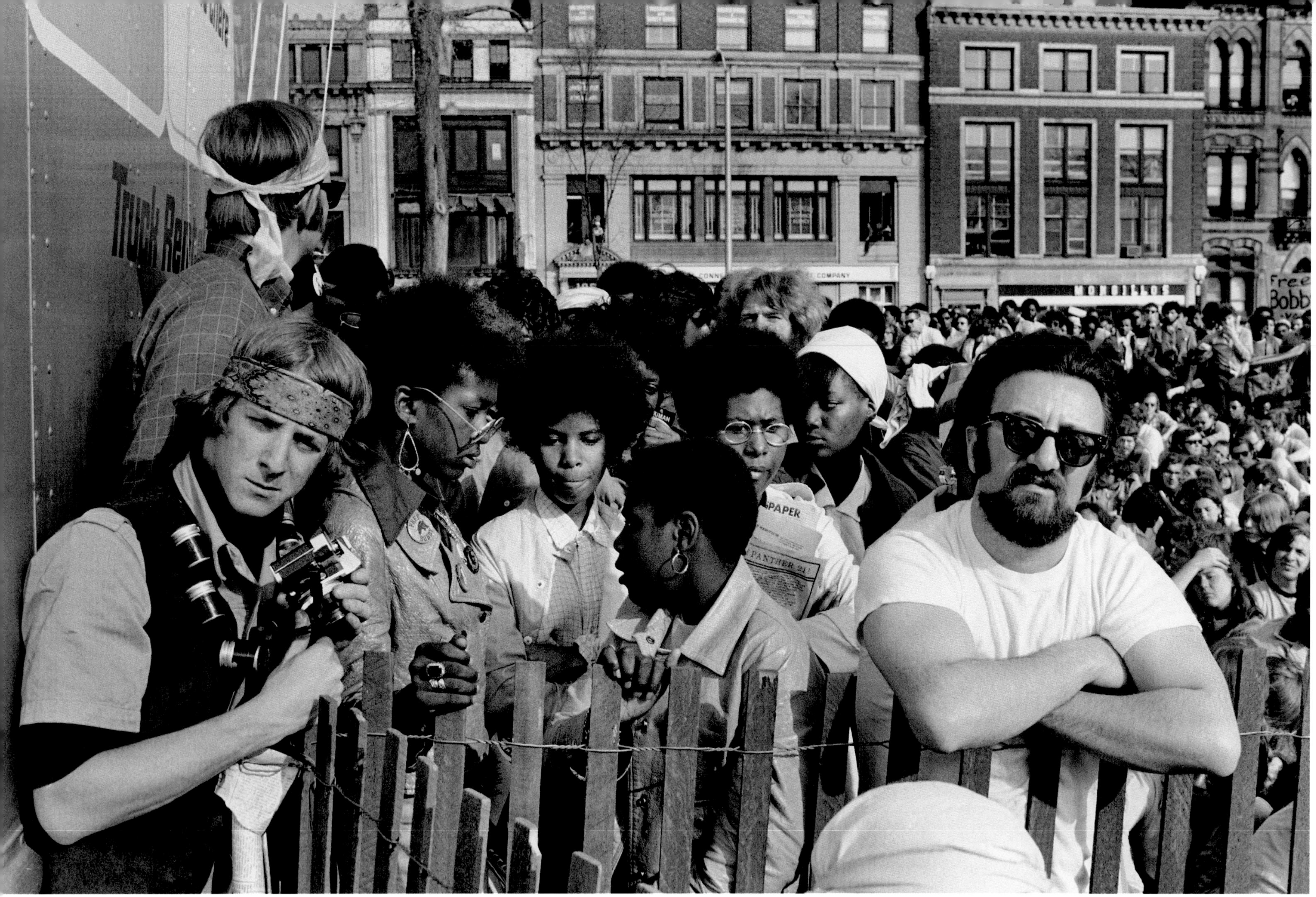
COMPANY
PANTHER 21

Crowd at a rally for the Black Panther Party
New Haven, CT, May 1-2, 1970

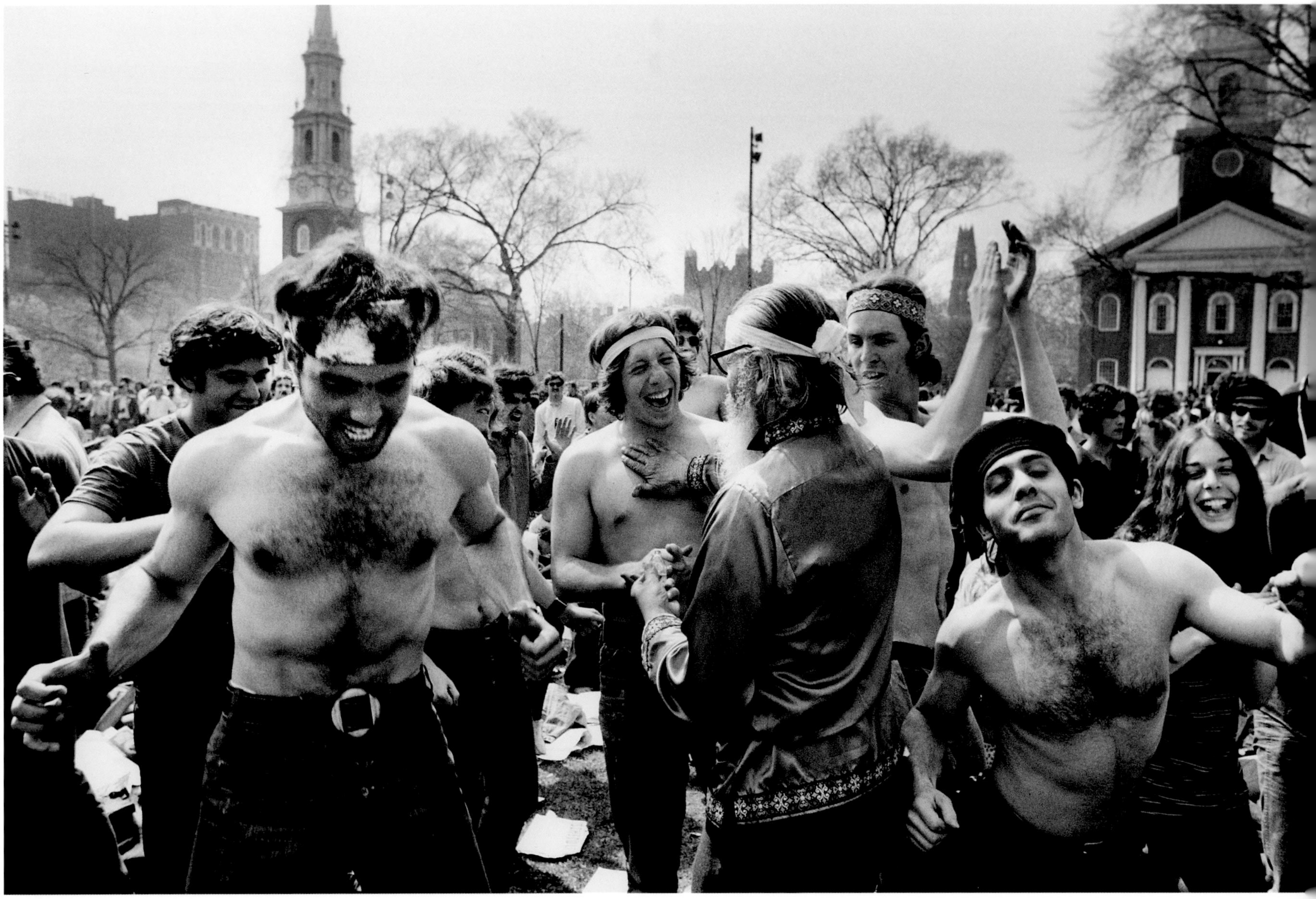

A crowd dances at a rally to free Black Panther Party Chairman Bobby Seale, New Haven Panther Party leader Ericka Huggins and other members of the Black Panther Party, after their arrest on murder charges, New Haven, CT, May 1, 1970

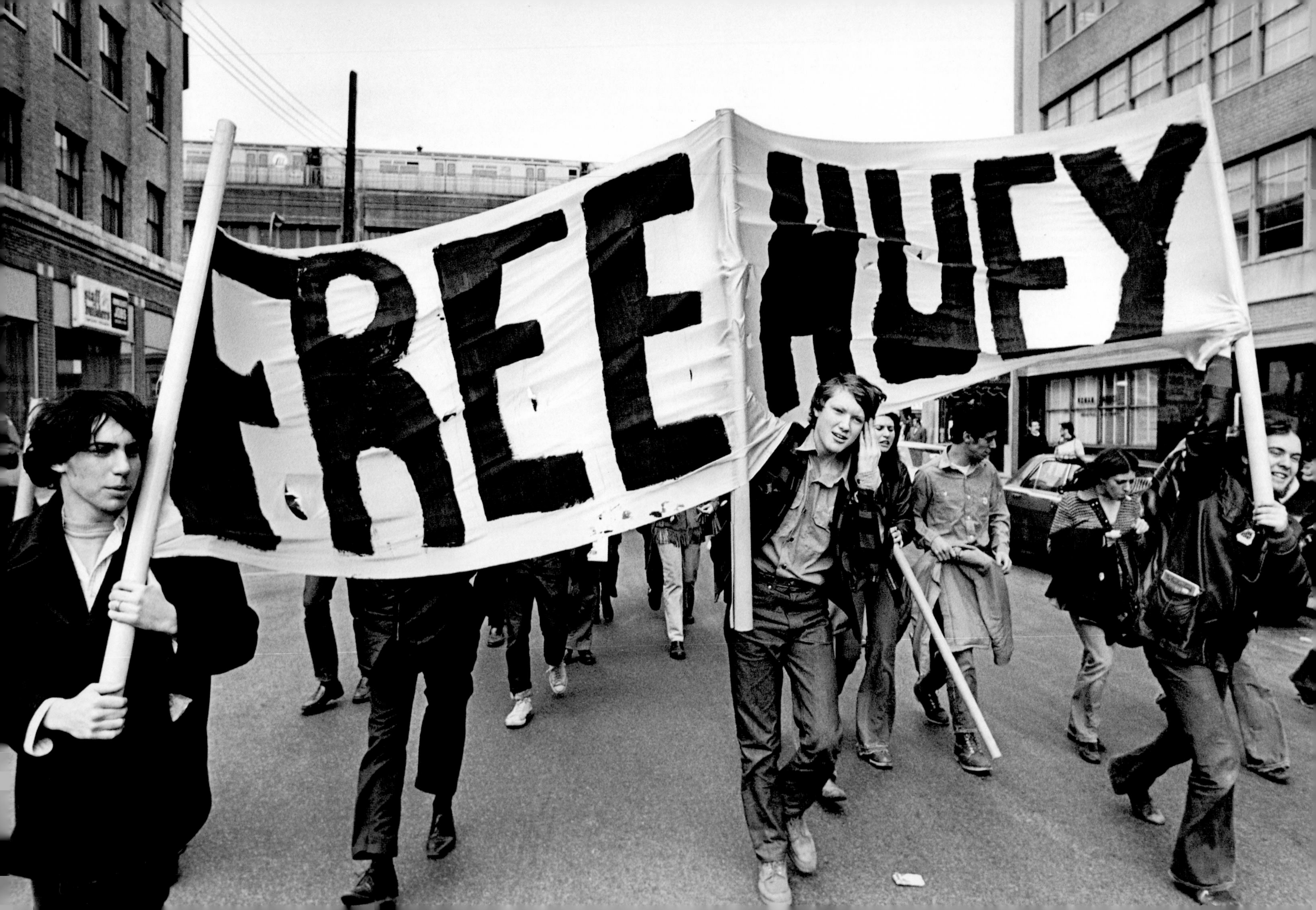
REE HUEY

The famous poster of Huey P. Newton and Bobby Seale holding up guns adorned walls throughout the 60s. Huey was charismatic, handsome and brilliant. The police kept trying to imprison or kill him with a series of charges that were later dropped or resulted in acquittals. At one point, he fled to Cuba for asylum. Like many of his peers, he finished high school illiterate. Somehow he managed to teach himself to read and shortly thereafter enrolled in Oakland's Merritt College. By founding the Black Panther Party with Seale, a schoolmate, he not only helped Black Americans assert their dignity in the face of police harassment, he also underscored their inherent humanity to the rest of the world. He went on to start neighborhood school programs where children were taught about black power and worked to shift the Panthers' focus to community service. Along with his party comrades, his voice and being inspired a generation to fight against racism. Sadly, Huey turned to hard drugs later in his life and was convicted of embezzlement from one of the Panther programs to support his habit. A drug dealer killed him in 1989.

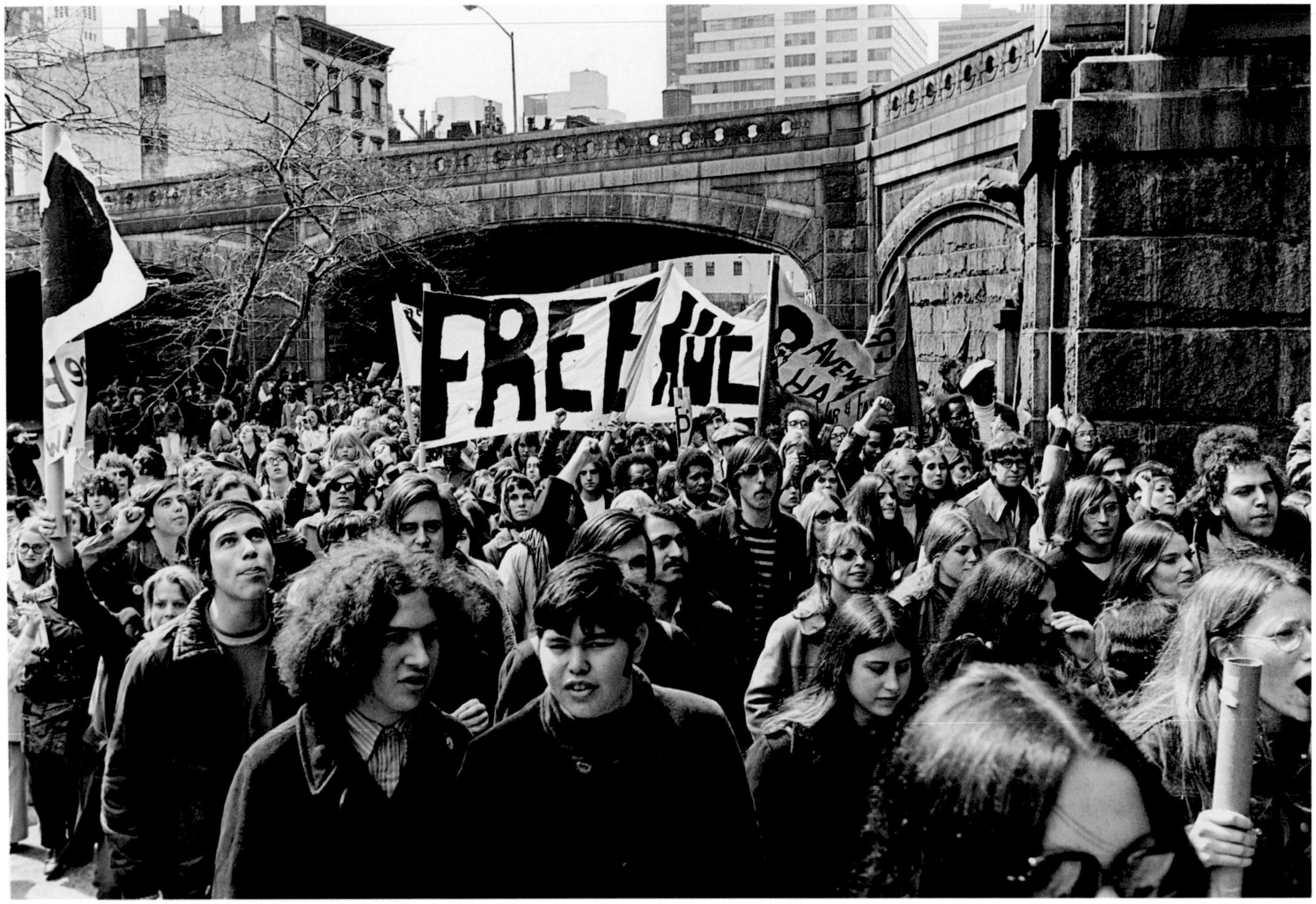
FREE

Demonstrators march in support of the Black Panther Party, New York City, April 4, 1970

Left to right: Black Panther Party lawyer Charles Garry, Panther leader Elaine Brown and Panther Minister of Defense Huey P. Newton at Yale University, New Haven, CT.

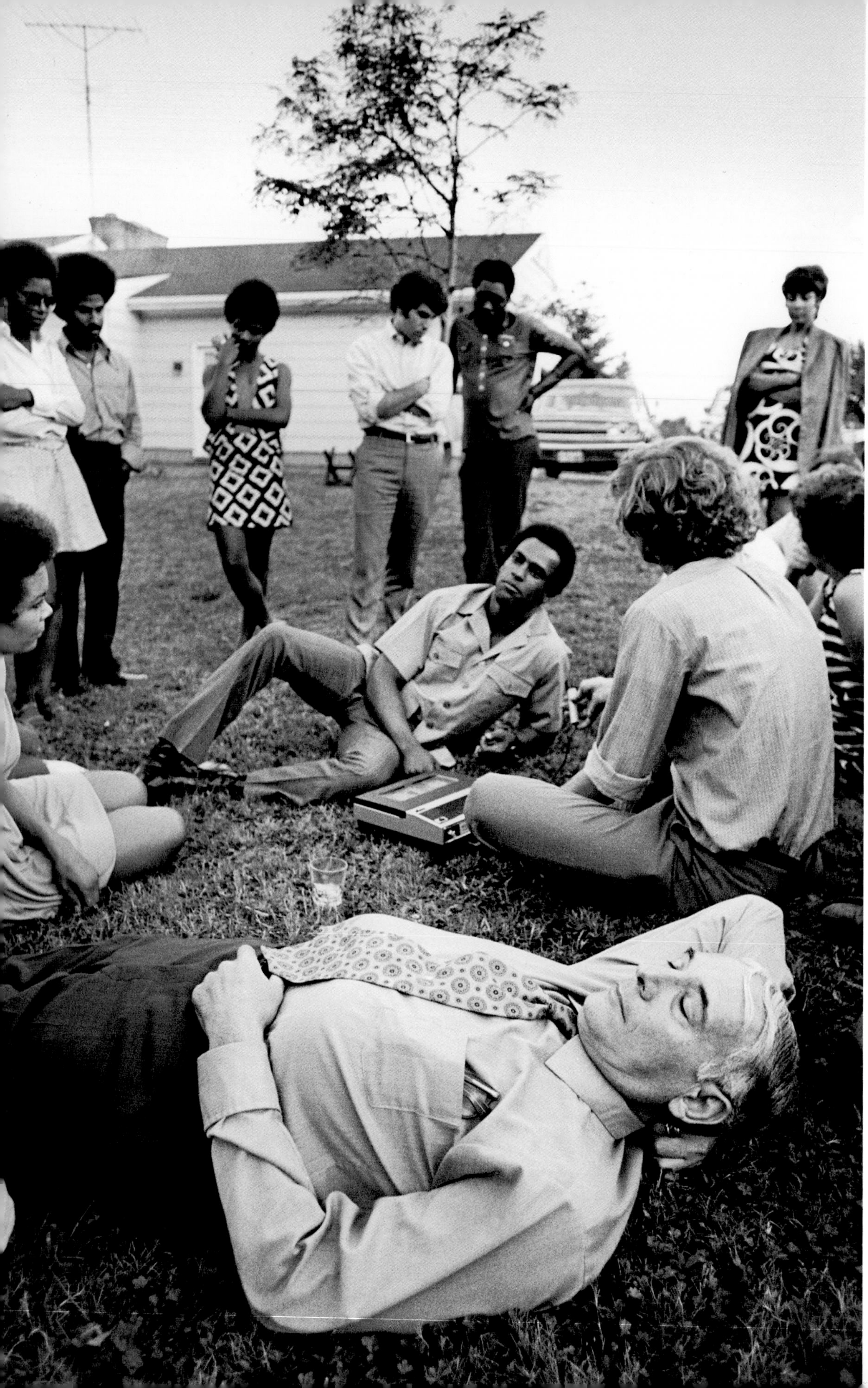

Left and Right: Black Panther lawyer Charles Garry rests on the grass while Minister of Defense Huey P. Newton does an interview with Liberation News Service, Yale University, New Haven, CT

Huey P. Newton speaks during the Revolutionary People's Party
Constitutional Convention, Philadelphia, PA, September 7–9, 1970

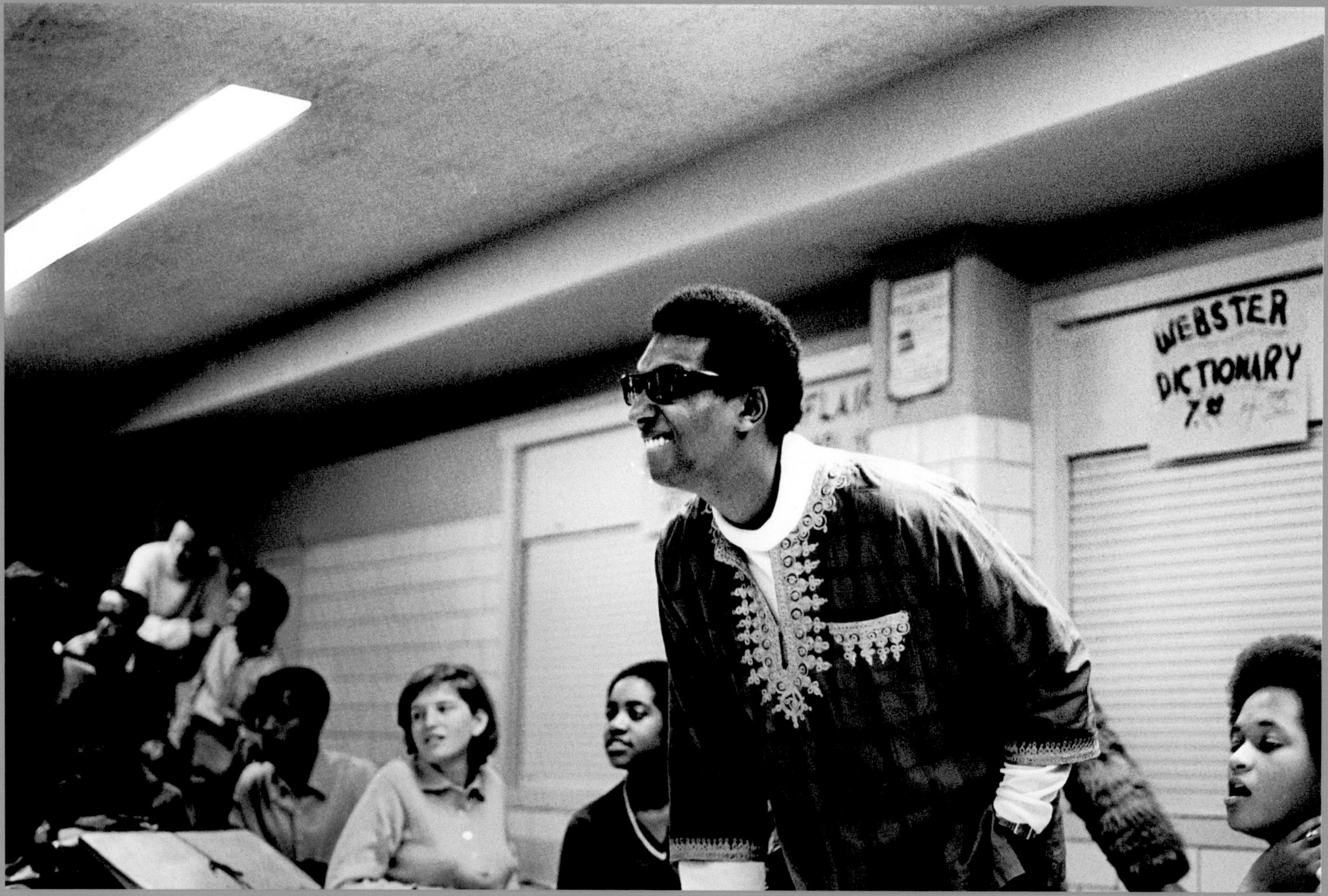
WEBSTER
DICTIONARY

Stokely Carmichael speaks at his (and David Fenton's) alma mater,
Bronx Science High School, New York City, December 1968

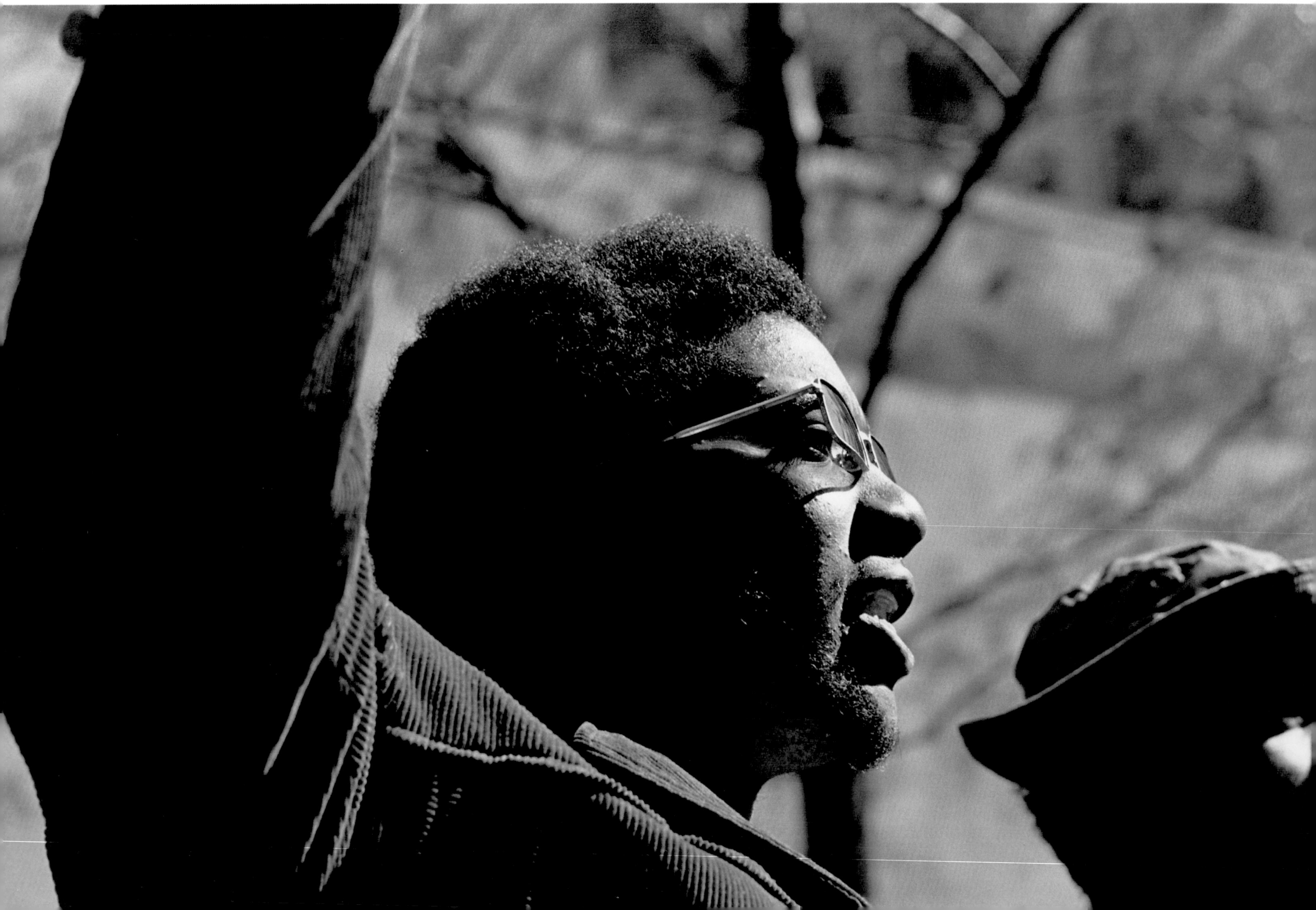

Fred Hampton

Fred Hampton speaks at the Days of Rage, Chicago, IL, October 11, 1969

The FBI murdered Black Panther Fred Hampton while he slept. This is not an inflammatory statement—it's a fact. Fred was only 21 years old when he was assassinated. He was the head of the Panther's Chicago chapter. I remember him as a spellbinding orator. The FBI decided to "neutralize" him (their word), and put an informant, William O'Neal, into his immediate entourage. On the night of December 3, 1969, O'Neal put a sleeping pill into Hampton's drink and at 4:45 am, the FBI and police stormed his apartment, spraying automatic gunfire into Hampton's bedroom. After pushing into his room, they fired two shots point blank into his head. One of the greatest potential black leaders was dead.

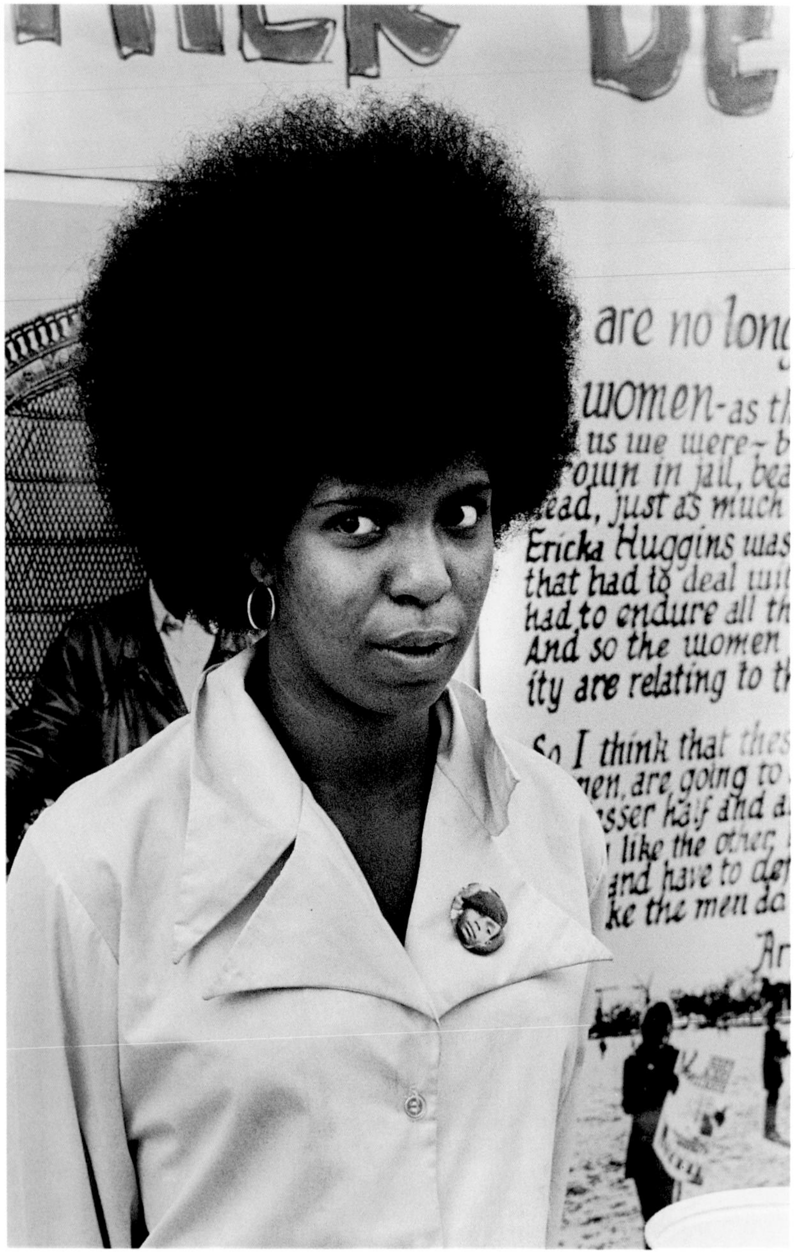
are no
women-as
just as much
Ericka Huggins
that had to deal
had to endure all
And so the women
are relating to
So I think that
are going to
like the other
and have to
the men do

A woman at a Black Panther rally, New Haven, CT, May 1–2, 1970

Black Panther Minister of Information Eldridge Cleaver, New York City, October 17, 1968

Black Panther Party Chairman Bobby Seale (left) and Panther Party Chief of Staff David Hilliard hold a press conference outside Panther Party headquarters, Oakland, CA, August, 1969

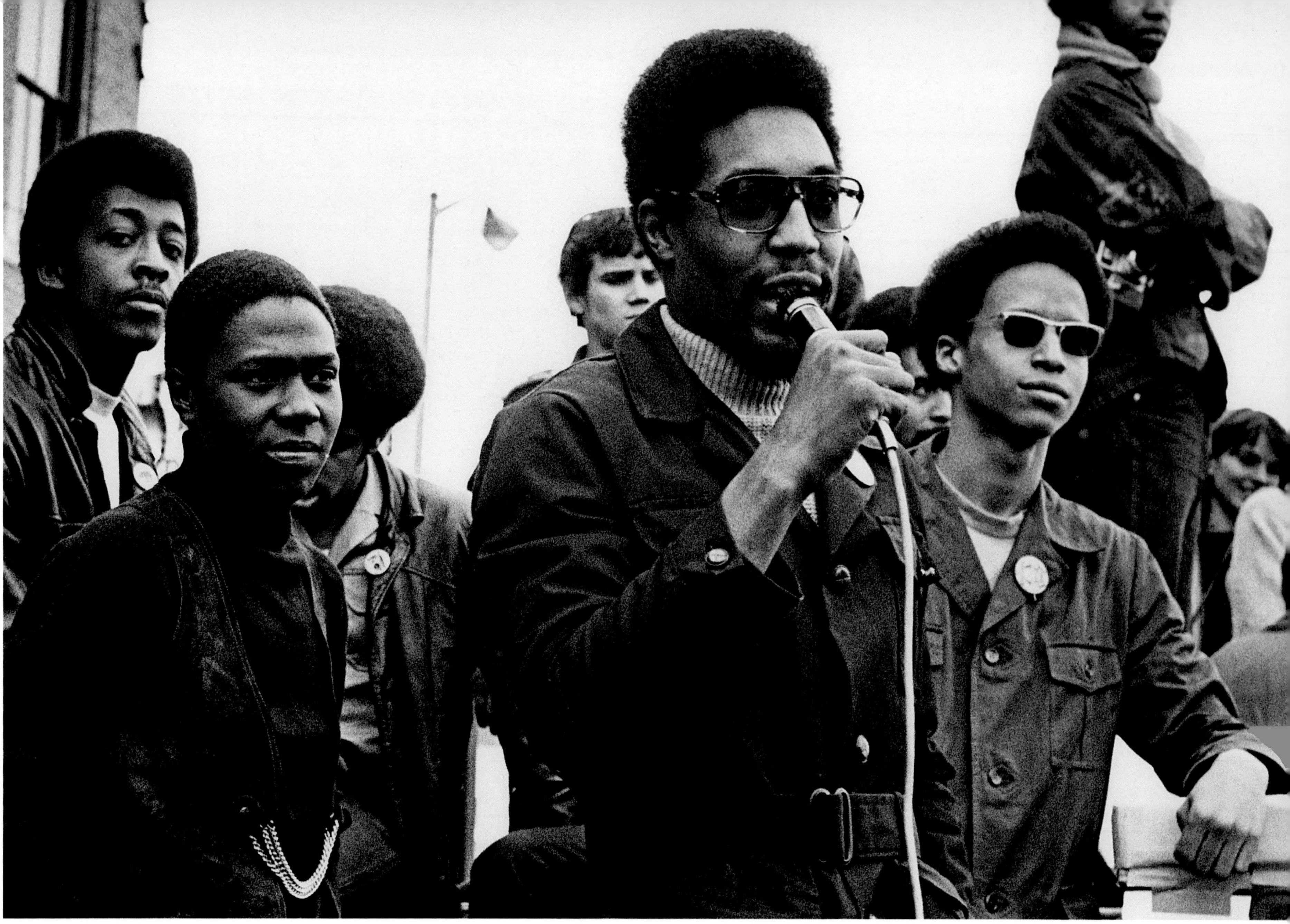

Black Panther Dhoruba Bin–Wahad, a co–defendant in the Panther 21 case, speaks at a rally in support of the Panther 21. Co–defendants Afeni Shakur (mother of Tupac Shakur) and Jamal Joseph stand to his left and right. New York City, April 4, 1970

Jamal Joseph, the youngest co–defendant in the Panther 21 case, New York City, June 18, 1970

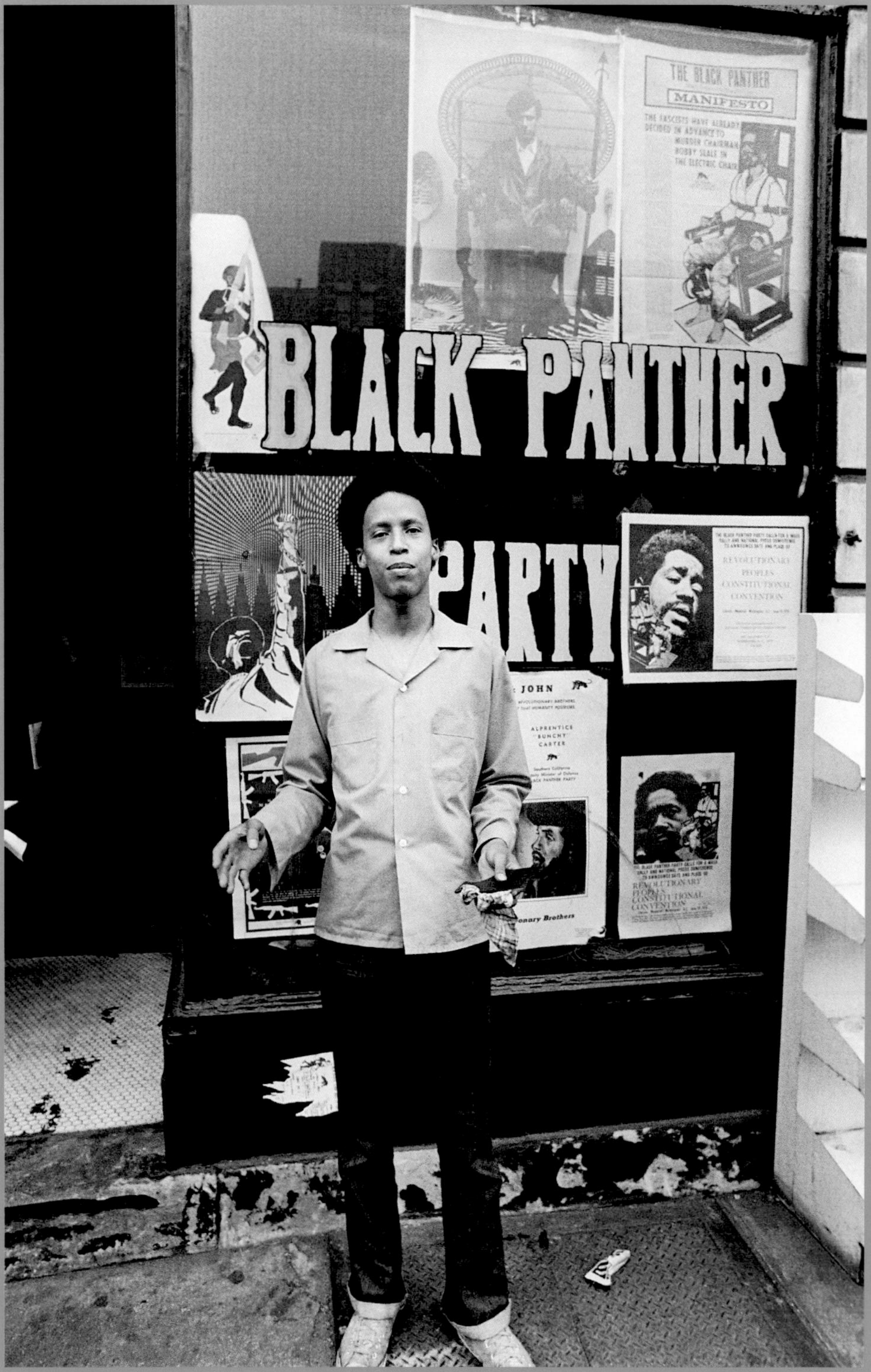
THE BLACK PANTHER
MANIFESTO
THE FASCISTS HAVE ALREADY DECIDED IN ADVANCE TO MURDER CHAIRMAN BOBBY SEALE IN THE ELECTRIC CHAIR
BLACK PANTHER
PARTY
REVOLUTIONARY PEOPLES CONSTITUTIONAL CONVENTION

Jamal Joseph at Black Panther Party headquarters in Harlem, NY, June 18, 1970

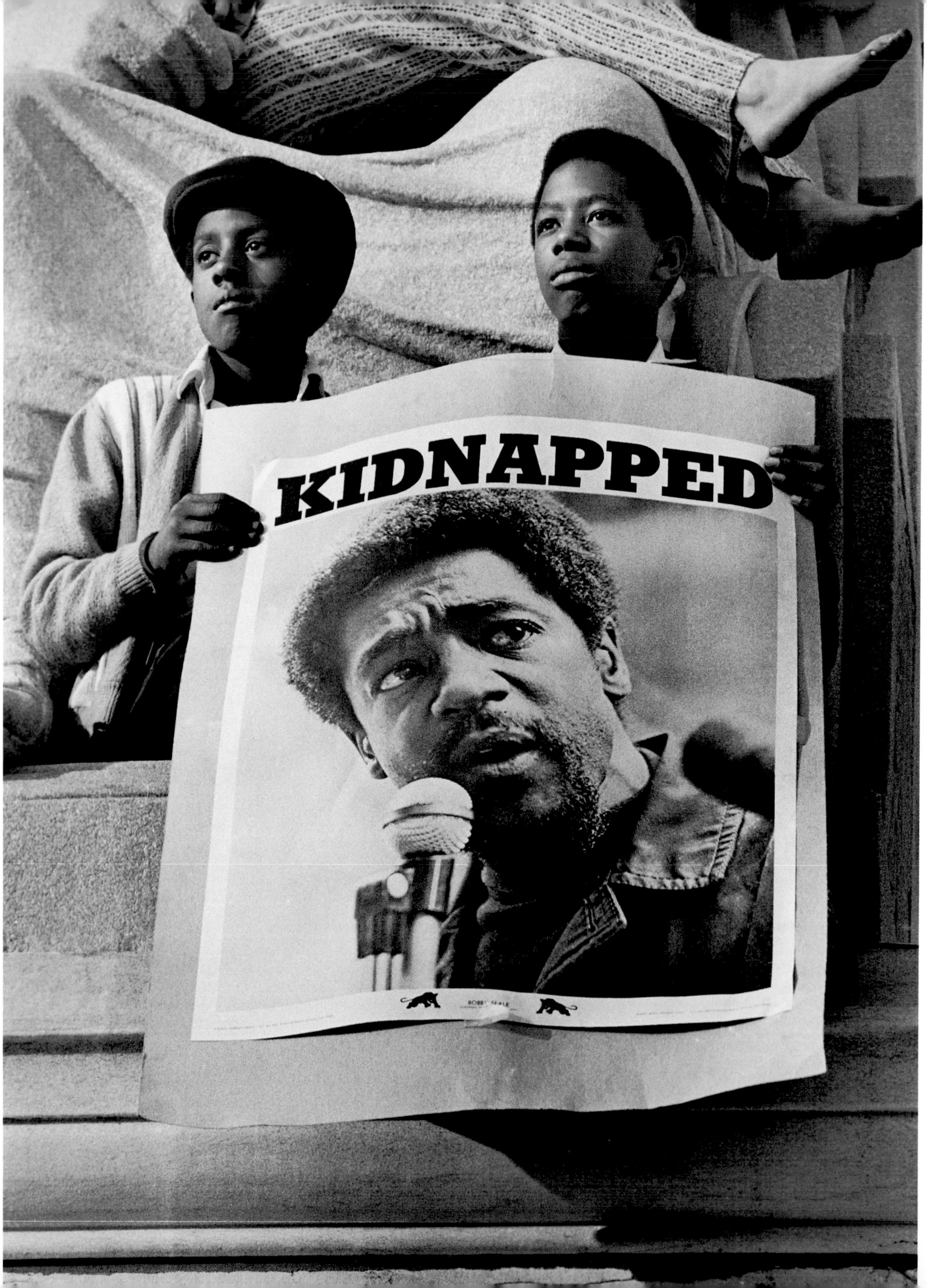
KIDNAPPED
BOBBY

Kidnapped in New Haven

Two boys at a rally in support of Black Panther Party Chairman Bobby Seale and other Panthers, New Haven, CT, May 1, 1970

Yale University was the site of one of the largest demonstrations ever held on behalf of the Black Panther Party. It was part political protest, part countercultural festival and went on for two days. Party Chairman Bobby Seale had been arrested and imprisoned without bond on charges of kidnapping and murdering a police informant, along with twelve other members of the New Haven Panther chapter. With no physical evidence, except that he had coincidentally been in New Haven the night before the murders (giving a speech at Yale), Seale was charged.

This was just after Fred Hampton's murder by the FBI and Seale's gagging during the Chicago 7 conspiracy trial. The Yale campus erupted. The entire student body voted to strike in support of the Panthers and most of the faculty agreed. The president of Yale, Kingman Brewster, declared his support for the Panthers, which contributed to his eventually being fired. The National Guard was called out and used so much tear gas in the streets that all the daffodils blooming around the campus died.

Many celebrity activists turned out for the rally, including Dr. Benjamin Spock, French writer Jean Genet, poet Allen Ginsberg and several of the Chicago 7 defendants including Abbie Hoffman, Jerry Rubin, David Dellinger and Tom Hayden. Hillary Rodham Clinton, then a Yale Law School student, monitored the trial for fairness along with other law students, on behalf of the ACLU.

While they were in jail, I wrote to Seale and Panther Ericka Huggins to contribute two introductions to my book, the original *Shots: Photographs from the Underground Press*. They agreed and wrote from prison.

Seale remained in prison until he and Huggins were acquitted on all charges in May of 1971. The police had over–reached against the Panther leadership again. The three Panthers who confessed to the murder of the informant were later convicted.

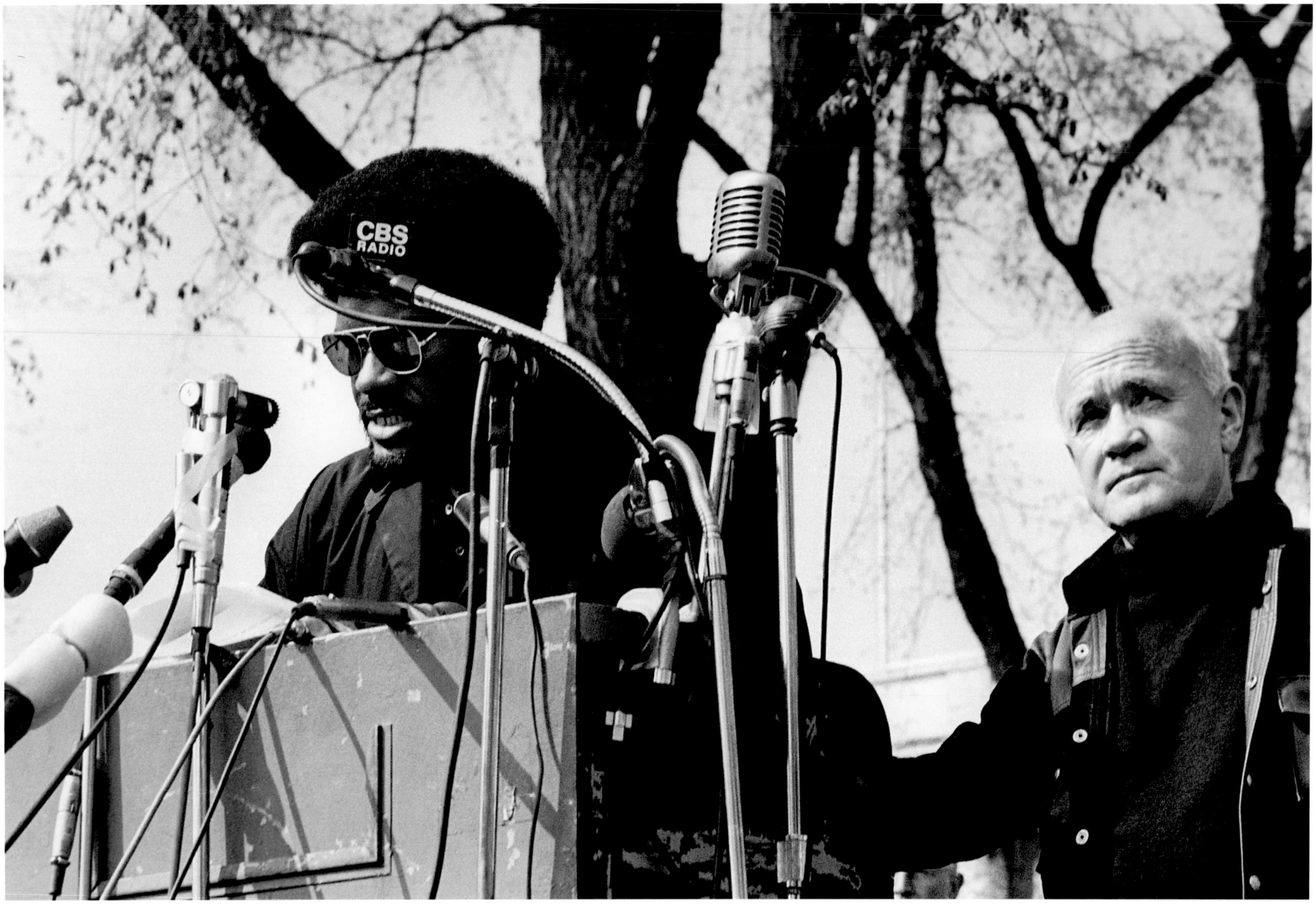
CBS
RADIO

Elbert "Big Man" Howard, Deputy Minister of Information for the Black Panther Party, and French writer Jean Genet at a rally in support of the Black Panthers, New Haven, CT, May 1–2, 1970

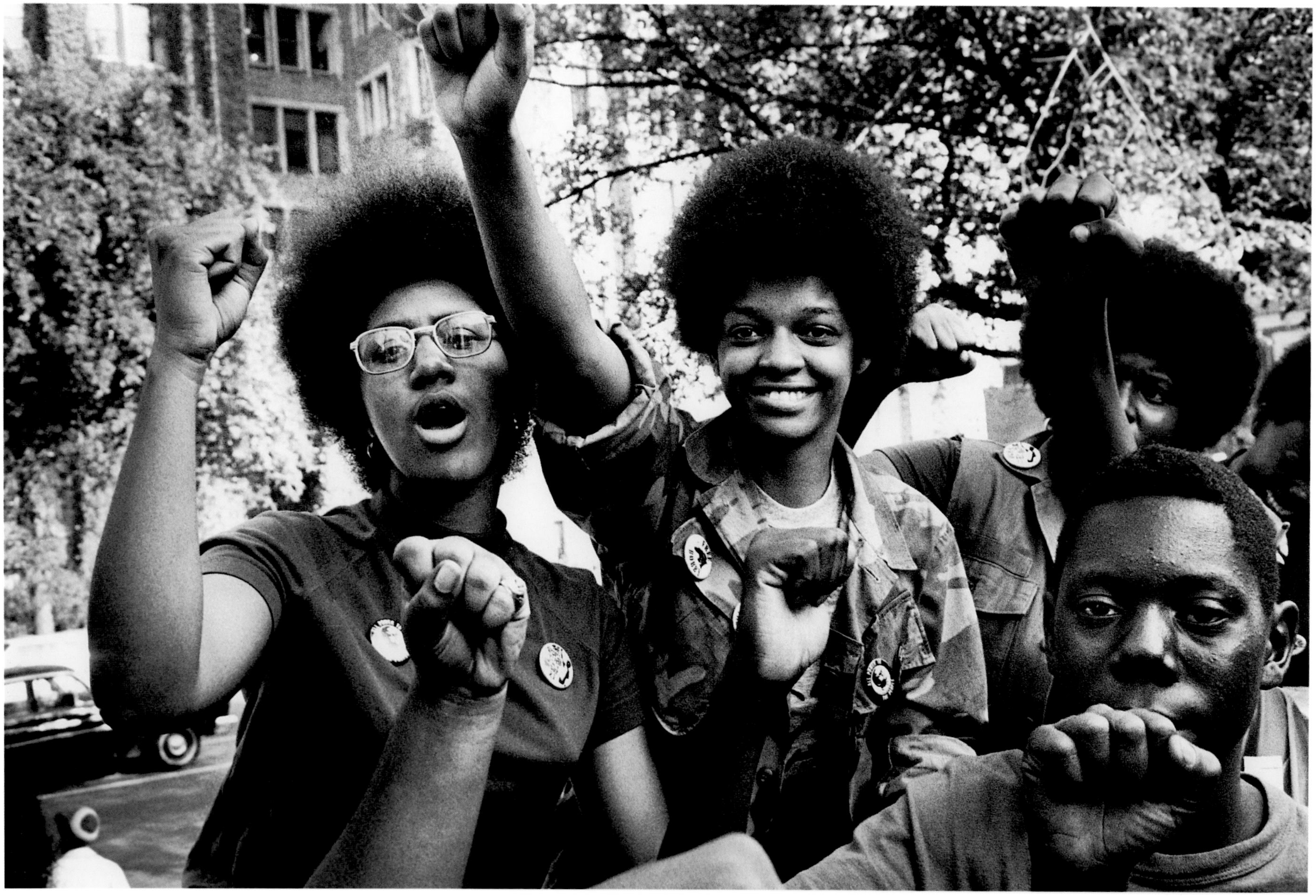

Attendees of the Revolutionary People's Party Constitutional Convention, a Black Panther–sponsored event to further coalition among activist groups, Philadelphia, PA, September 7–9, 1970

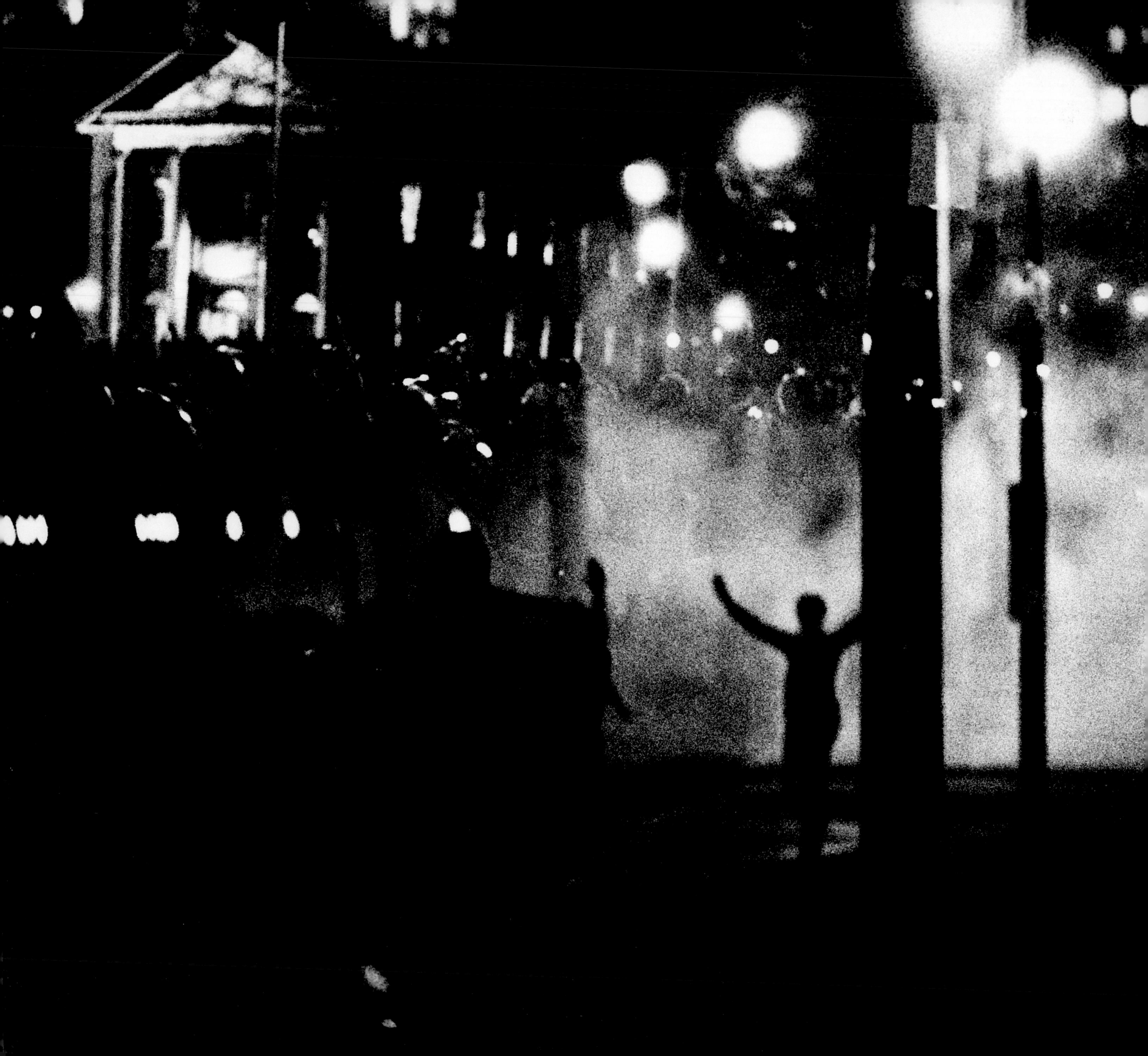

*A protestor runs through tear gas during demonstrations for the
Black Panther Party, New Haven, CT, May 2, 1970*

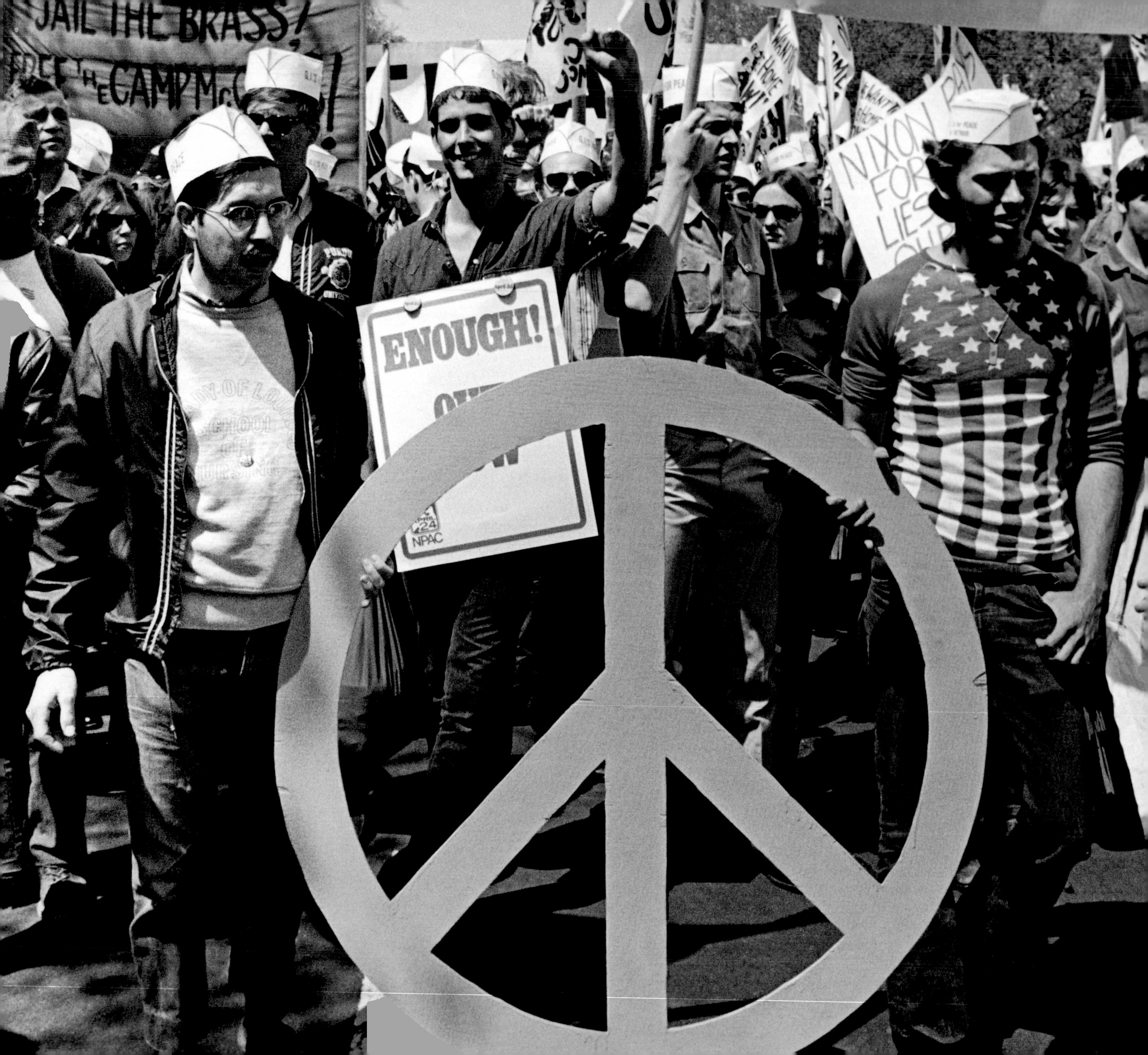

JAIL THE BRASS!
ENOUGH!
NPAC
NIXON

PROTESTS, RALLIES
& RIOTS

SDS

Members of Students for a Democratic Society (SDS) and the Progressive Labor Party (a small faction within SDS) caucus at the annual SDS Convention before their official split. Chicago, IL, June 18–22, 1969

Students for a Democratic Society (SDS) served as the backbone of much of the antiwar movement. This photograph was taken at their June 1969 convention in Chicago, where a crazy communist faction, the Progressive Labor Party, was booted out of SDS. I remember these dogmatic crazies waving Mao's Little Red Book in unison as they chanted slogans. It was my first experience of left wing sectarianism. The leadership of SDS went to Bernardine Dohrn, pictured addressing the convention on the next page. She was deeply charismatic, and soon after took the Weatherman faction underground to plant bombs to protest the war. See? The war made everybody crazy.

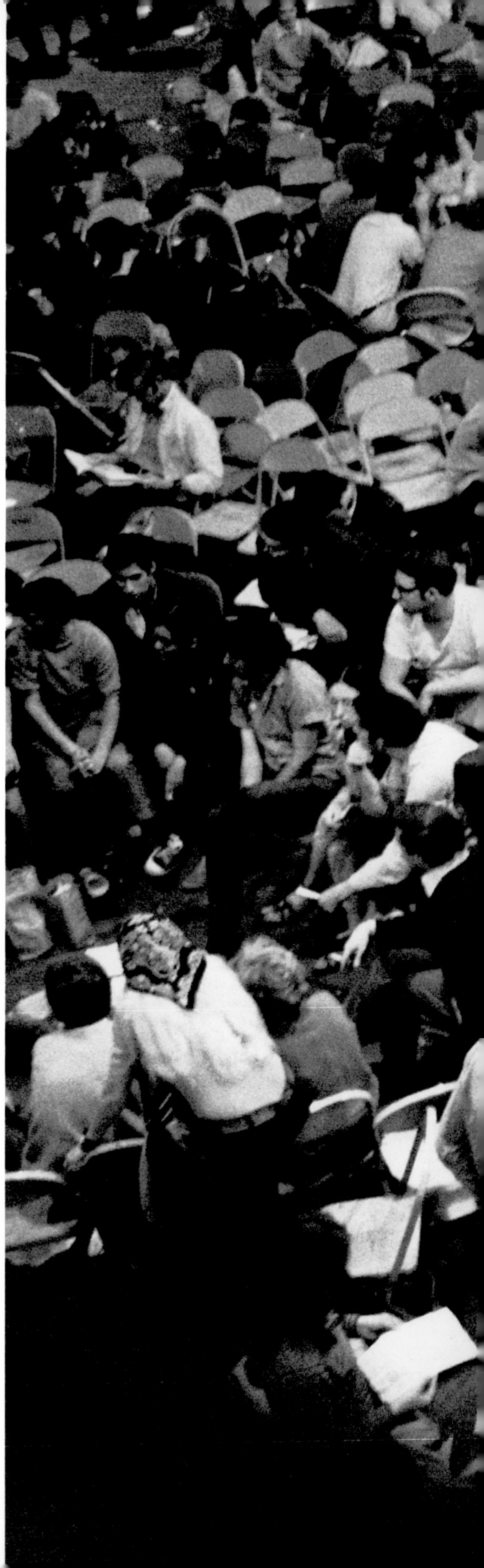

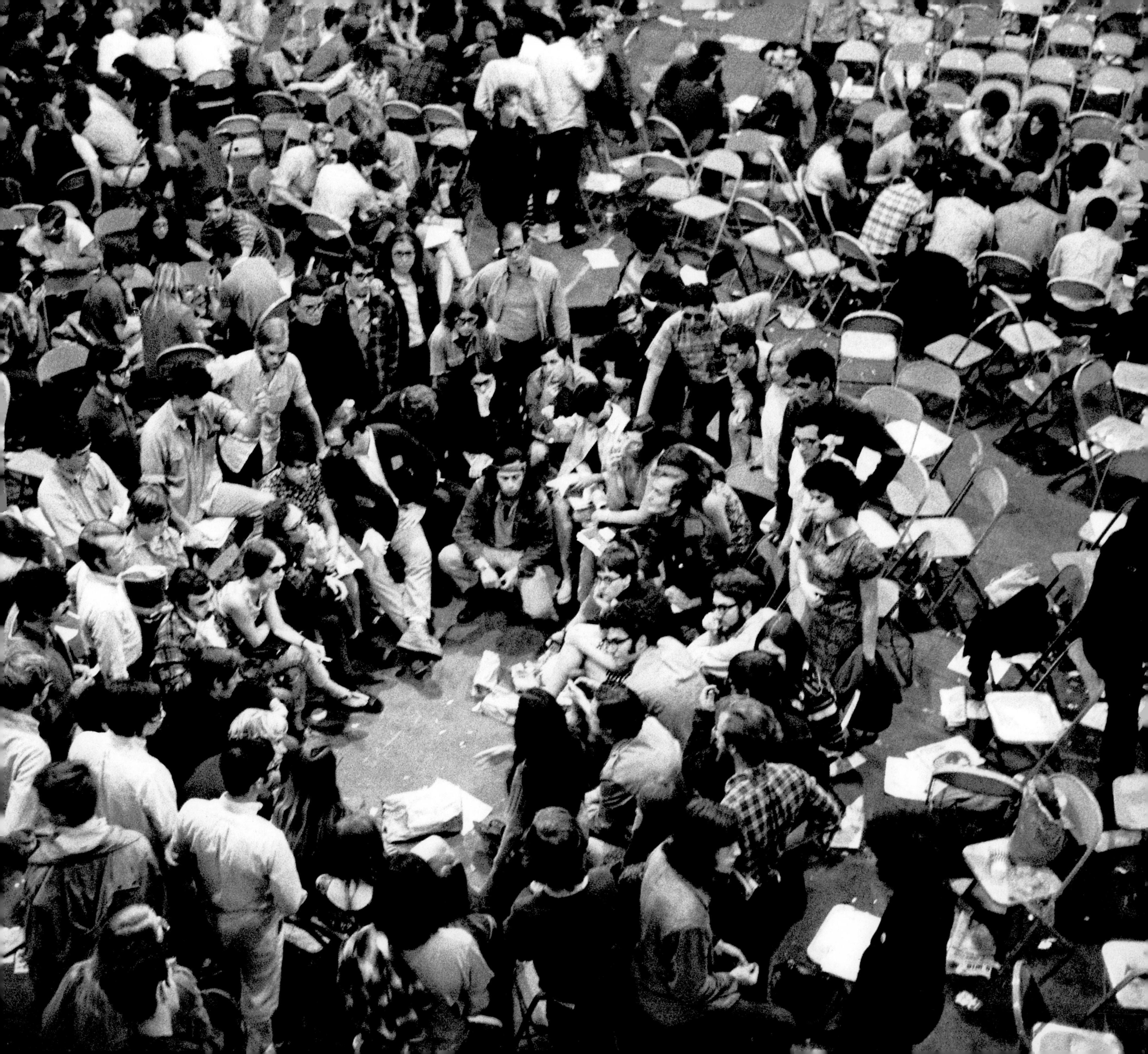

Bernardine Dohrn, who later became a leader of the Weather Underground, addresses the crowd at the Students for a Democratic Society (SDS) Convention, Chicago, IL, June 1969

William Kunstler, Chicago 7 attorney, Pittsburgh, PA, October 22, 1970

D.C. Demonstrations

Protestors in the Reflecting Pool during an antiwar march, Washington, D.C., May 9, 1970

You won't see people naked in the Reflecting Pool on the mall in D.C. today. You won't see them there at all. And certainly not with a Viet Cong flag.

Throughout the 60s, there were major antiwar demonstrations in Washington several times a year. Some of them combined militant protest with hippie love fests. *"Make love, not war"* was the slogan. So while demonstrating in the Reflecting Pool, this couple made out.

What I remember most vividly about these demonstrations was how exhausting they were to photograph. Imagine 400,000 people marching. I had to keep running back and forth from the start of the march to the finish and back again to get the best shots, and frequently had to put on a gas mask and wade through clouds of tear gas, or policemen using their clubs against demonstrators. I watched demonstrators pick up tear gas canisters billowing smoke and throw them with bare hands back at the police.

In one famous incident, protestors gathered in front of the Justice Department. We could see Nixon's Attorney General John Mitchell, of Watergate infamy, at his office window. Suddenly, a phalanx of police in riot gear closed off the street. We ran the other way. Another police line closed off the only exit. Tear gas rained. There was no escape. The cops came toward us clubbing away. It wasn't the only time I was grateful to have a police press pass shielding me.

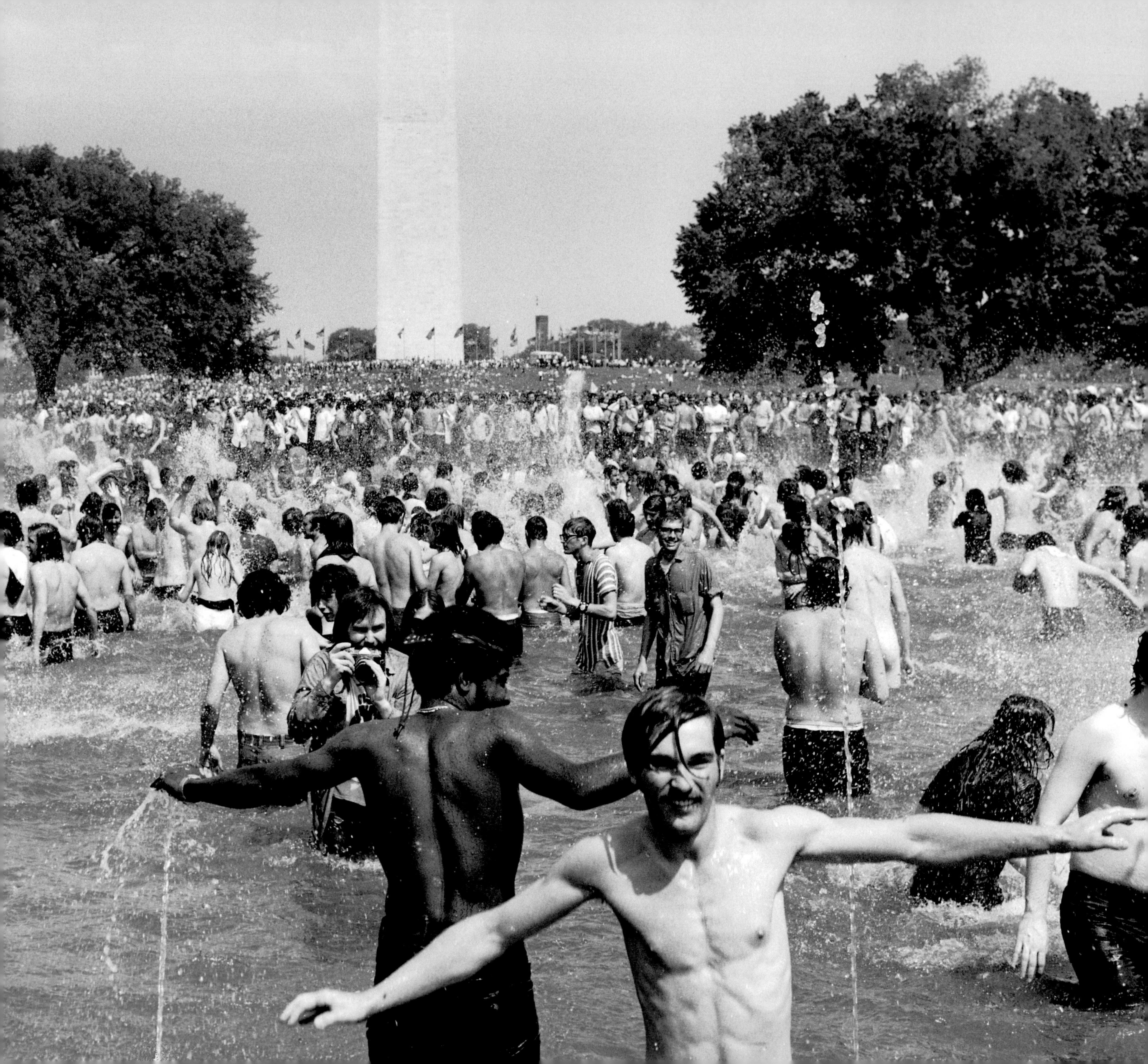

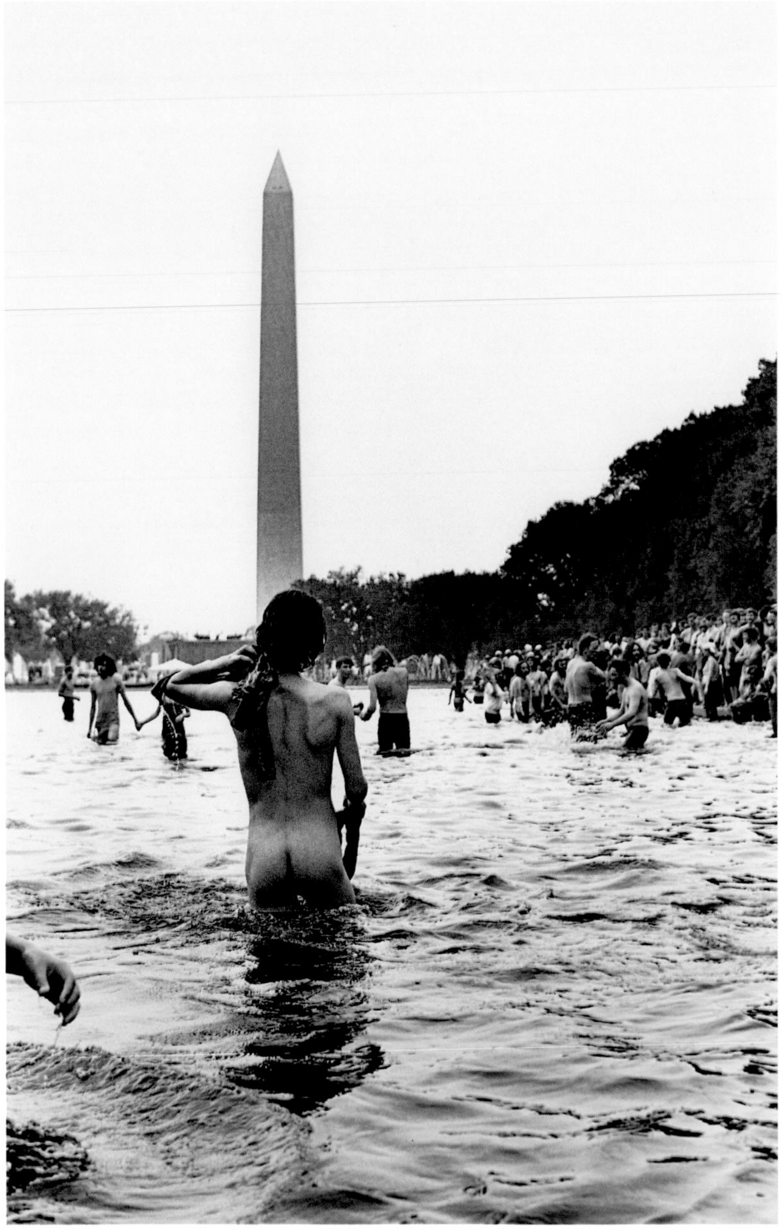

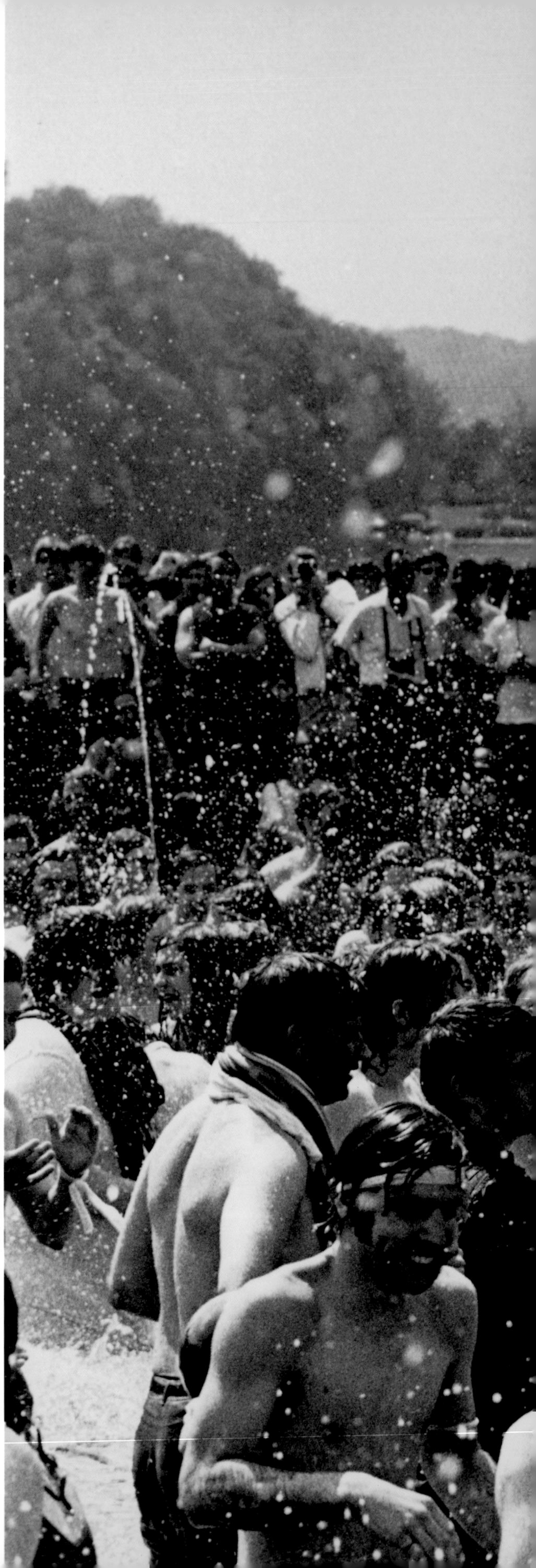

A naked protestor in the Reflecting Pool at the "Honor America Day Smoke–In," where activists smoked marijuana on the Mall to protest "Honor America Day," a celebration of the July 4th Holiday. July 4, 1970

Protestors in the Reflecting Pool during an antiwar march, Washington, D.C., May 9, 1970

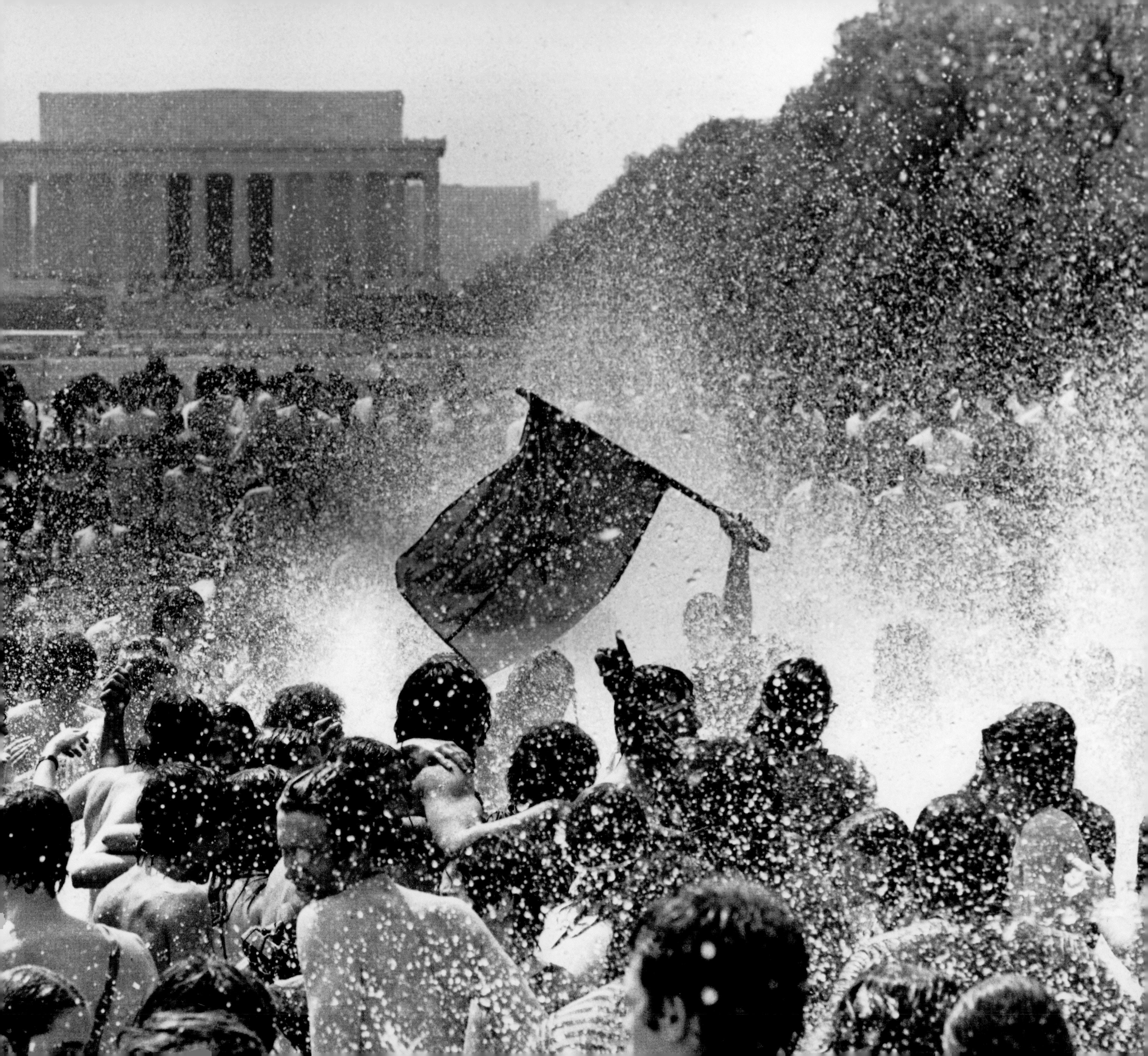

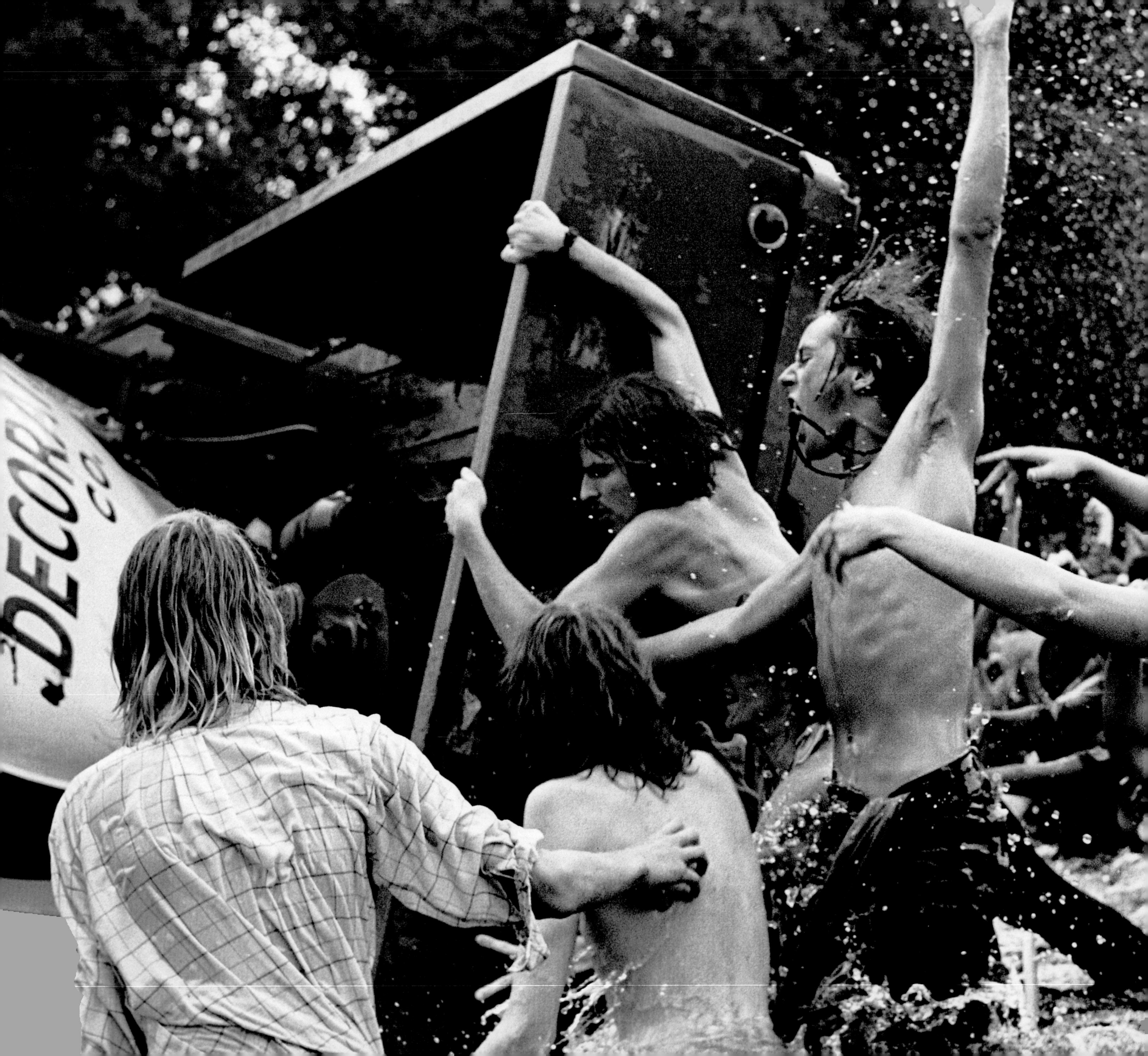
DECOR
CO

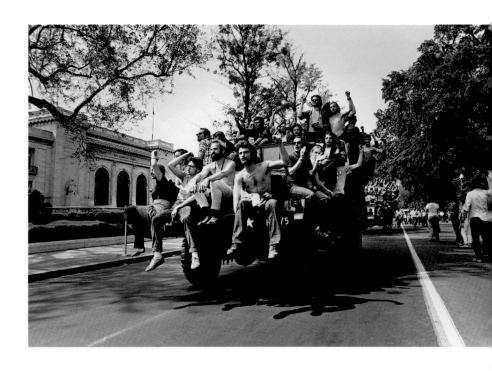

Protestors overturn a truck in the Reflecting Pool during
the "Honor America Day Smoke-In."
Washington, D.C., July 4, 1970

Protestors ride through the streets during an antiwar march,
Washington, D.C., May 9, 1970

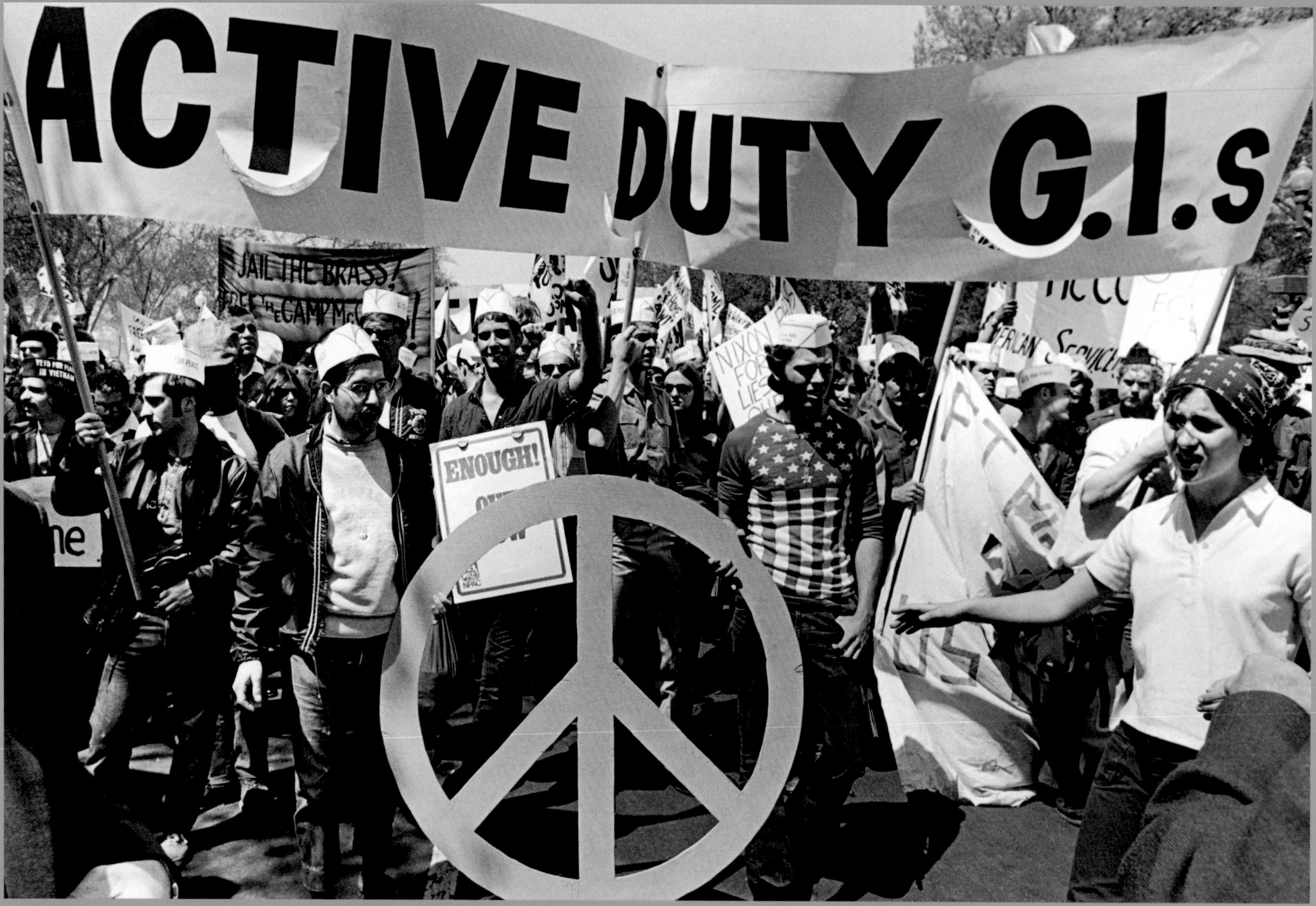
ACTIVE DUTY G.I.s
JAIL THE BRASS!
ENOUGH!

Active duty soldiers protest the war in Vietnam, Washington, D.C., April 24, 1971

The antiwar "May Day Protests" of 1971, which ran from May 1-6 in Washington, D.C. led to more than 13,000 arrests including those pictured here behind the fence. The courts declared these mass arrests illegal and freed the protestors.

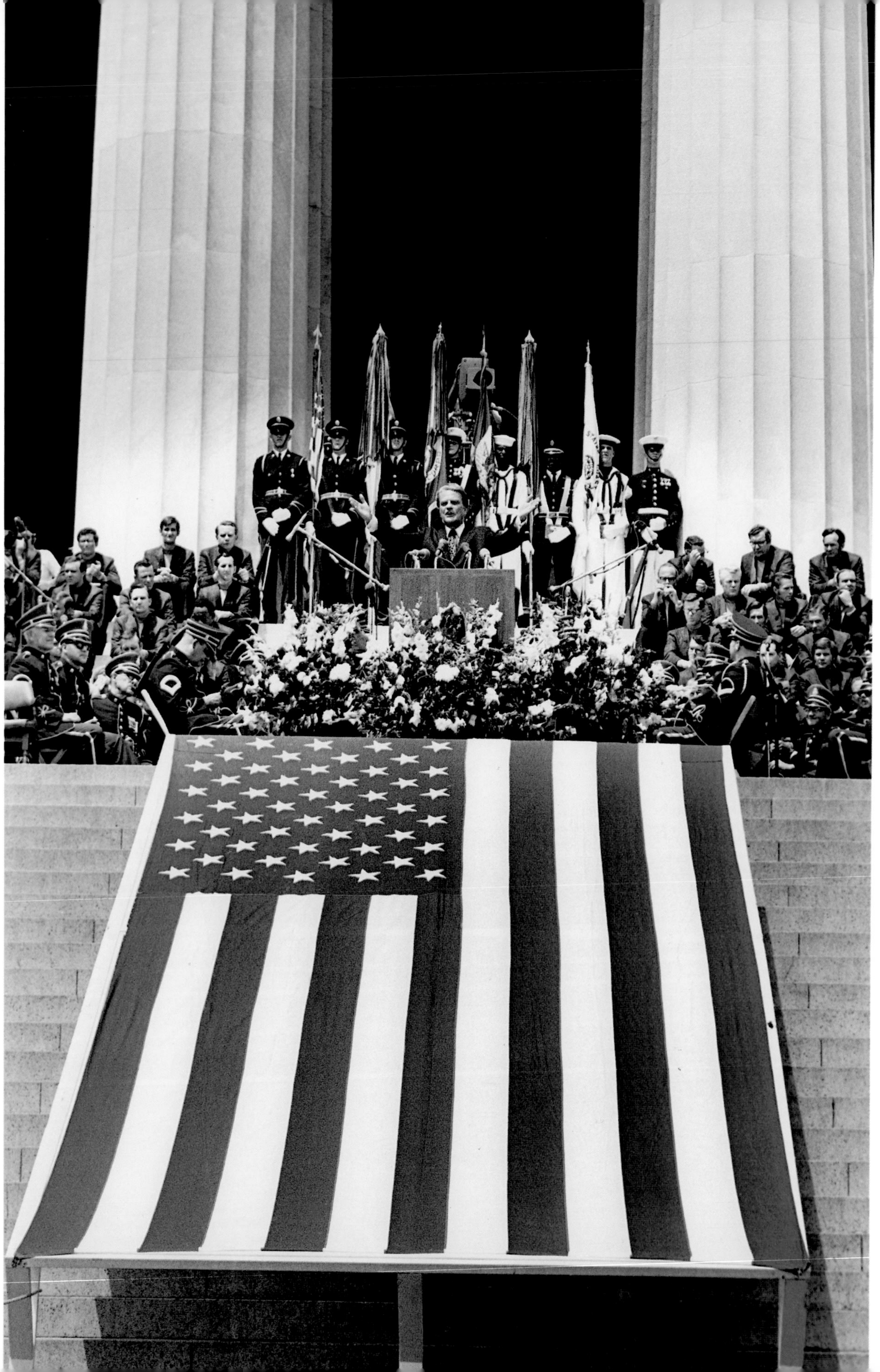

The Reverend Billy Graham speaks to supporters during "Honor America Day." Washington, D.C., July 4, 1970

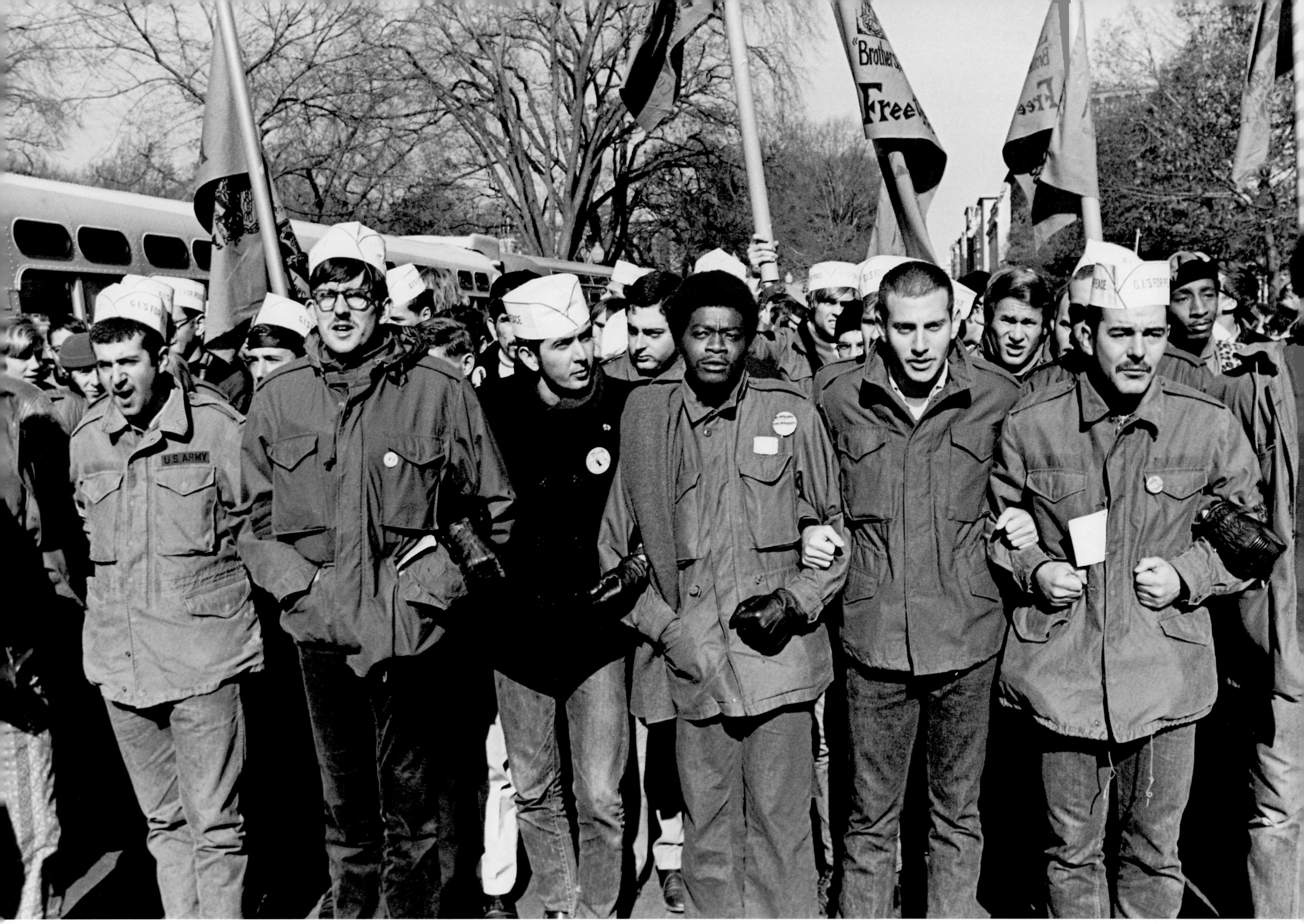
U.S.ARMY

A group of active duty "GIs for Peace" march,
Washington, D.C., April 24, 1971

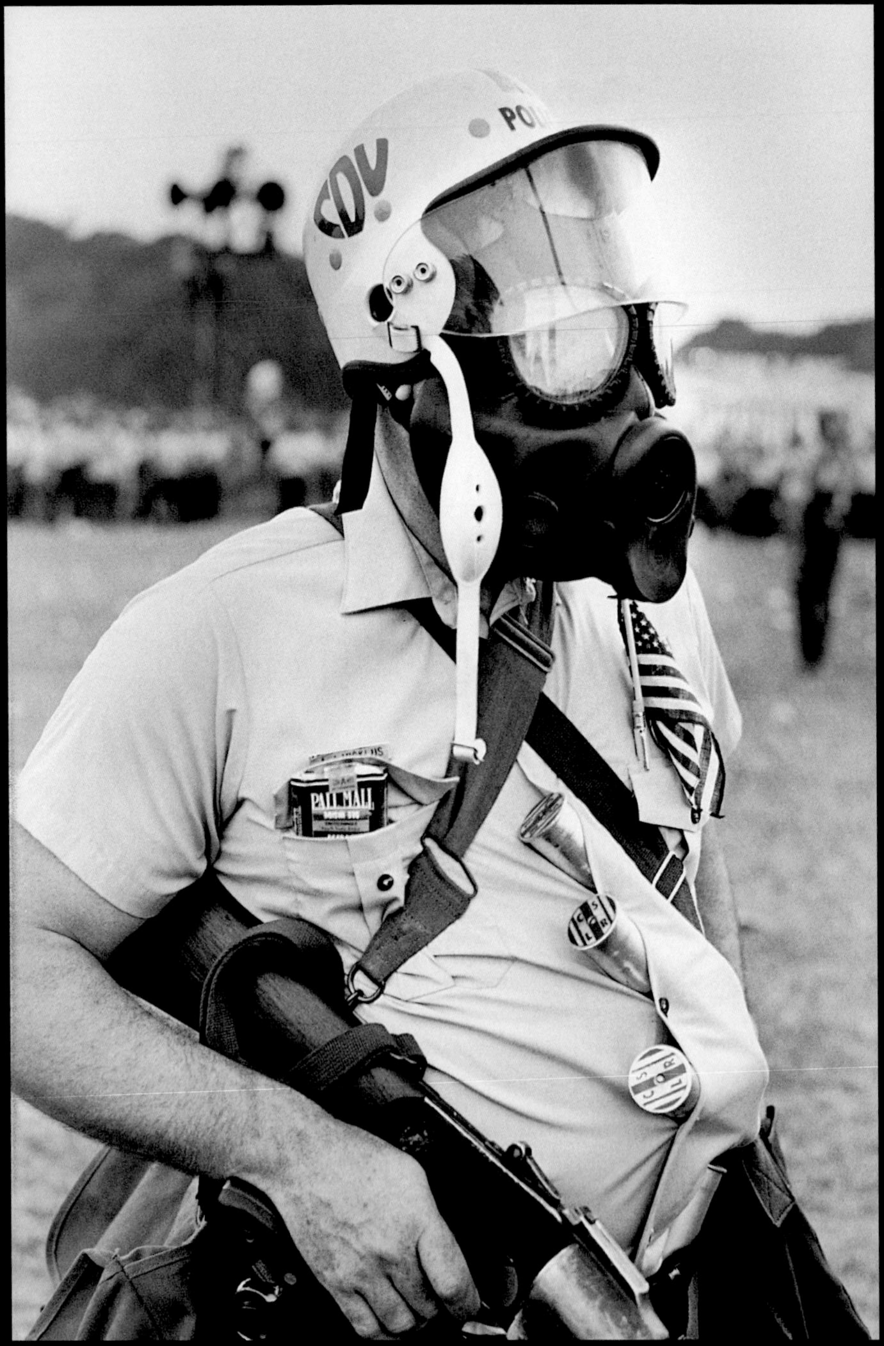
PALL MALL

A policeman in riot gear during "Honor America Day" (note the tear gas bullets in his shirt.)
Washington, D.C. July 4, 1970

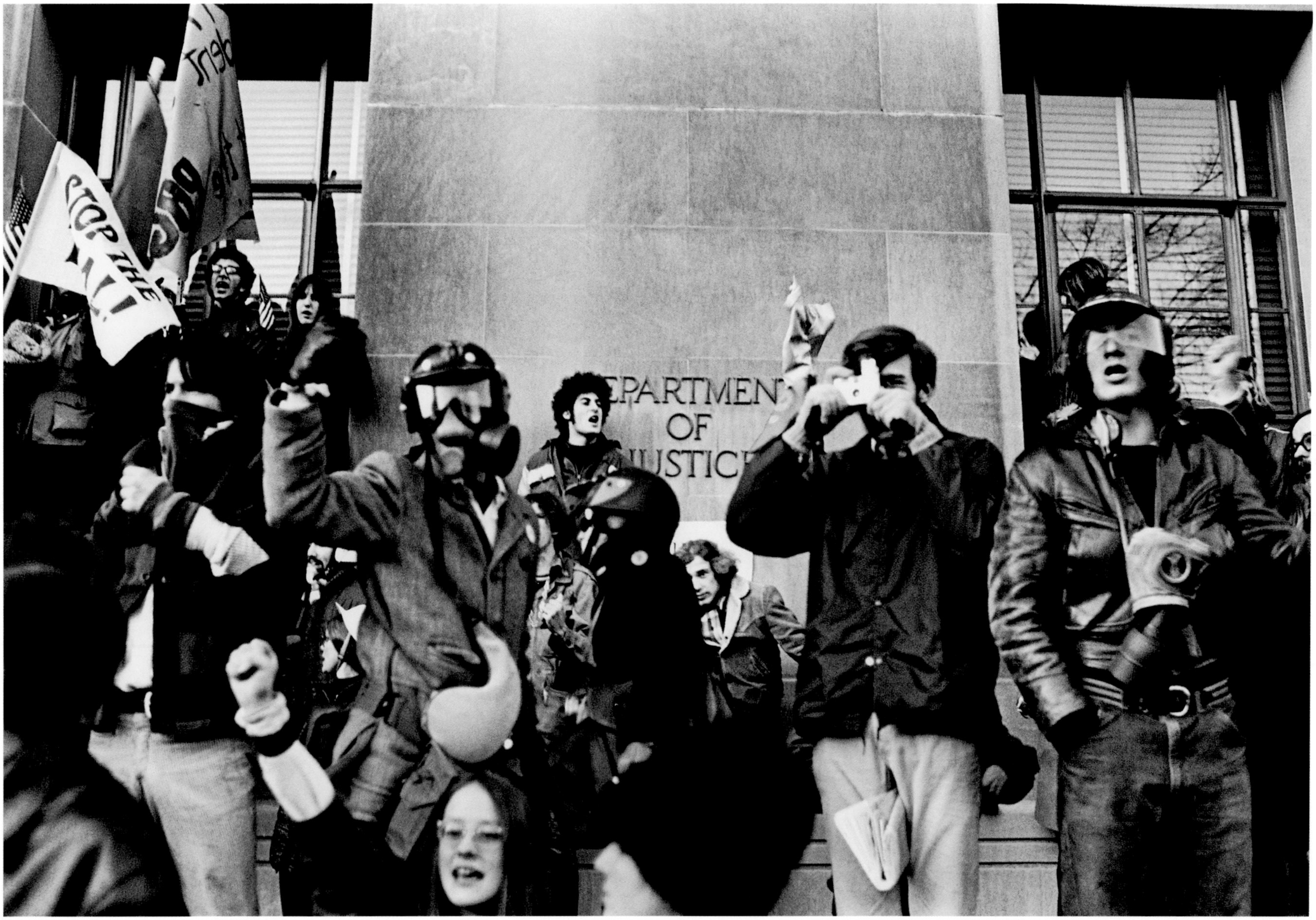
STOP THE
DEPARTMENT
OF
JUSTICE

Demonstrators in front of the U.S. Department of Justice during the National Mobilization to End the War, Washington, D.C., November 15, 1969

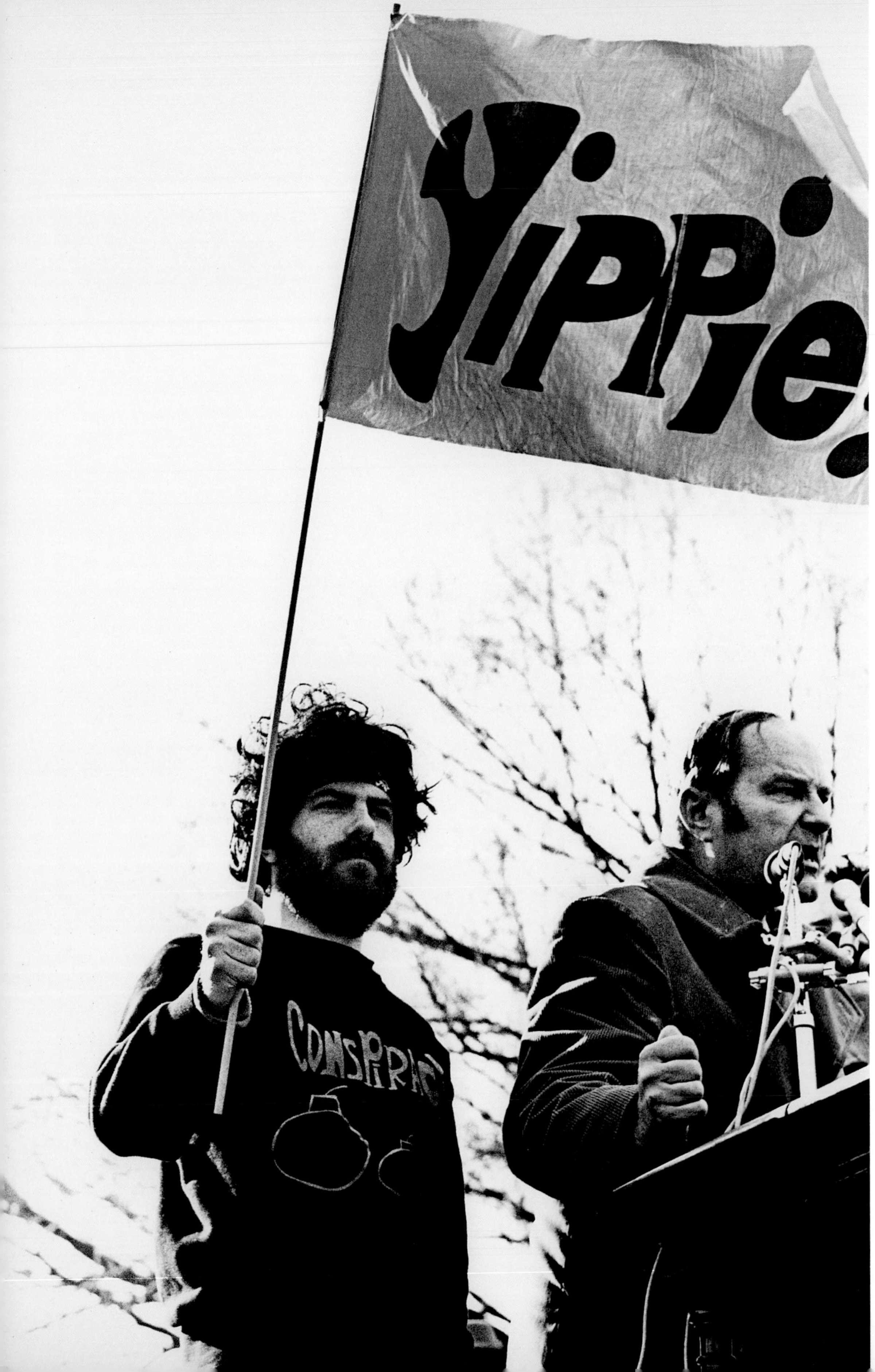
YIPPIE!
CONSPIRAC

Jerry Rubin and David Dellinger at the National Mobilization to End the War, Washington, D.C., November 15, 1969

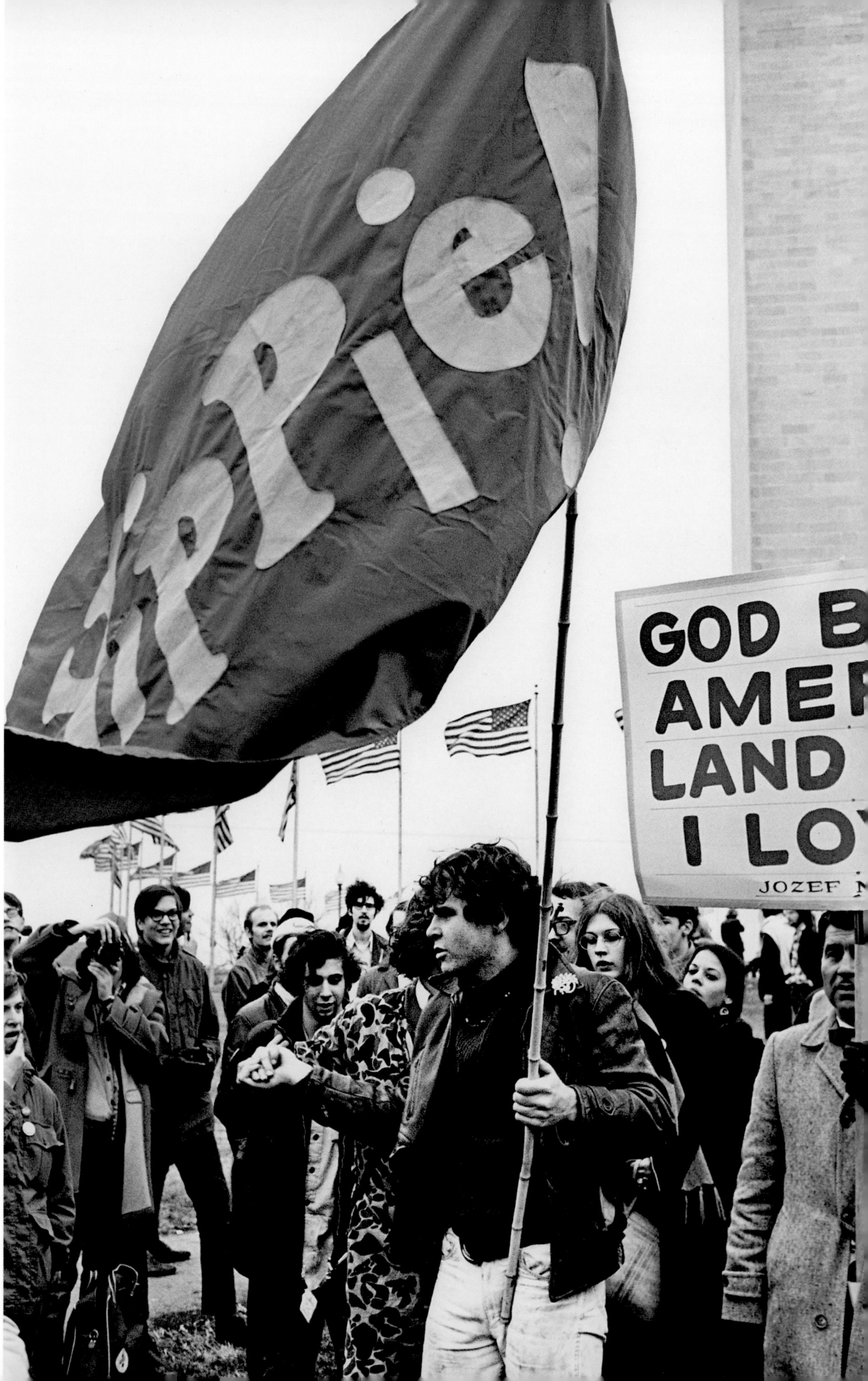
GOD B
AMER
LAND
I LO
JOZEF N

Yippies demonstrate during the inauguration of President Richard M. Nixon, Washington, D.C., January 18–21, 1969

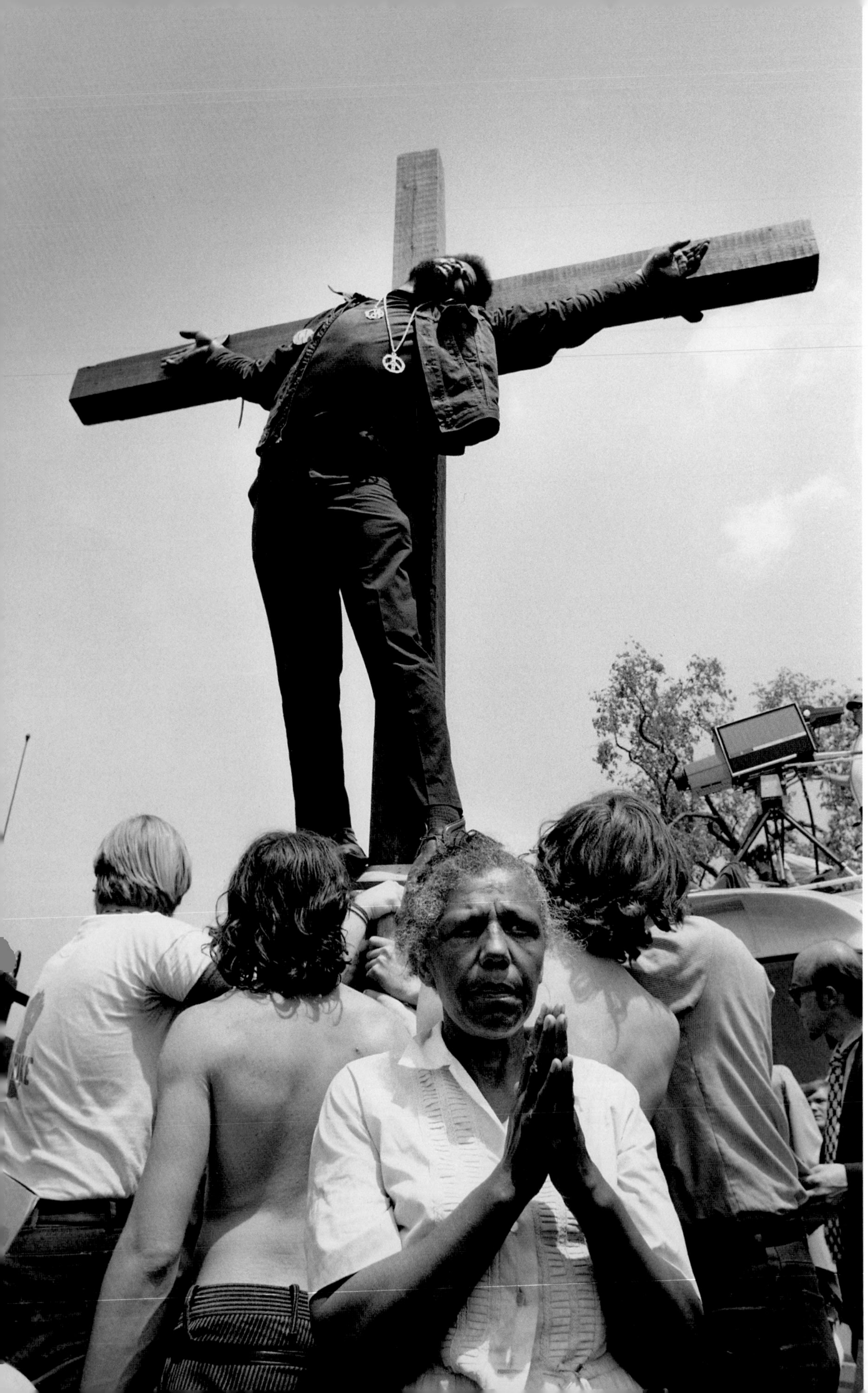

Street Theatre

A mock crucifixion during an antiwar rally, Washington, D.C., May 9, 1970

There were always colorful characters at protests: the black man on the cross, the Bread and Puppet Theatre with their Nixon and Agnew masks, the pro–war demonstrators, or the soldiers guarding the White House secretly flashing us "V" signs in opposition to the war.

One time, Nixon protected the White House by surrounding it with a chain of buses. A group of excessively militant demonstrators urged the crowd to attack the building. Some cooler heads narrowly prevailed to avoid this. I don't think those buses would have been enough had they failed.

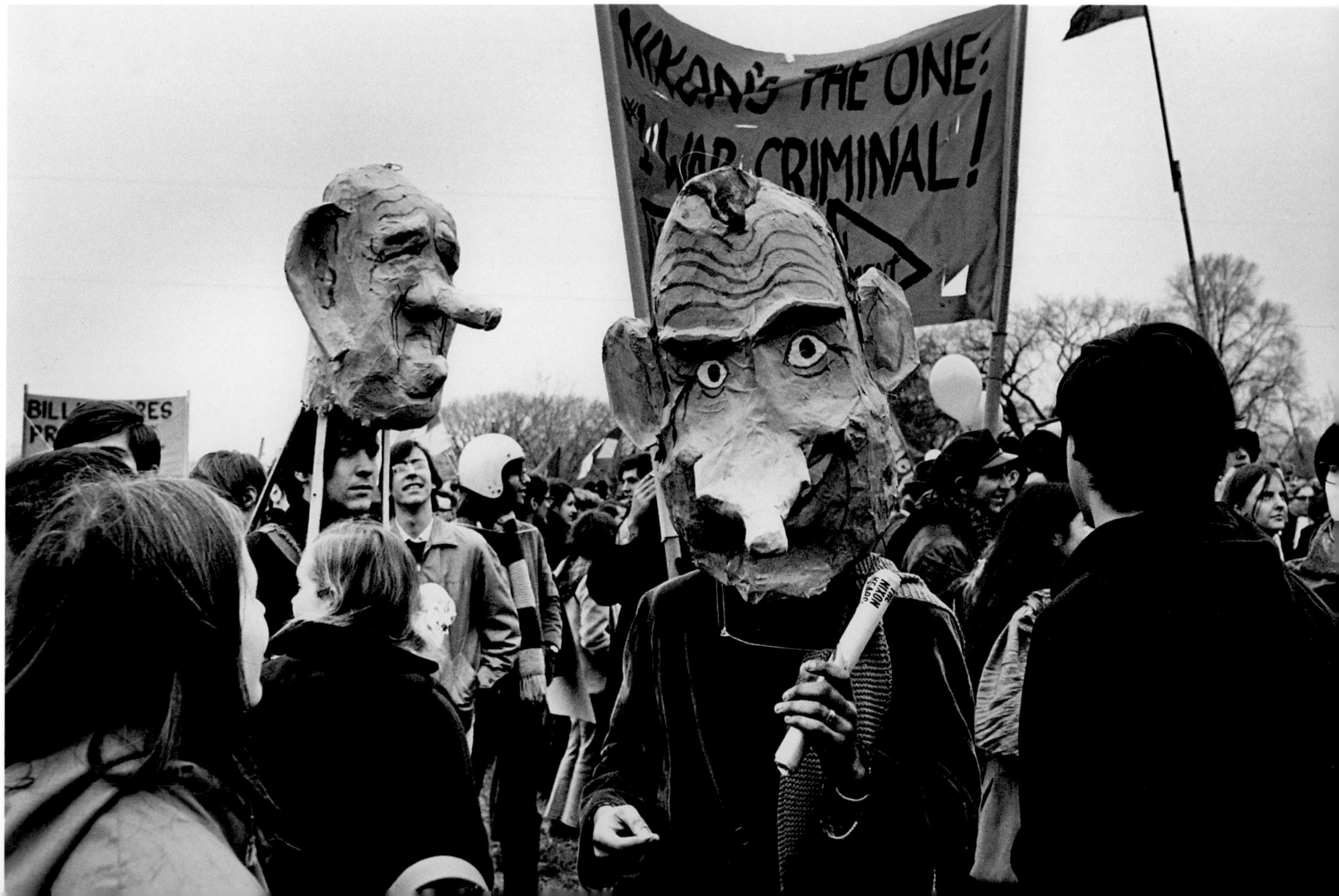
THE ONE:
CRIMINAL!

Protestors dress up as President Richard M. Nixon during his inauguration, Washington, D.C., January 18–21, 1969

Richard M. Nixon at a rally in his honor at Madison Square Garden, New York City, October 31, 1968

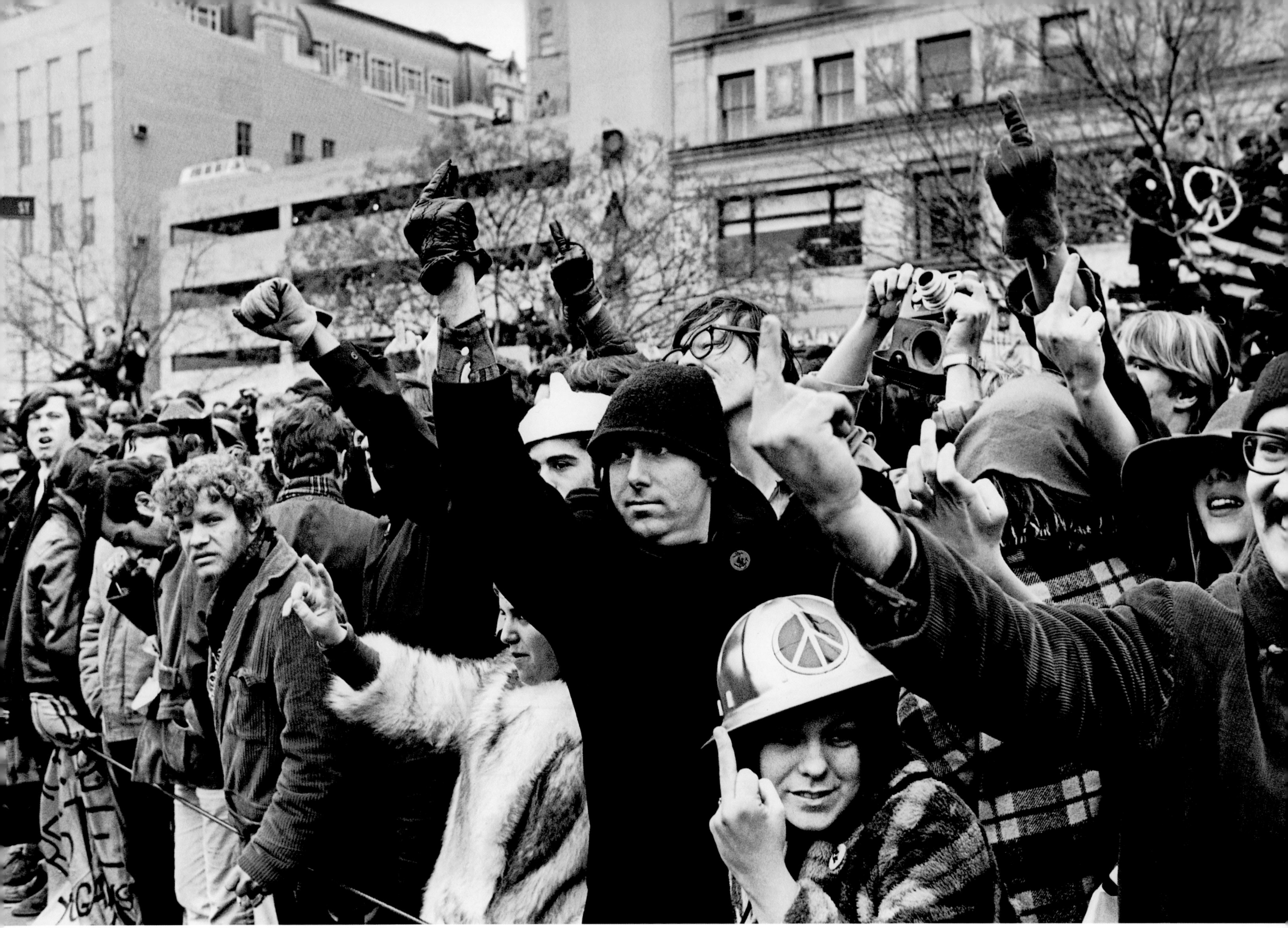

Demonstrators at President Richard M. Nixon's inauguration, January 18–21, 1969

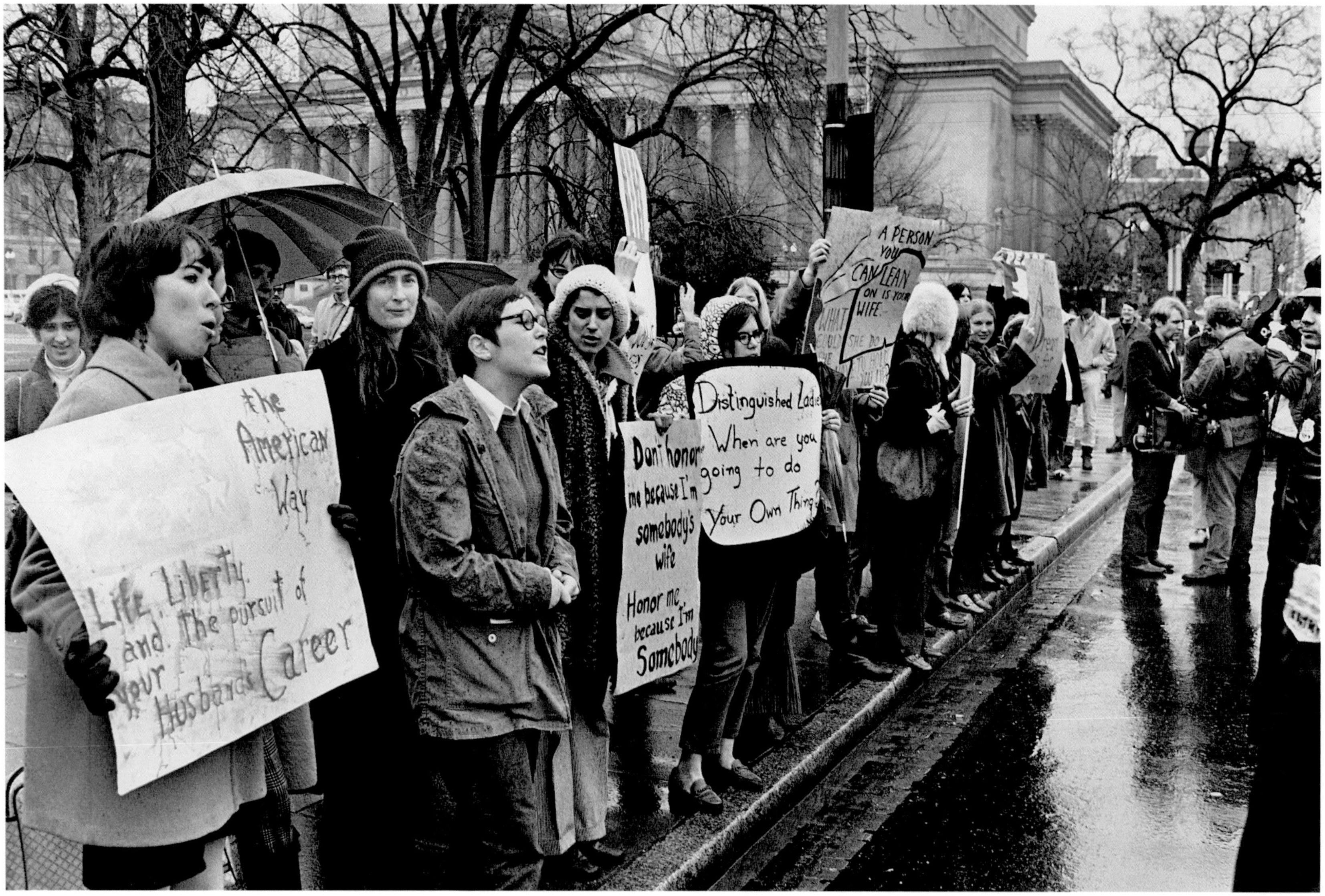
the American Way
Life, Liberty, and the pursuit of your Husband's Career
Don't honor me because I'm somebody's wife
Honor me, because I'm Somebody
Distinguished Ladies
When are you going to do Your Own Thing?
A PERSON YOU CAN LEAN ON IS YOUR WIFE

Left and Right: *Women protest during President Richard M. Nixon's inauguration, Washington, D.C., January 18–21, 1969*

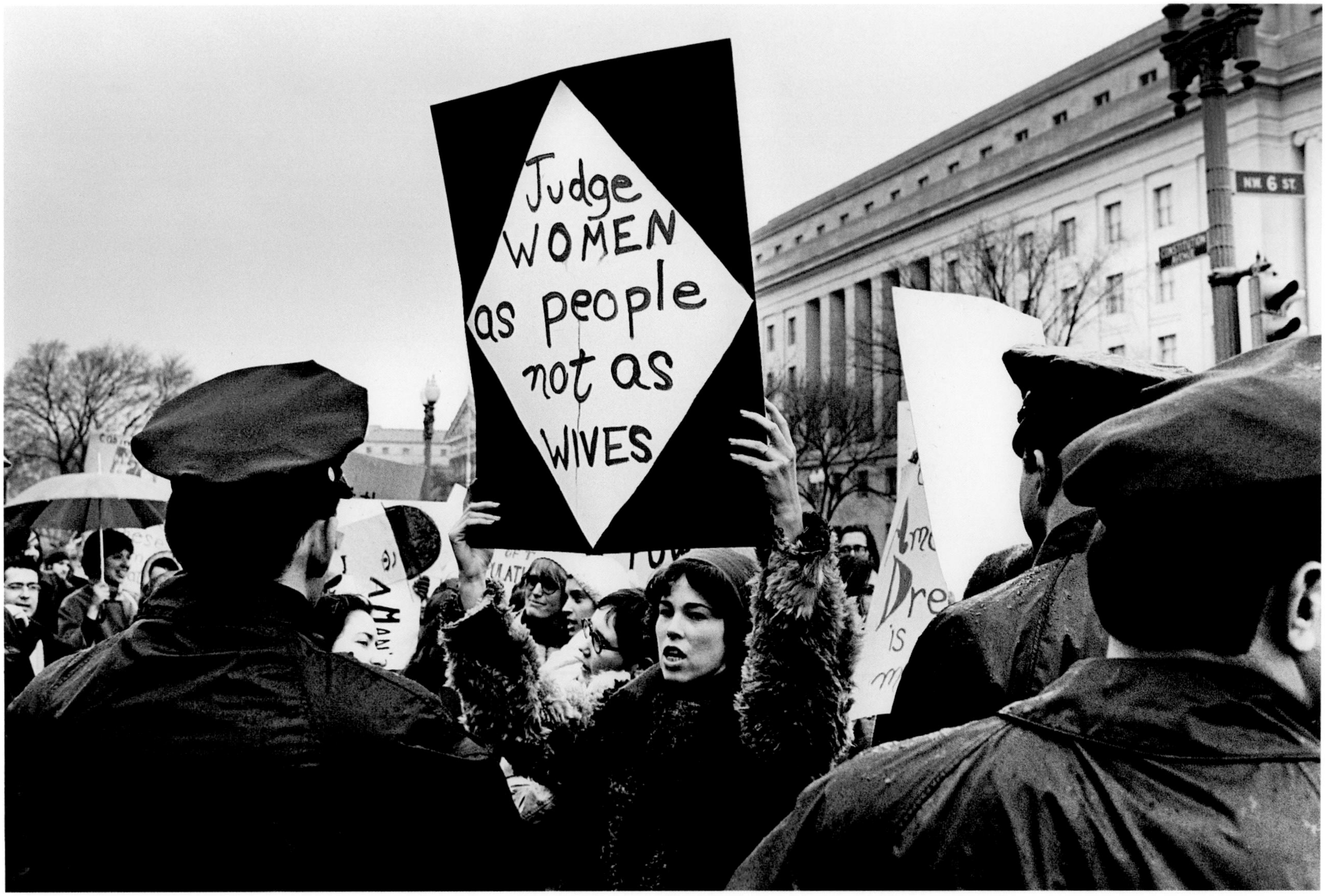
Judge
WOMEN
as people
not as
WIVES

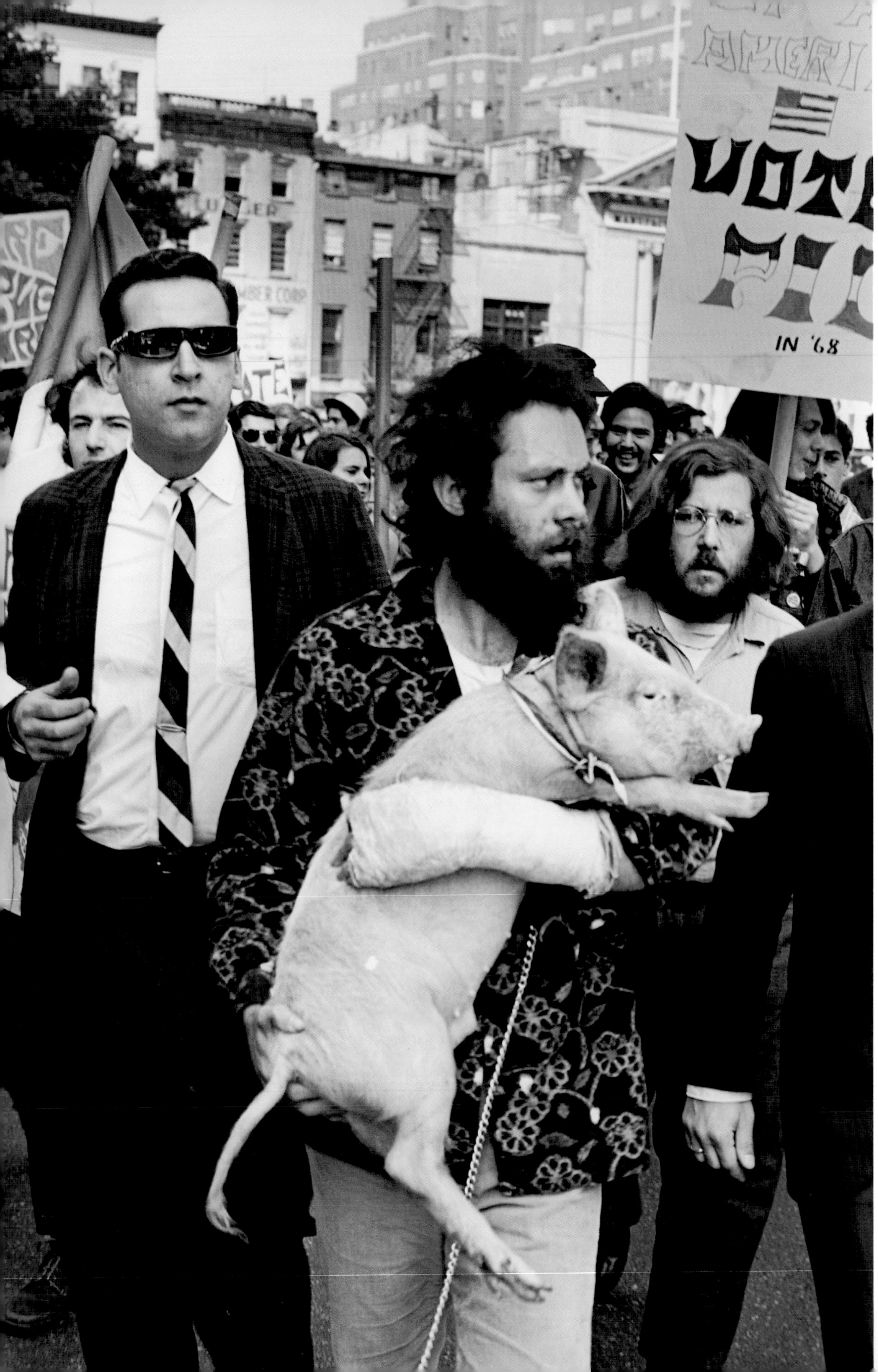
VOT
IN '68

Pig for President

Yippies march through the streets with "Pigasus," their chosen "candidate" for President, New York City, September, 1968

The Youth International Party, or YIPPIE!, fooled the media to no end. It wasn't a party, and it didn't have any members. It was five or ten theatrical protestors led by Abbie Hoffman and Jerry Rubin who managed to get themselves taken very seriously by the authorities. The TV news treated the Yippies as though they were real. In 1968, the Yippies ran a Pig for President, "Pigasus," pictured here. The sign in the back says "Vote Pig in '68."

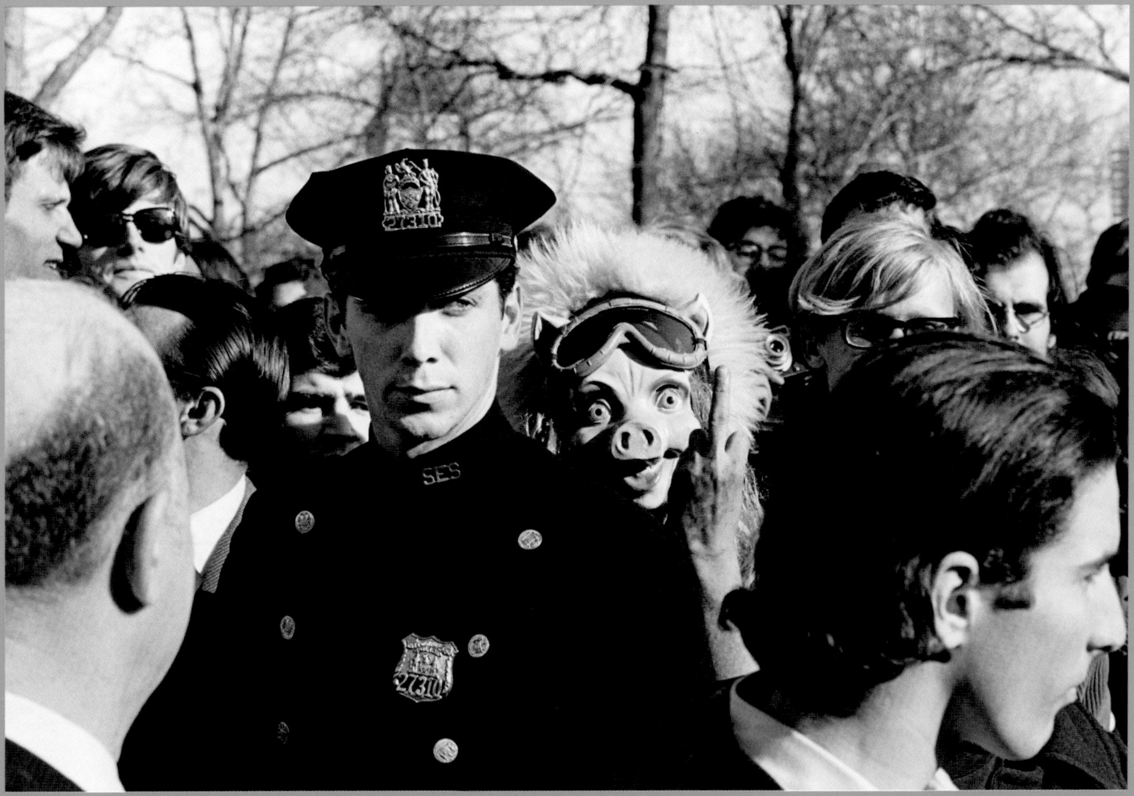
27310
SES
27310

A protestor in a pig mask stands behind a policeman at a Central Park Peace March, New York City, April 5, 1969

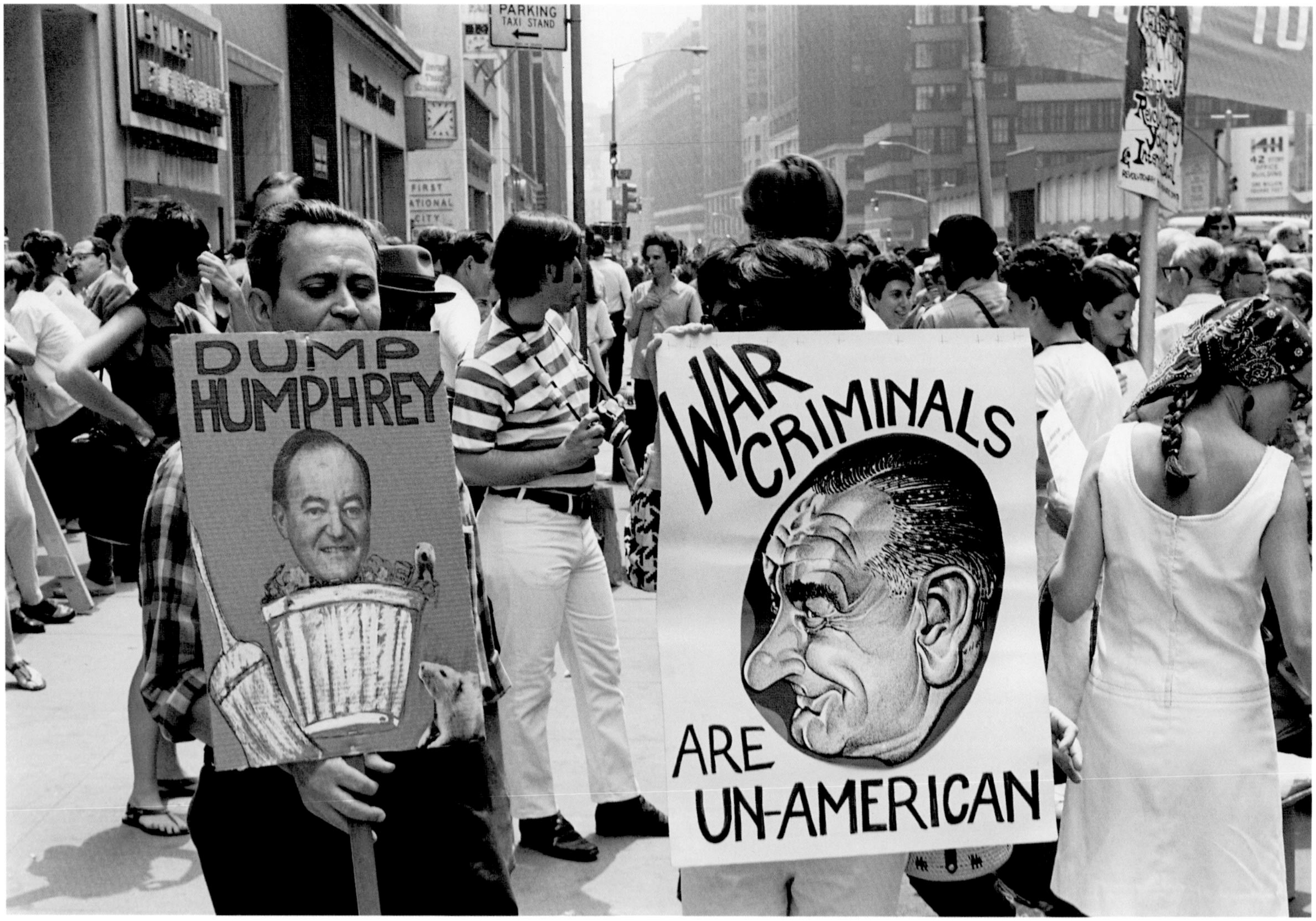
PARKING
TAXI STAND
DUMP
HUMPHREY
WAR
CRIMINALS
ARE
UN-AMERICAN

Protestors at an antiwar rally, New York City, Fall 1968

Soldiers stand guard during the inauguration of President Richard M. Nixon, Washington, D.C., January 18–21, 1969

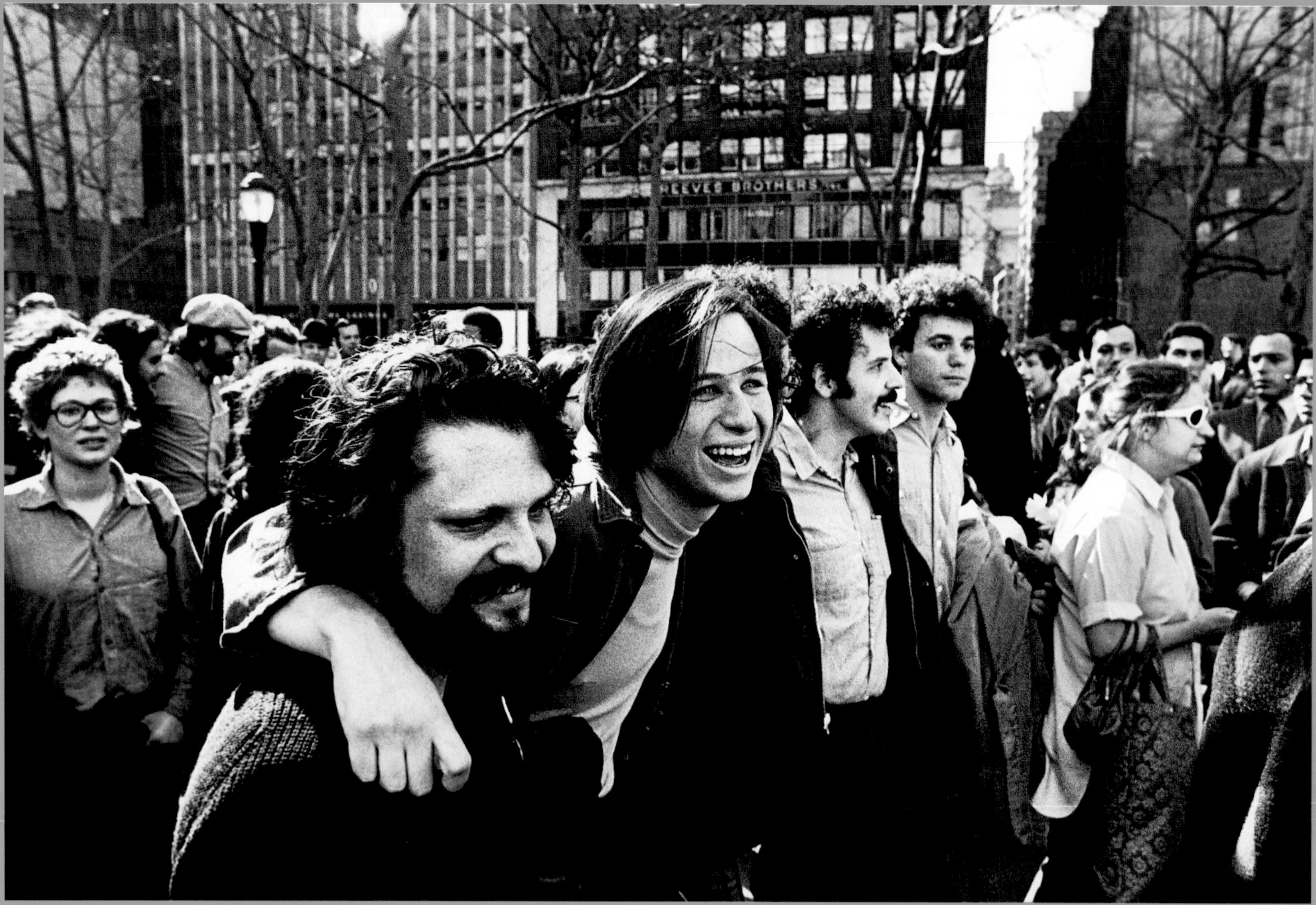
EEVES BROTHERS

Participants in an early gay liberation protest, New York City, April 15, 1970

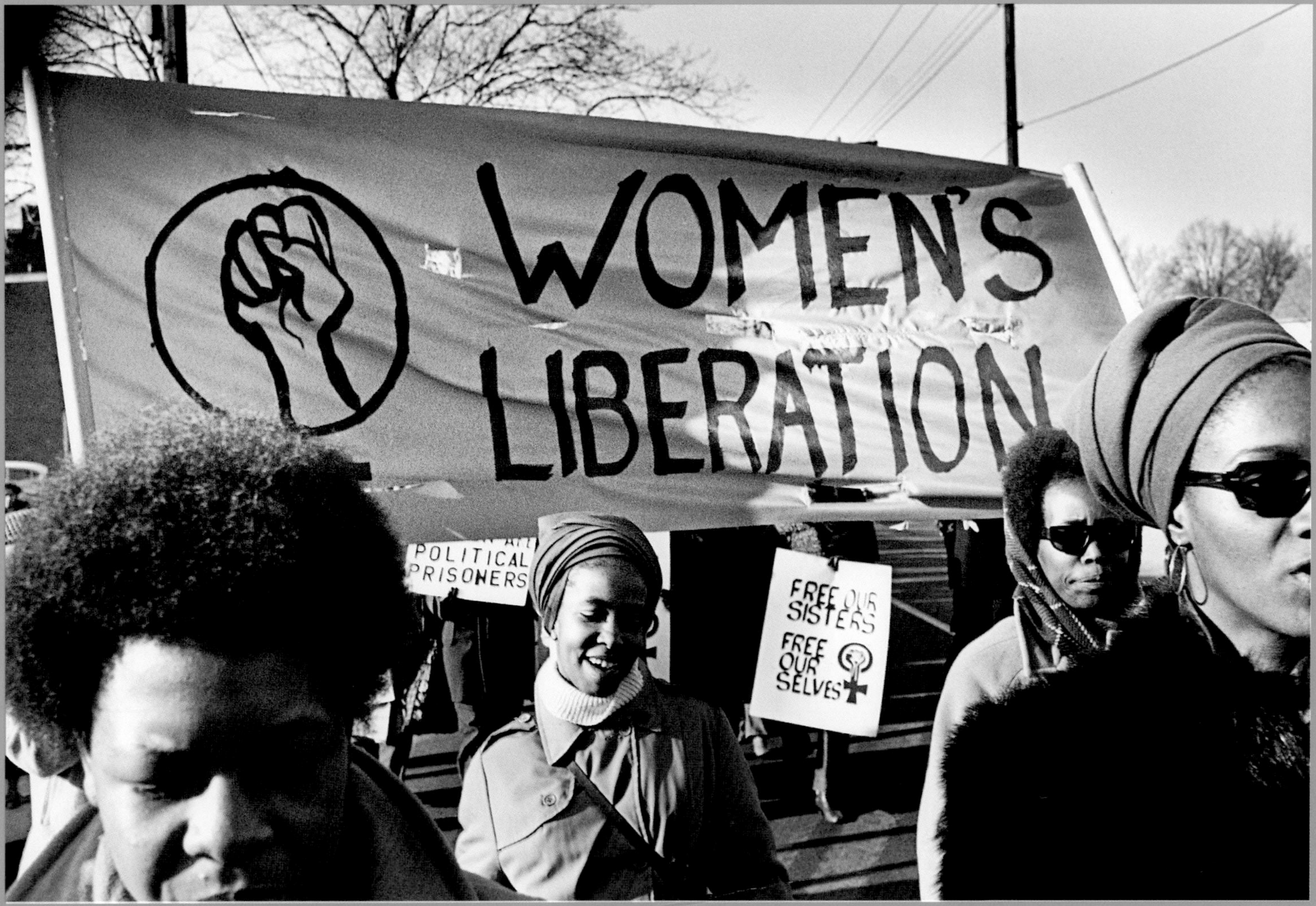
WOMEN'S LIBERATION
POLITICAL PRISONERS
FREE OUR SISTERS FREE OUR SELVES

Women rally for their rights during a protest in support of the Black Panther Party, New Haven, CT, November, 1969

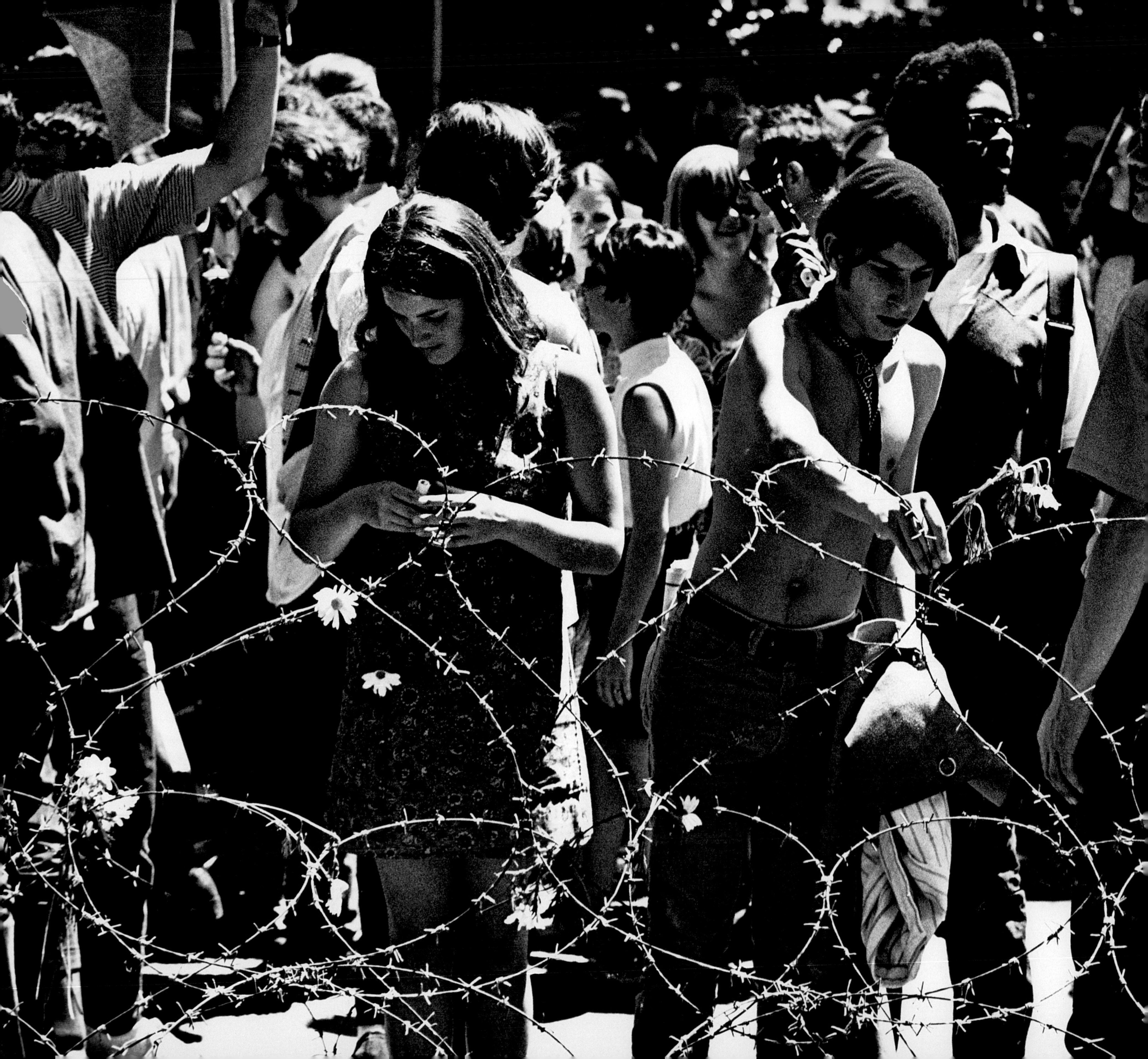

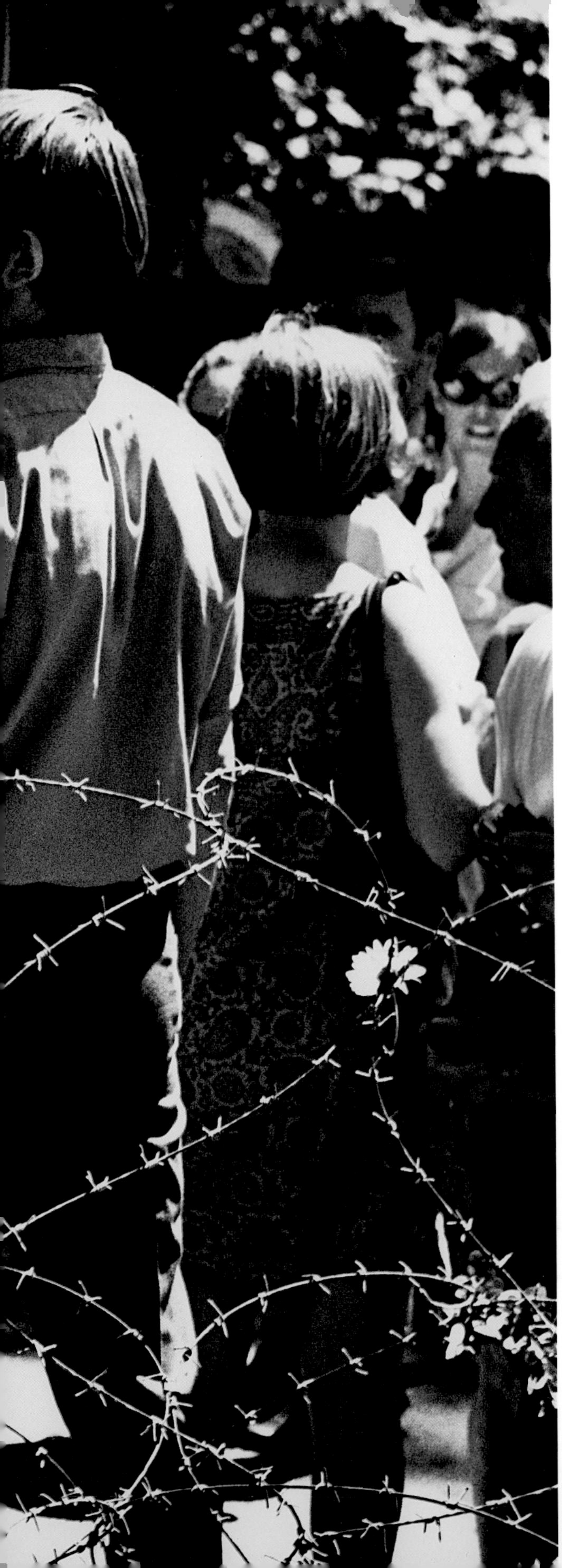

People's Park, Berkeley, CA

Demonstrators place flowers in the fence at People's Park, Berkeley, CA, May 30, 1969

I will forever associate Berkeley with tear gas.

Every time I flew out there to photograph a riot (they had lots of them), there was tear gas everywhere. Berkeley activists were particularly skilled at throwing tear gas canisters back at the police, especially at the Alameda County Sheriffs, who wore distinctive dark blue uniforms and were known as the "Blue Meanies" (from the Beatles film *Yellow Submarine*).

My first cross–country trip assignment was to shoot the People's Park demonstrations. In April 1969, Berkeley residents and students spontaneously turned a small piece of abandoned land into a community park. The University fenced it off, resulting in massive protests. Governor Ronald Reagan declared a state of emergency and called out the National Guard. The police actually killed one bystander, James Rector, who was watching the demonstration from a nearby roof. National Guard helicopters sprayed the streets with tear gas and 1,000 people were arrested.

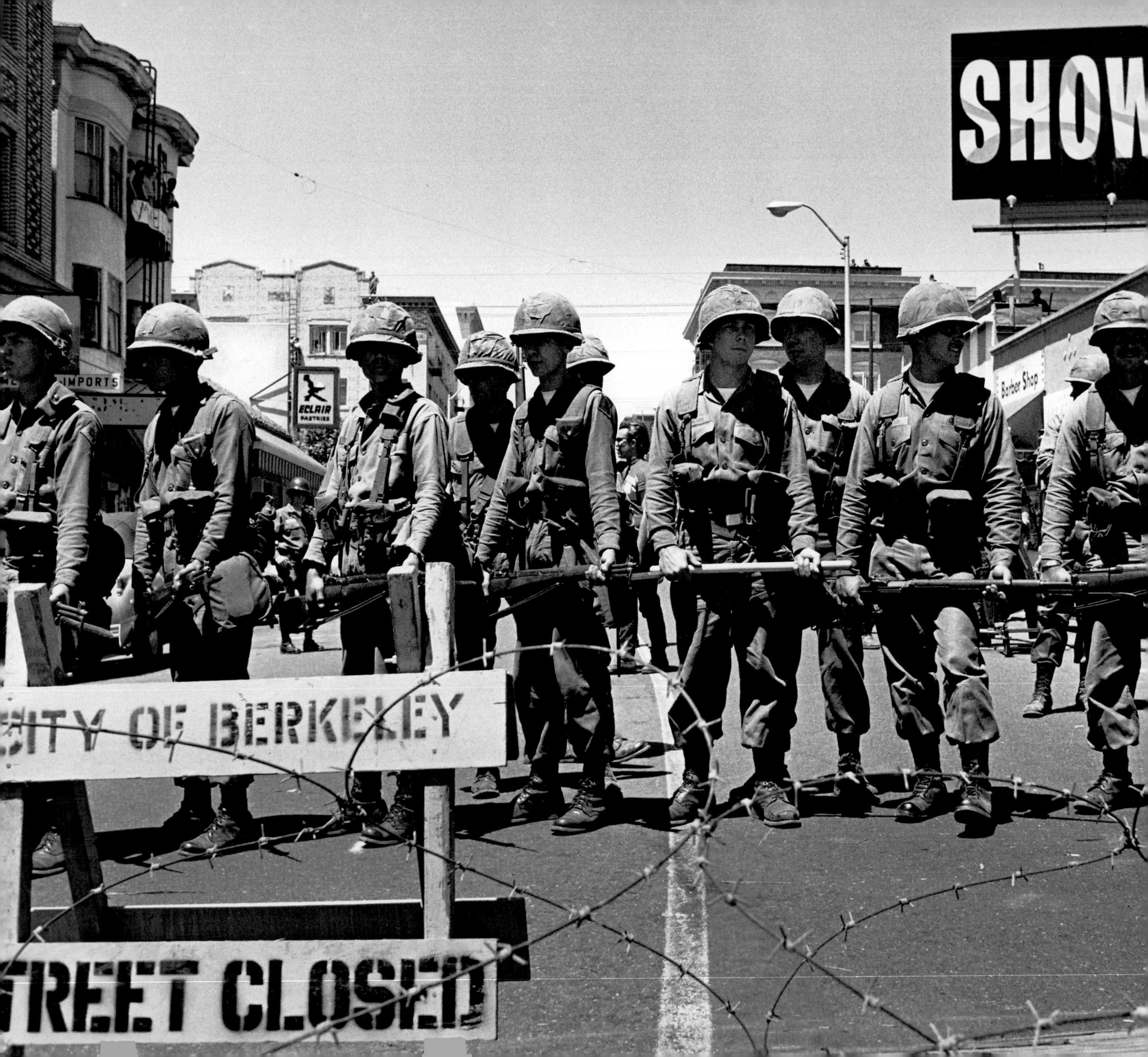
SHOW
IMPORTS
ECLAIR
PASTRIES
Barber Shop
CITY OF BERKELEY
STREET CLOSED

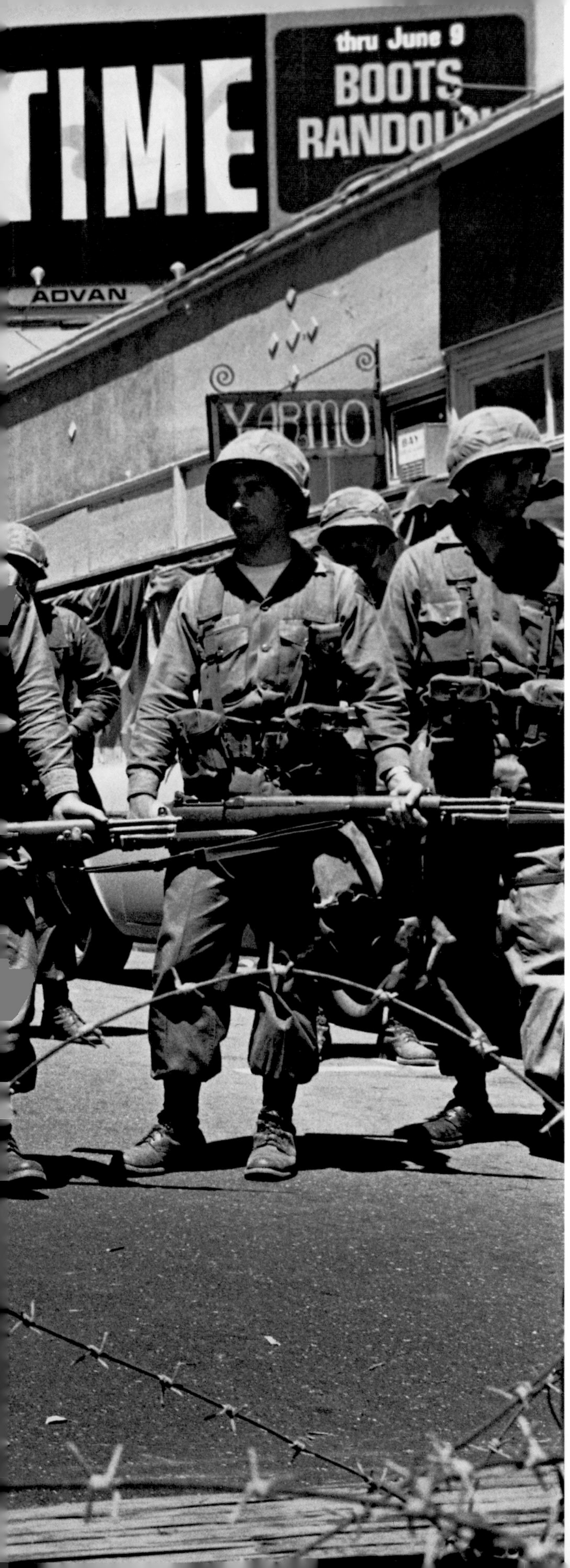
TIME
thru June 9
BOOTS
YARMO

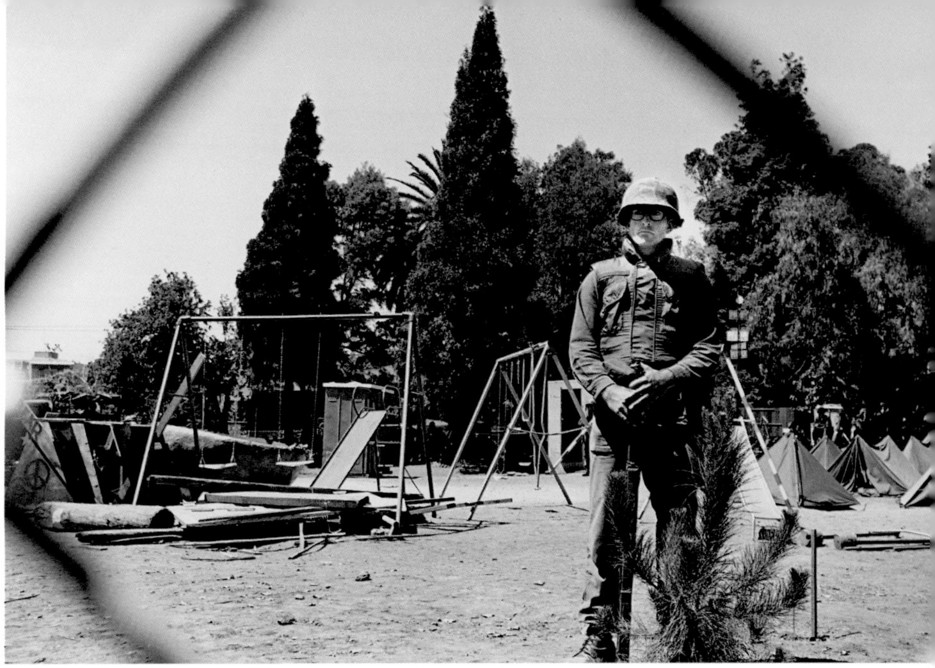

Left: California National Guard troops close off the streets around People's Park.

Above: A California National guardsman helps protect People's Park from the people. Berkeley, CA, May 30, 1969

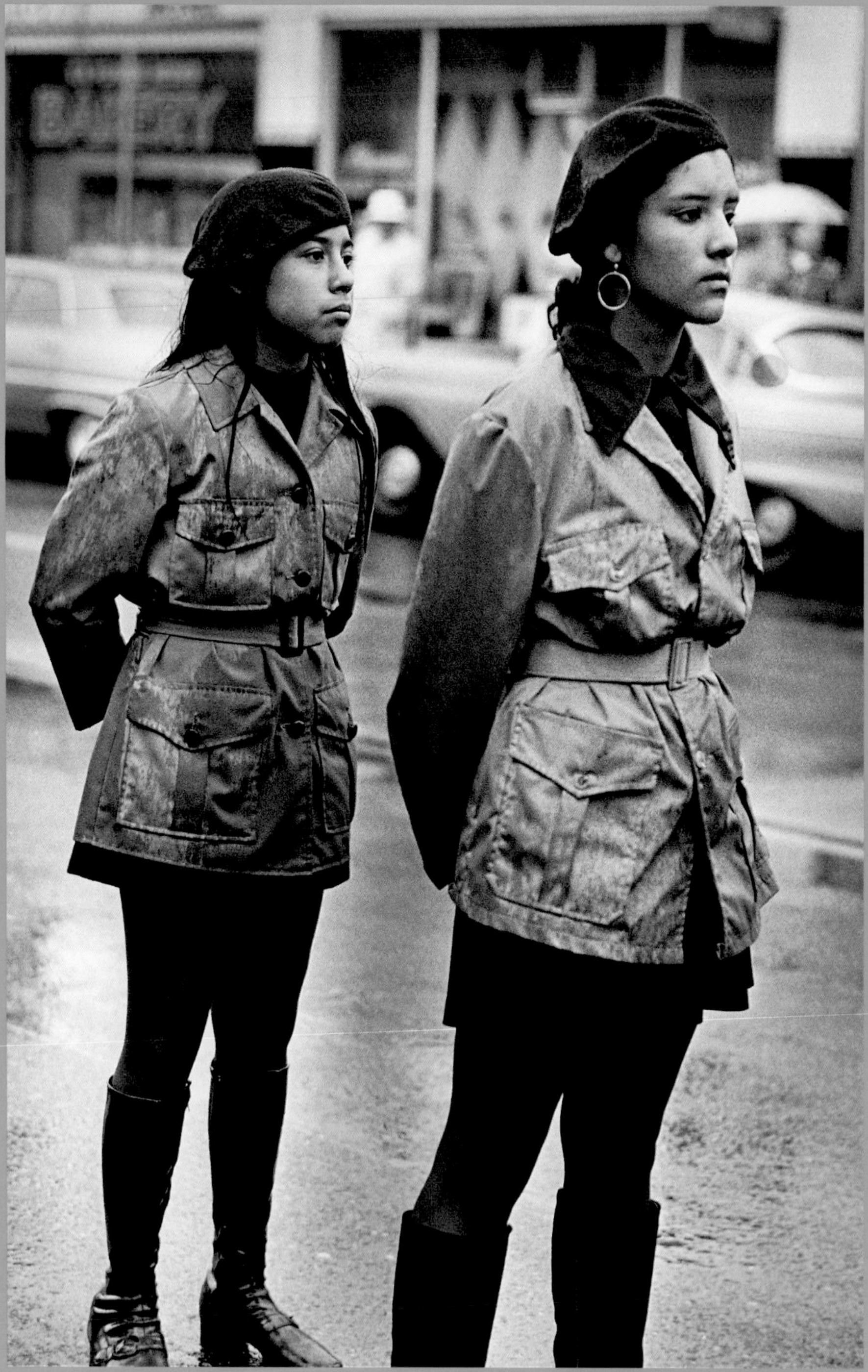
BAKERY

Two members of the Brown Berets, a Chicano organization, at a Chicano Moratorium march, Los Angeles, CA, February 28, 1970

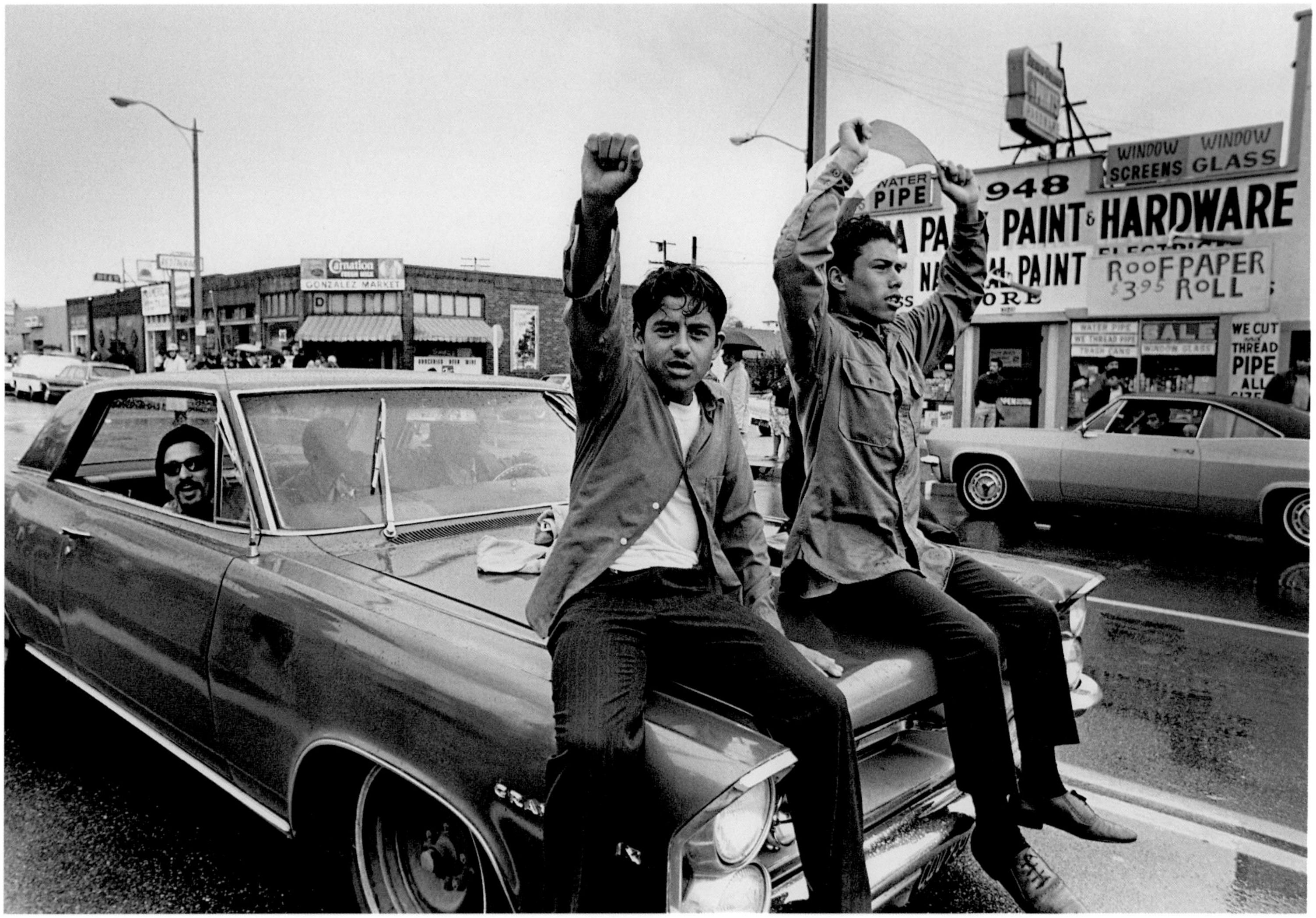
WATER PIPE
948
PAINT
HARDWARE
WINDOW SCREENS
WINDOW GLASS
ROOF PAPER $3.95 ROLL
WE CUT and THREAD PIPE
SALE
Carnation
GONZALEZ MARKET

Protestors at the Chicano Moratorium, Los Angeles, CA, February 28, 1970

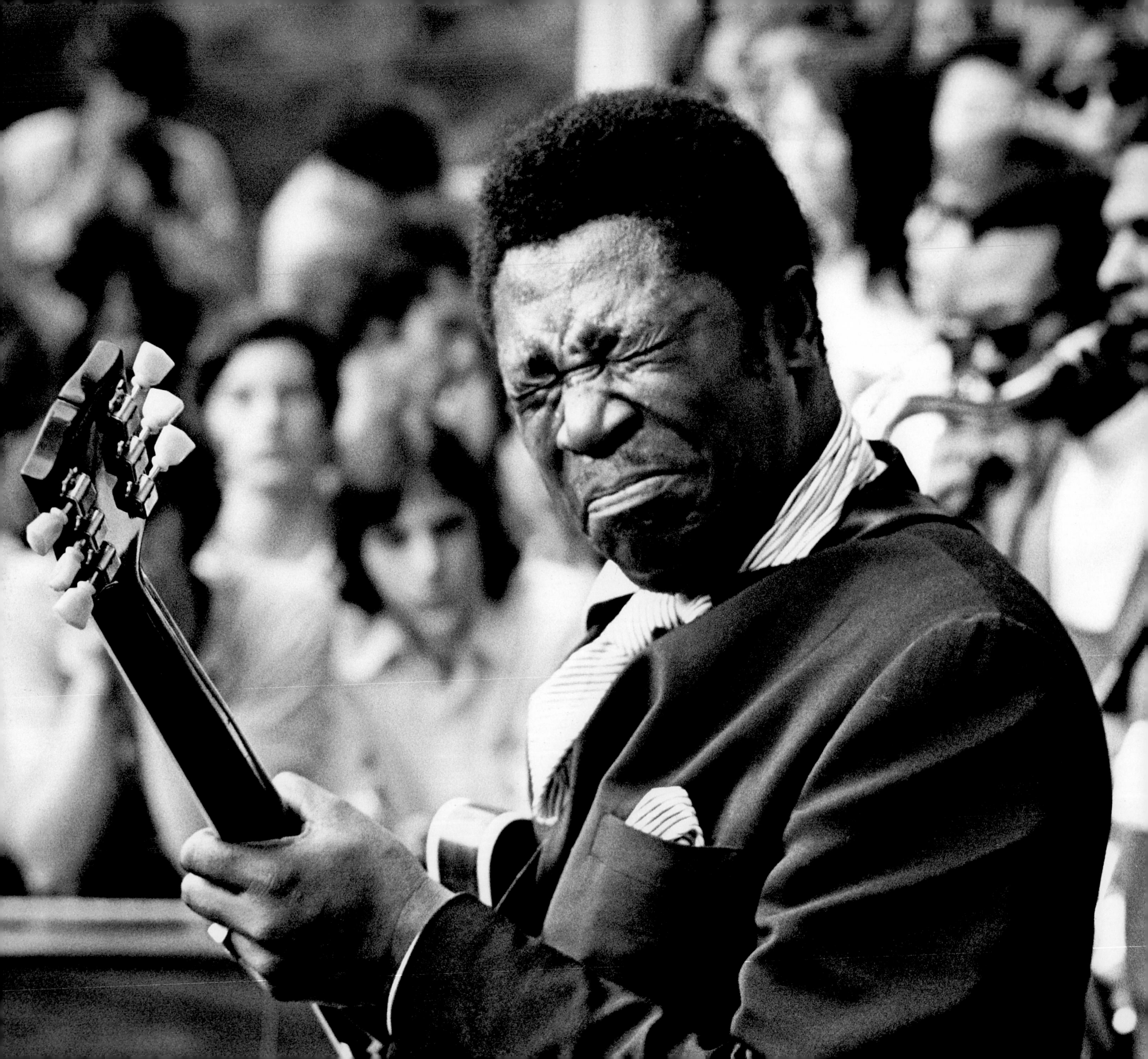

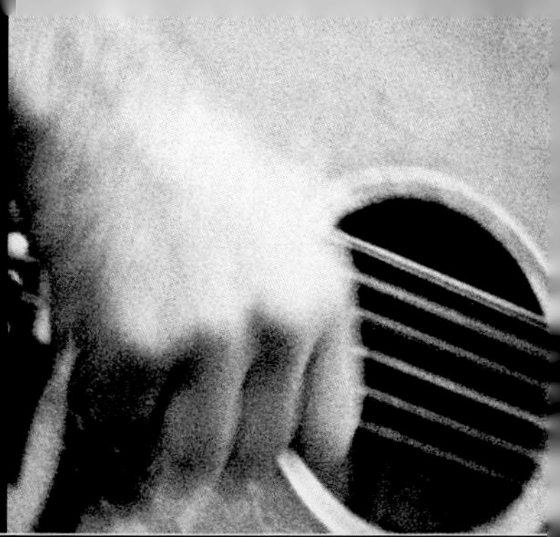

4

WHAT'S THAT SOUND?

What's That Sound?

Janis Joplin at the Fillmore East, New York City, February 11, 1969

When I wasn't photographing riots, I was shooting rock stars. It was a lot safer than dodging tear gas grenades.

My most prized possession, other than my Leica cameras, was a free press pass to the Fillmore East, the main showplace for 60s acid–rock and blues on New York's Lower East Side. I went almost every weekend to photograph acts such as *Big Brother and the Holding Company* (with Janis Joplin), *Country Joe and the Fish*, *Sly and the Family Stone*, the *Grateful Dead*, *Buffalo Springfield*, the *Byrds*, *Jefferson Airplane*, *Creedence Clearwater Revival*, *Bob Marley and the Wailers*, blues greats like B.B. King and Howlin' Wolf, Rod Stewart's U.S. premiere with

Most rallies featured musicians protesting the war, ranging from Phil Ochs to Charles Mingus and everything in between. Pete Seeger and Peter, Paul and Mary sang at almost every demonstration.

It's hard to imagine now how important the music was to the protest movement and the birth of the counterculture, but it was essential. The music created a cross–cultural, unified identity among young people that hasn't been seen since. Country Joe sang that "It's one, two, three, what are we fighting for. Don't ask me, I don't give a damn, next stop is Vietnam." The Rolling Stones' *Street Fighting Man* became something of a militant anthem. We knew every

My personal favorite was a ditty sung by The Fugs: *Kill, Kill, Kill for Peace.*

The music of that era changed me forever. I was a classical music kid until I heard *Revolver* and *Rubber Soul* by the Beatles. In the third row center for one of Jimi Hendrix's first concerts in America, I was forever blown away by a wall of Sun amplifiers and feedback. But the moments I will never forget were when Janis Joplin belted the blues—no one has approached her raspy, gutsy power since. Watching her guzzle Southern Comfort on stage, I wondered how long she could keep it together. She and Hendrix both died of overdoses soon after.

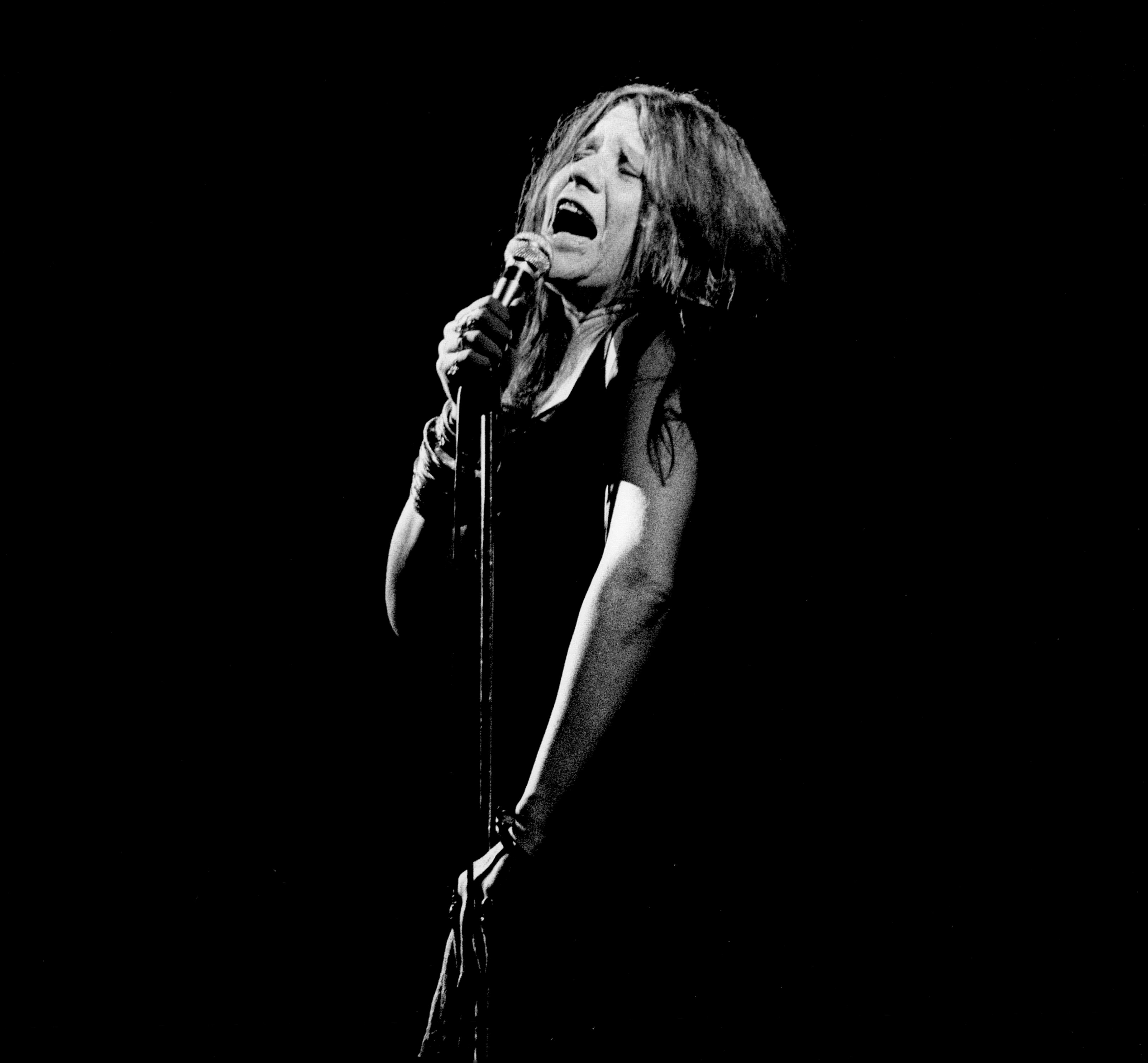

Janis Joplin (in sequence) performs at the Fillmore East, New York City, February 11, 1969

John and Yoko

John Lennon and Yoko Ono at the "Free John Sinclair" rally, in support of Sinclair, a White Panther and manager of the band MC5, after his arrest for giving two joints to an undercover police officer. Jerry Rubin is playing congas. Ann Arbor, MI, December 10, 1971.

In 1971, I was working in Ann Arbor, Michigan, on a campaign to free John Sinclair from a ten–year prison sentence he received for giving two joints of marijuana to an undercover agent. Sinclair made his case a challenge to the constitutionality of the state marijuana laws, which classified it incorrectly as an addictive narcotic. Despite the constitutional challenge, Sinclair was kept in solitary confinement much of the time he was in prison. The Michigan Supreme Court even denied him bail pending appeal.

Then Jerry Rubin got John Lennon and Yoko Ono involved. They came to Ann Arbor to play a benefit concert for Sinclair, along with Stevie Wonder, Bob Seger, Archie Shepp and speakers like Rubin, Abbie Hoffman, Bobby Seale, Allen Ginsberg, Rennie Davis, Ed Sanders of The Fugs and others. It was the first time Lennon had played in the U.S. since the breakup of the Beatles. He wrote a song about Sinclair for the occasion. I handled the public relations for the concert, and learned first–hand the powerful effect rock and roll could have on politics.

The "Free John Sinclair" concert was on Friday night, December 10, 1971. It was broadcast all over the state, generating enormous amounts of news coverage. Such was the power of the Beatles myth that the Michigan Supreme Court released Sinclair on Monday morning after two years in prison. Clearly, music had set John free.

Buoyed by this success, Lennon, Rubin, Abbie and others started planning a nationwide concert tour to oust Richard Nixon from office. The White House responded by trying to deport Lennon on an old pot bust, which effectively silenced him for the duration.

In 1979, I built on the inspiration of the Sinclair concert to put together the No Nukes concerts at Madison Square Garden in New York, for which I was co–producer. We held five nights of benefit concerts against nuclear power, and made a record and a motion picture featuring Bruce Springsteen, Jackson Browne, Bonnie Raitt, the Doobie Brothers, Peter Tosh, Gil Scott–Heron, James Taylor, Carly Simon and others.

More recently, I helped MoveOn.org put together and promote the "Vote for Change" concert tour against President Bush with Springsteen, REM, Dave Matthews, Pearl Jam, the Dixie Chicks, and Bonnie, Jackson and James Taylor again.

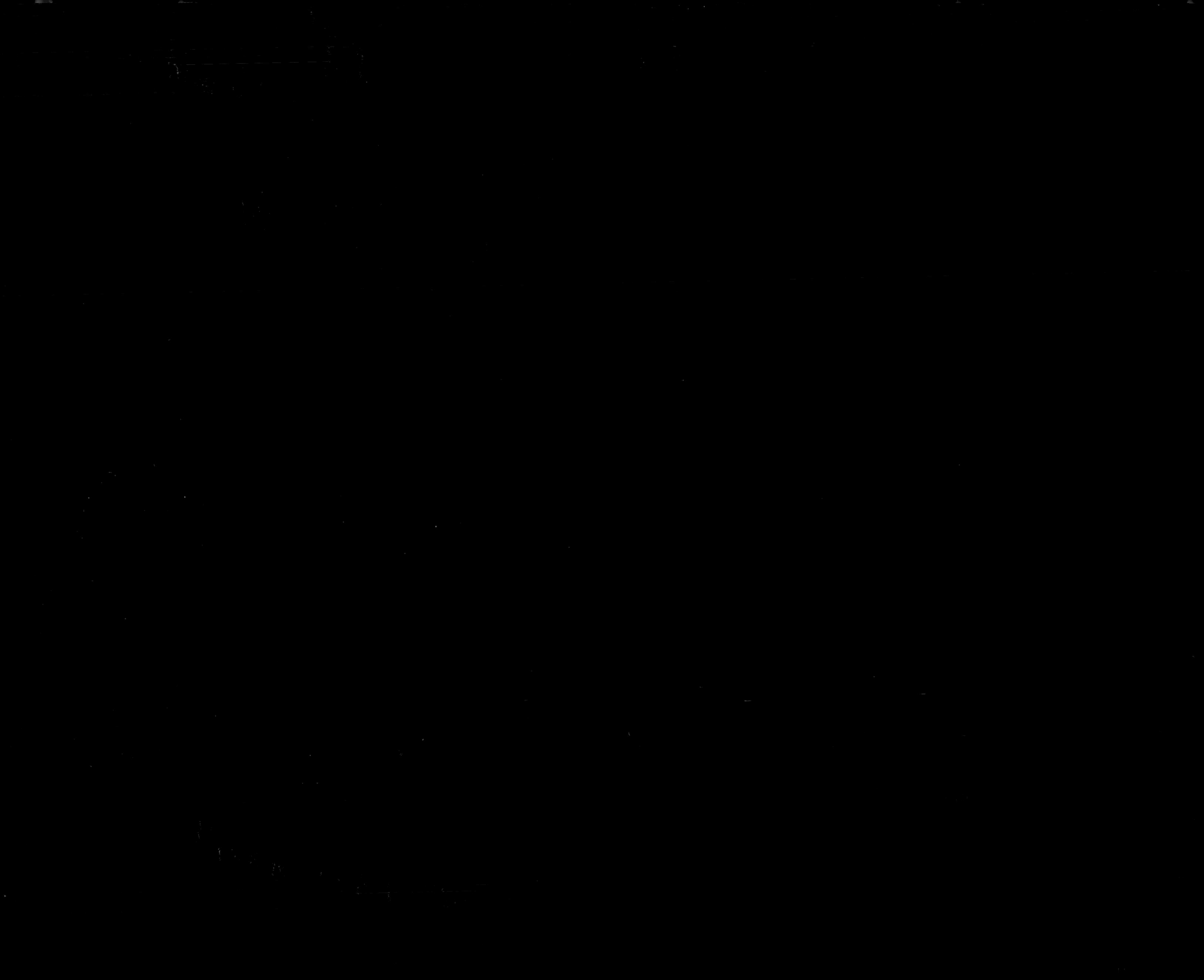

B.B. King performs in Central Park, New York City, June 13, 1969

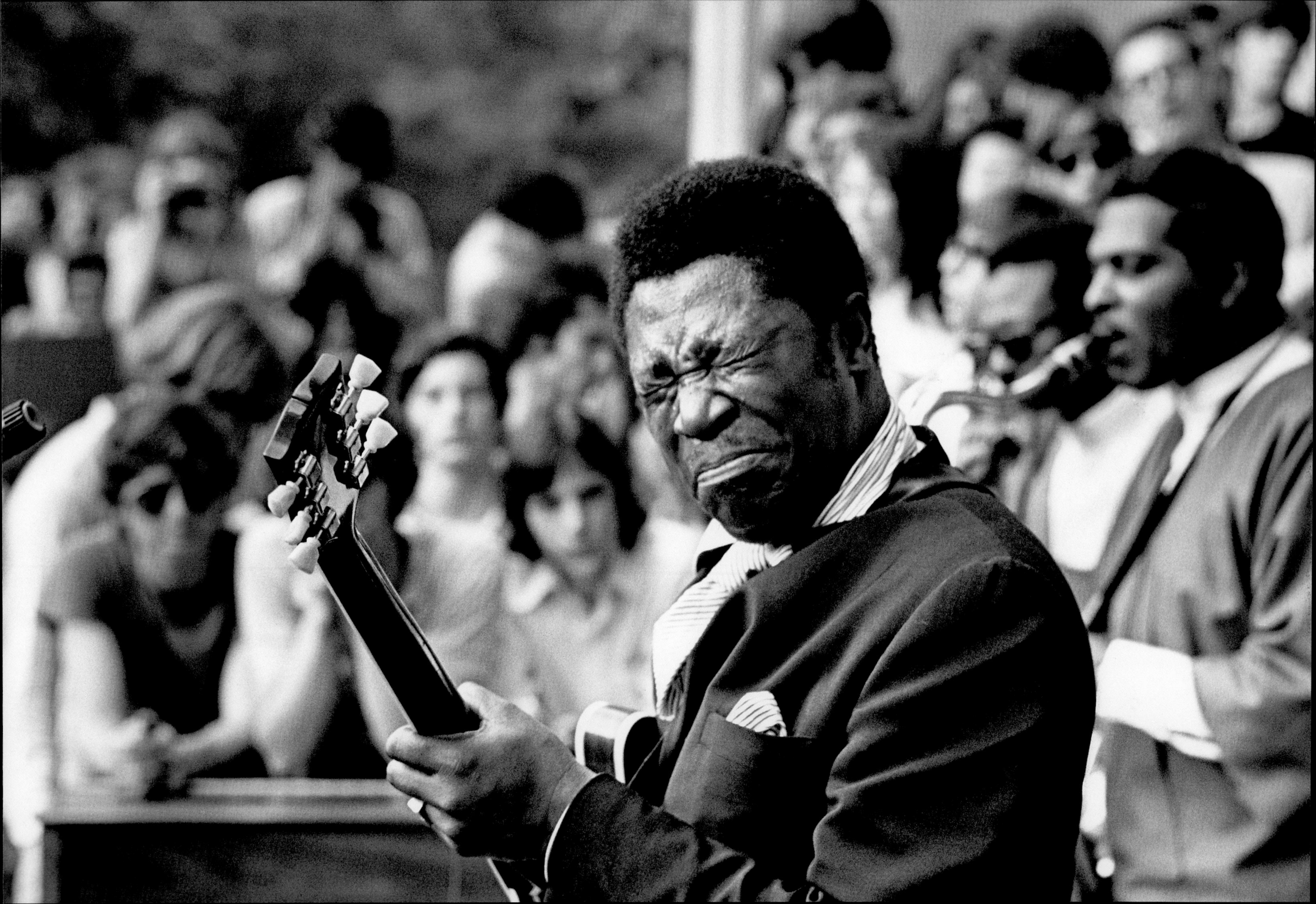

Jefferson Airplane performs in Central Park, New York City, May, 1968

Phil Ochs performs at a Central Park peace march, April 5, 1969

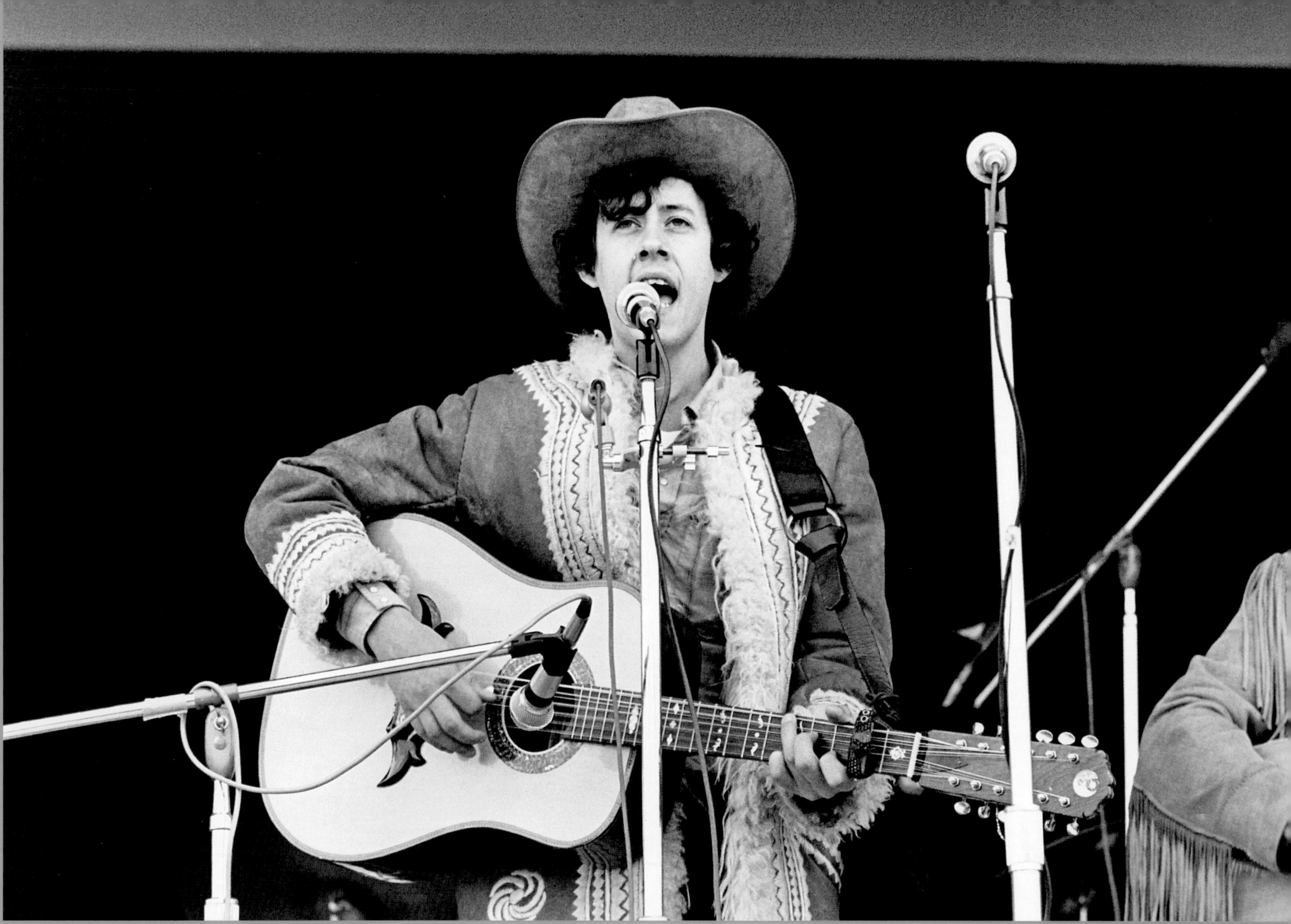

Arlo Guthrie performs at the National Mobilization to End the War, Washington, D.C., November 15, 1969

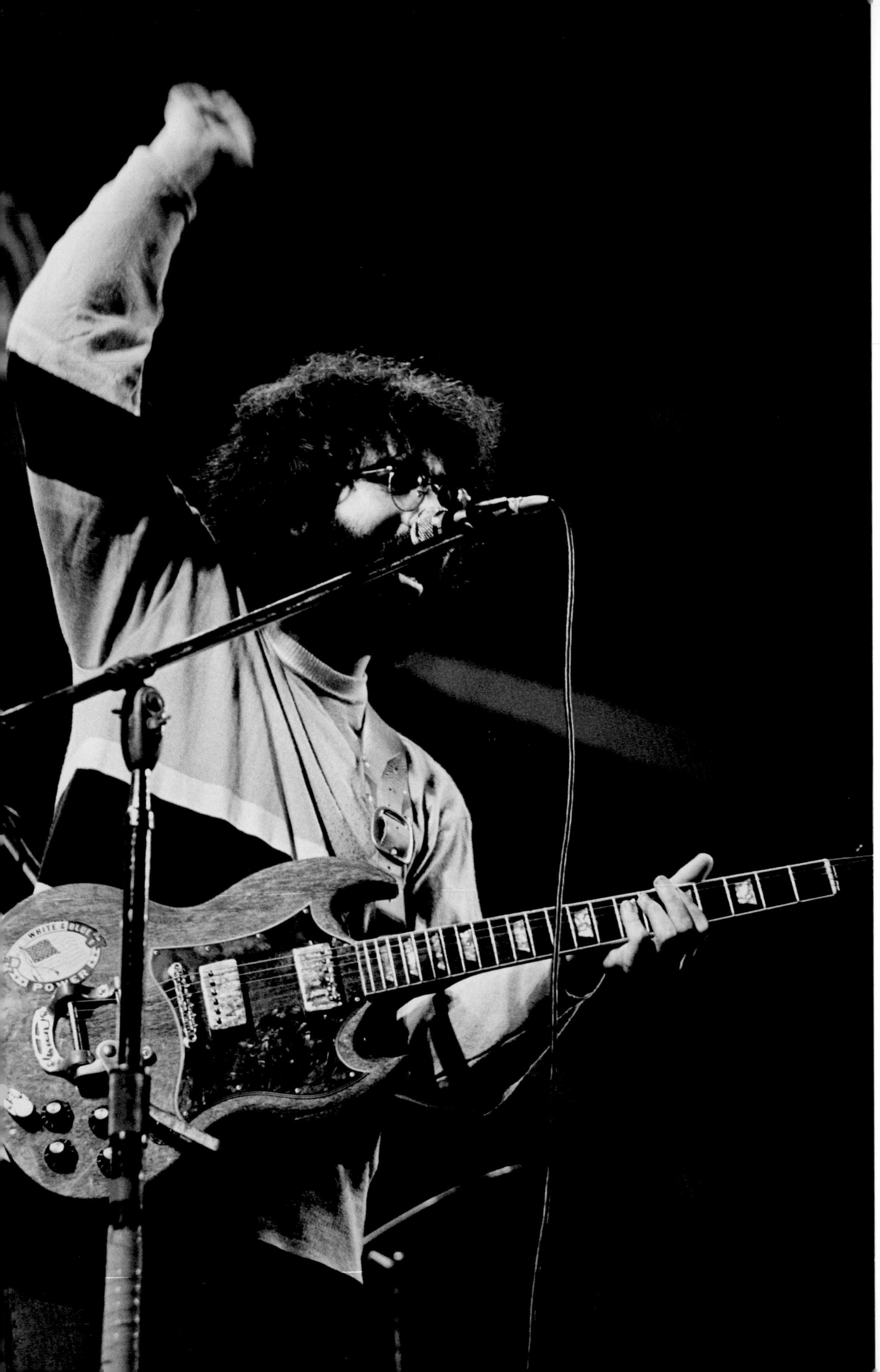

Jerry Garcia of the Grateful Dead *at the Fillmore East, New York City, February 11, 1969*

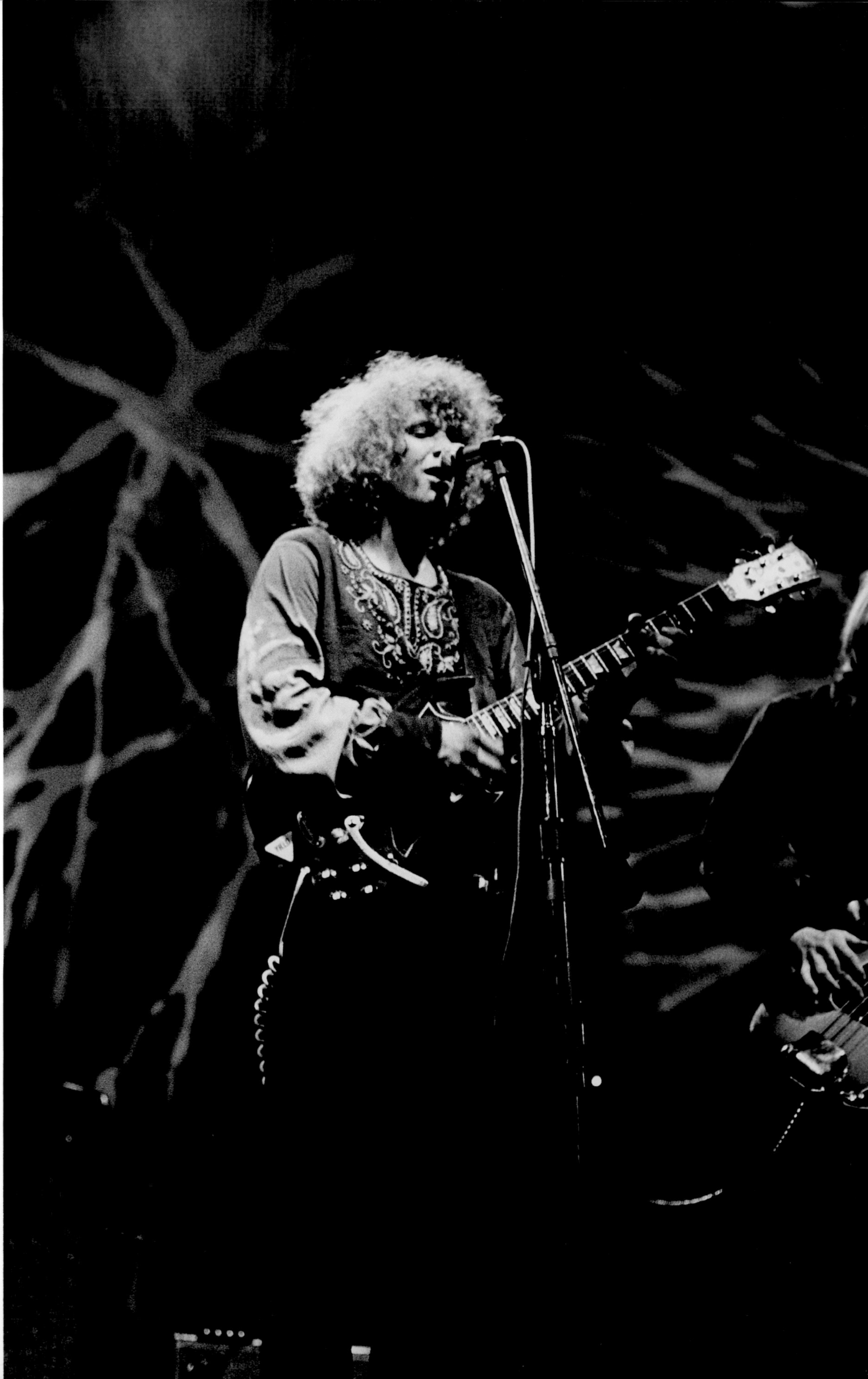

Berry Melton of Country Joe and the Fish *at the Fillmore East, New York City, September 28, 1968*

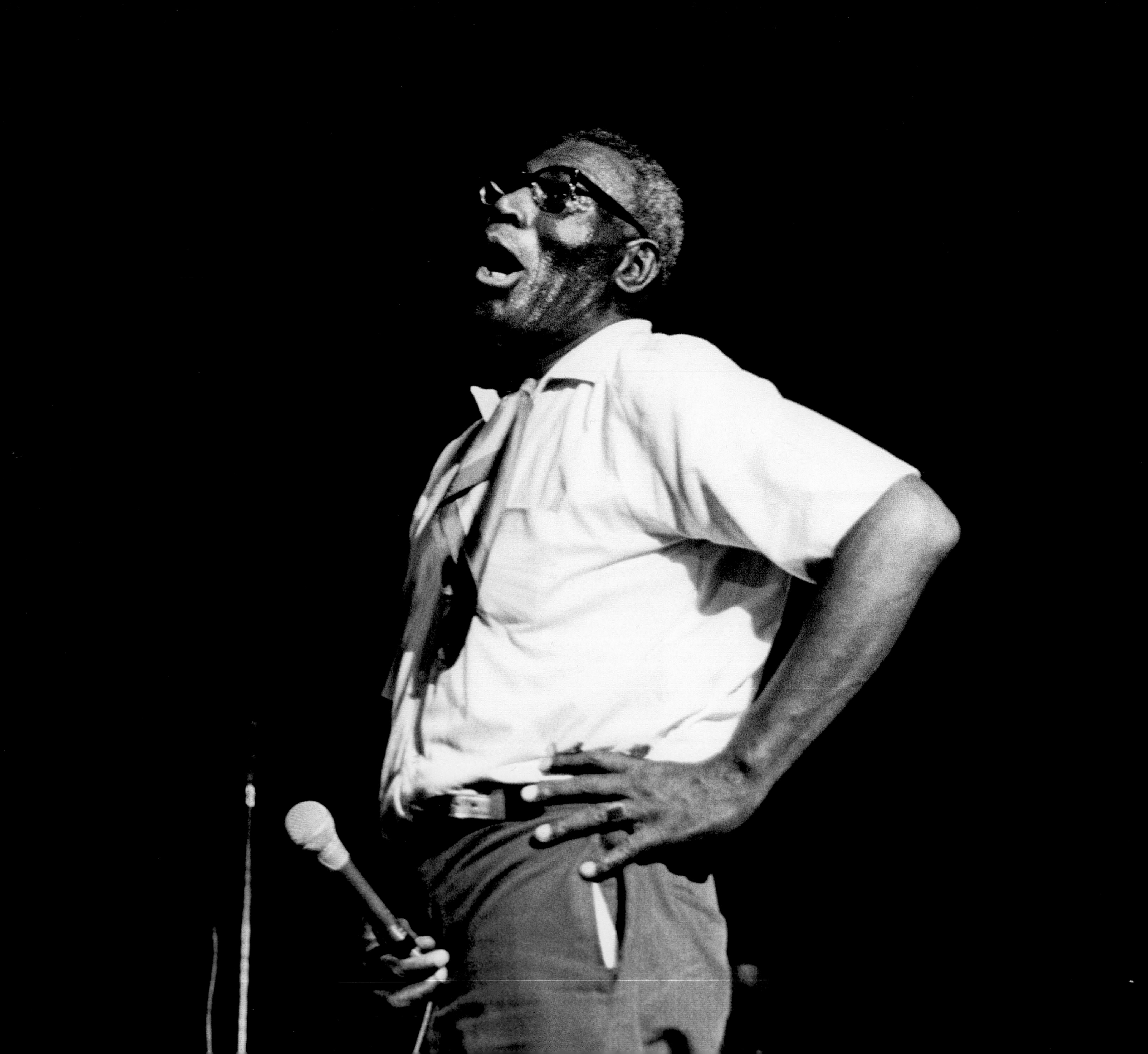

Howlin' Wolf performs at the Fillmore East, New York City, October 9–10, 1971

John Fogerty of Creedence Clearwater Revival, *in his recording studio Berkeley, CA, February 26, 1970*

Above and Right: The Rolling Stones *perform at Madison Square Garden, New York City, November 28, 1969*

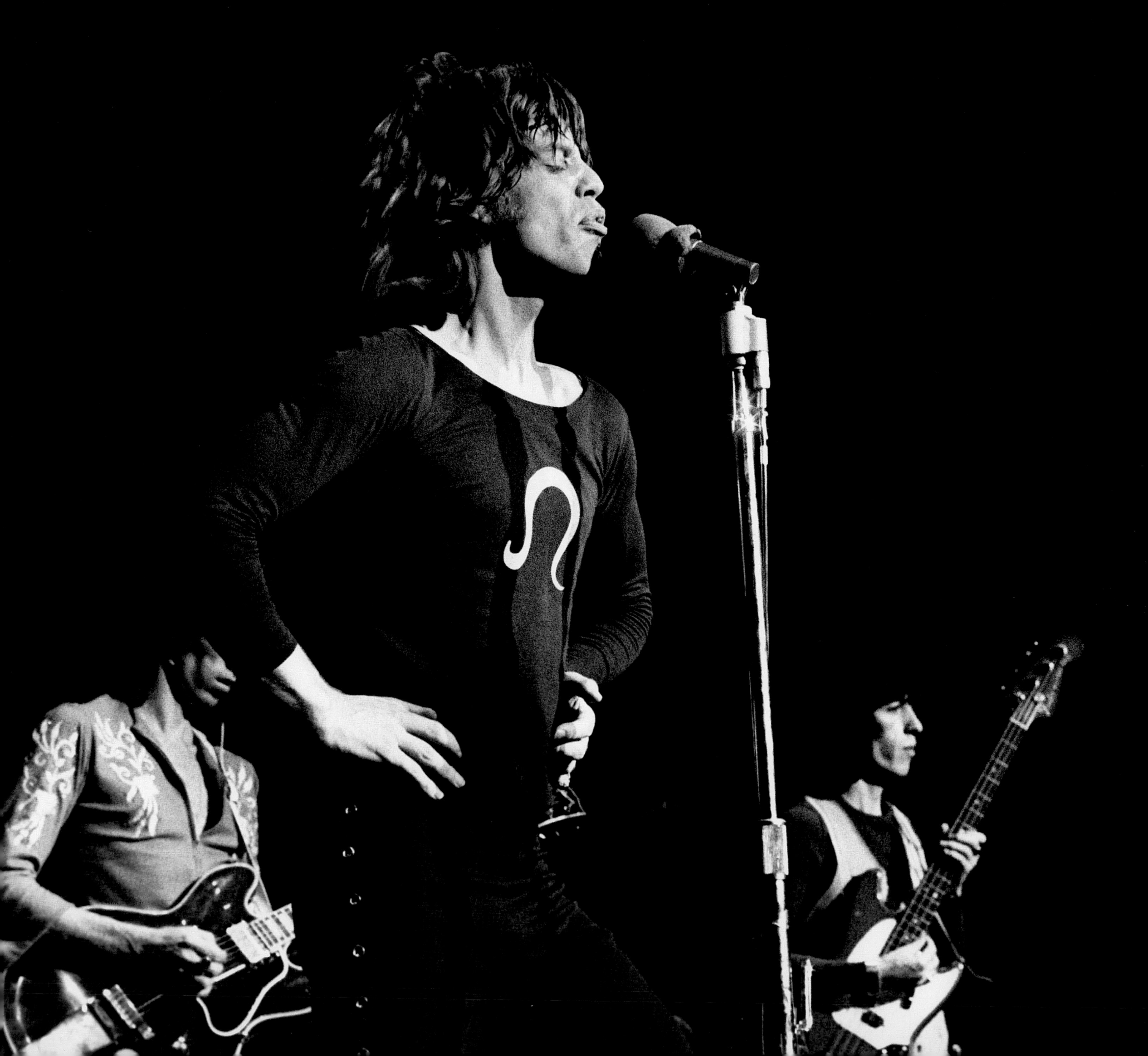

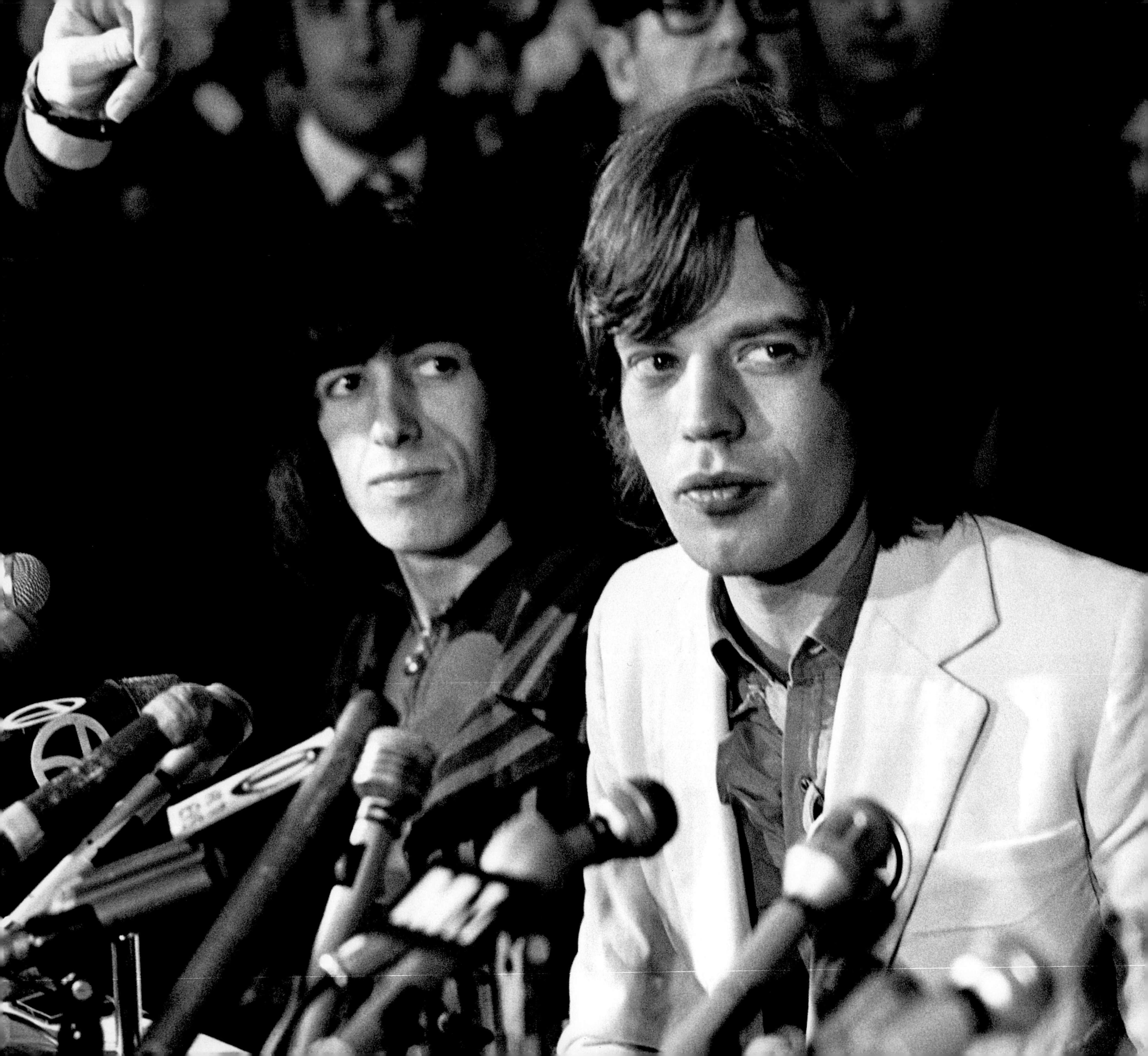

The Rolling Stones *(left to right: Bill Wyman, Mick Jagger and Keith Richards)*
hold a press conference, New York City, November 27, 1969

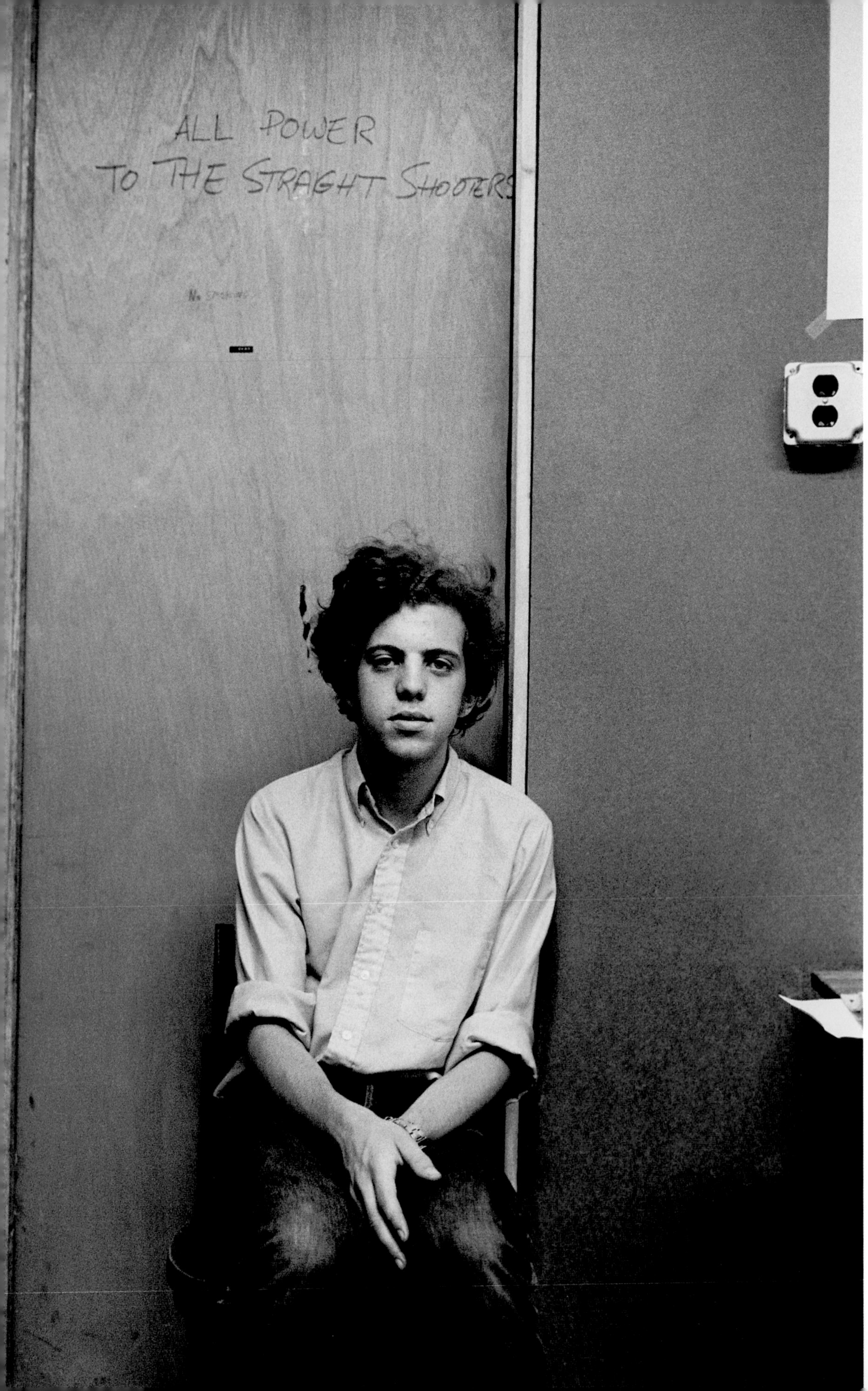
ALL POWER
TO THE STRAIGHT SHOOTERS

Liberation News Service

David Fenton at the Liberation News Service offices, New York City, May 21, 1970

This self–portrait was taken at the offices of Liberation News Service in the spring of 1970, when I had just turned 18.

I worked for LNS as a photographer and graphics editor for $25 a week plus free staff dinners. It was my university, political education and professional training all wrapped up in one.

LNS was a chapter of Students for a Democratic Society (SDS). Several of the staff had attended Columbia University and participated in the famous 1968 student strike. It was started by Ray Mungo and Marshall Bloom in 1967 to serve antiwar, underground newspapers throughout the world. They were later joined by Allen Young, a former *Washington Post* reporter who had quit over the *Post's* pro–government and distorted coverage of the war in Vietnam.

We worked out of a basement office on Claremont Avenue on the far Upper West Side of Manhattan near Columbia University, and distributed a "packet" of news and graphics twice a week, printed by hand at the offices. We'd stay up all night collating the packets and putting them in mail bags. Money came from subscribers and from a number of mainstream churches opposed to the war, including the Methodists.

LNS functioned as a collective. The entire group made all decisions. It was absurdly unwieldy, but forced us to develop a less hierarchical approach. There were a whole series of these alternative New York media institutions in the late 60s, including *New York Newsreel*, which made political documentaries, several newspapers including the *Rat* and the *New York Free Press* and the *Underground Press Syndicate*.

I first met Allen Young of LNS, who became a real mentor, through working on my high school antiwar newspaper, which used LNS material. He took me under his wing and taught me about Vietnam, Cuba, the Civil Rights movement, anticolonial wars of liberation, apartheid in South Africa and the CIA's totally counterproductive overthrow of governments from Guatemala to Iran. It was better than school for sure. And we had great parties.

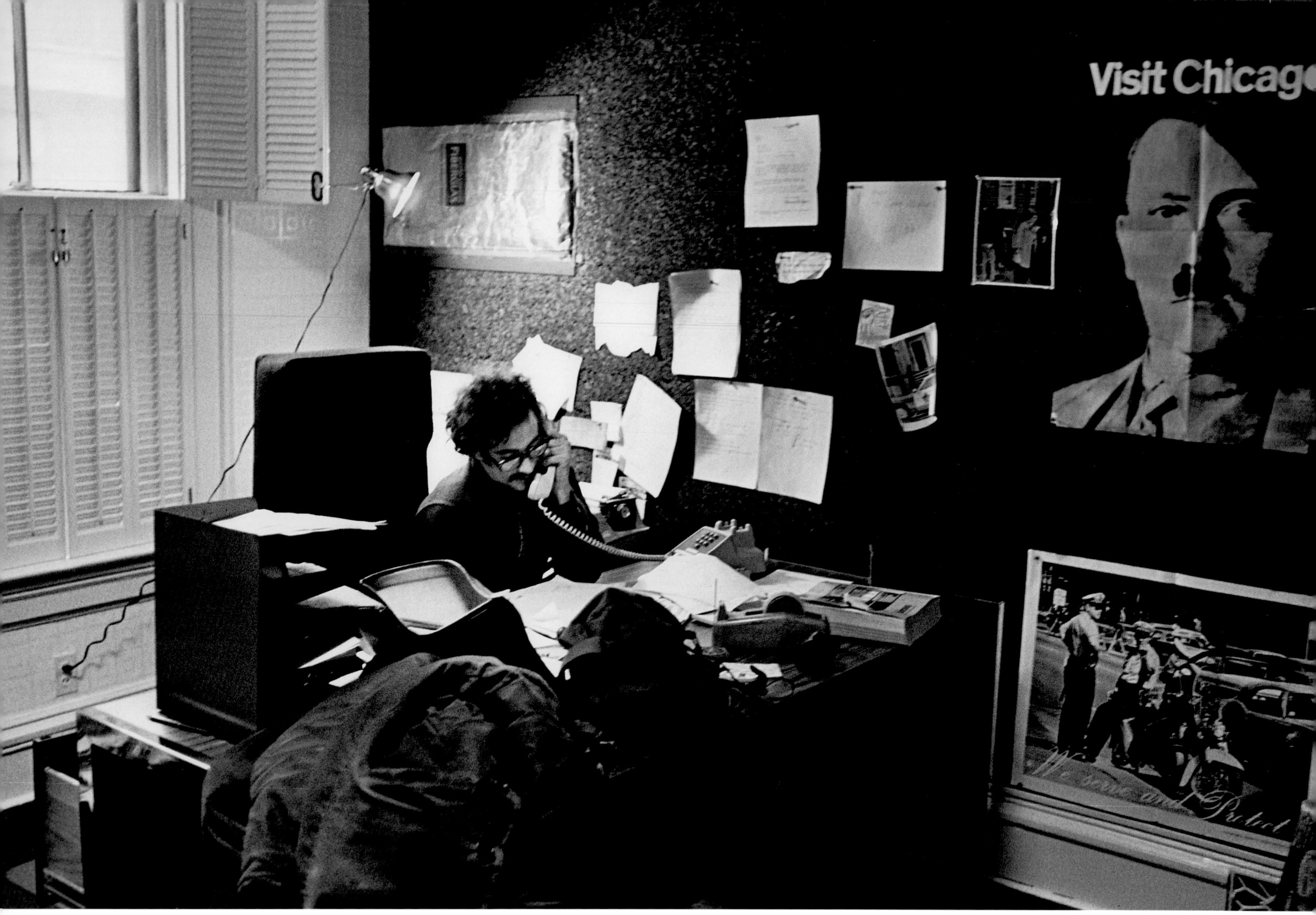
Visit Chicago

Mark Feinstein, a reporter for Liberation News Service, covers the Chicago 7 conspiracy trial, Chicago, IL, February 17, 1970

LNS had a huge impact in enlarging the antiwar movement and helping to turn elites against the war. But, after a decade, it succumbed to factionalism and sectarianism, typical tendencies of the Left, disbanding in 1981. I eventually moved to Ann Arbor, Michigan after being told to stop taking photographs by several female members who were resentful of my minor celebrity.

Allen Young, a member of Liberation News Service at the National Mobilization to End the War, Washington, D.C., November 15, 1969

Members of the Liberation News Service, New York City, October 12, 1969

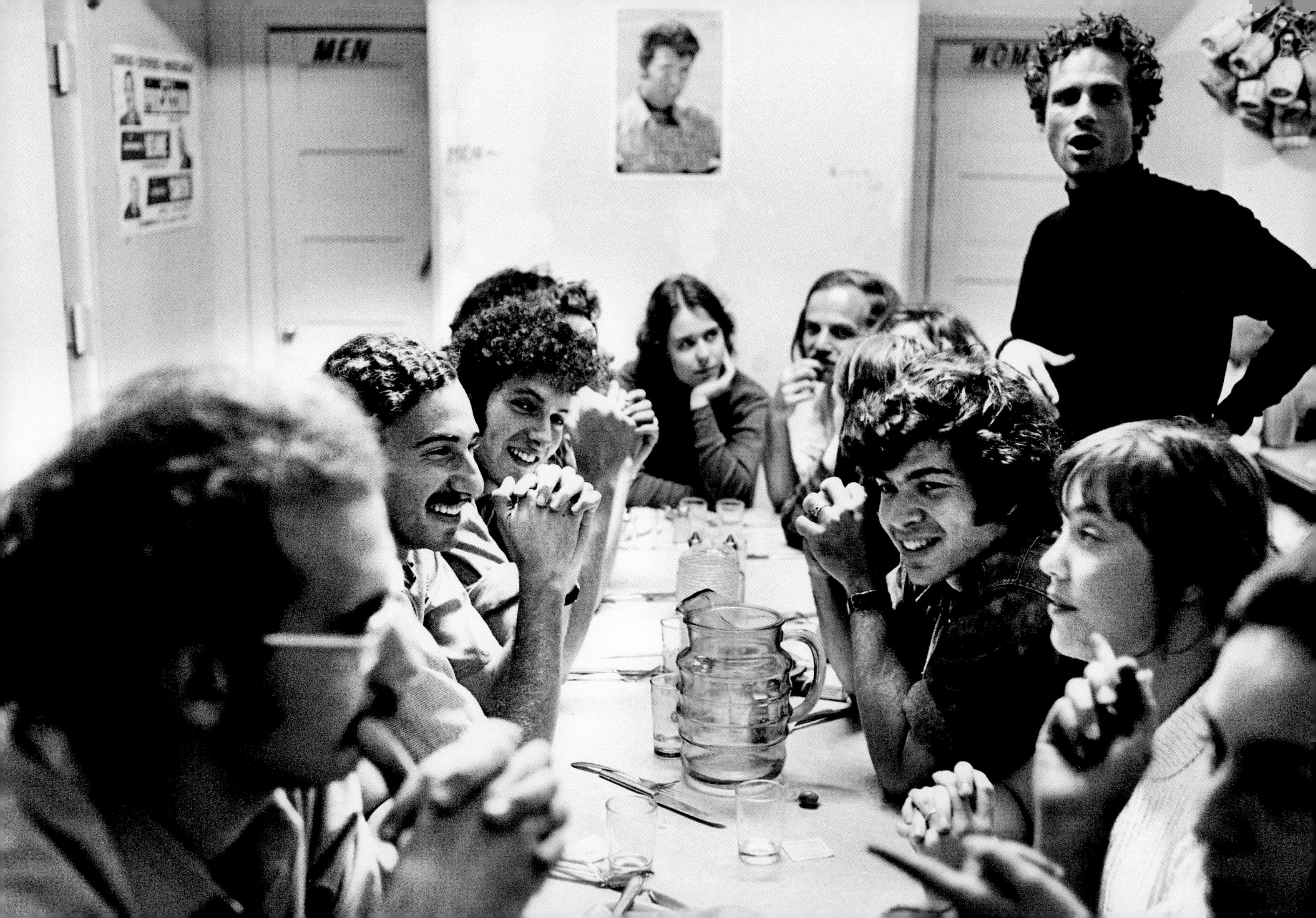
MEN

The Whole World Was Watching
Afterword by Chris Murray

The spirit of protest was alive and well in America during the 1960s and early 1970s. Fueled by the outrage over the tragedy of the Vietnam War and a burning desire for social justice, organizations such as the Black Panther Party, the Young Lords and the antiwar movement emerged. Following the extraordinary courage and conviction of the Civil Rights movement, their impact was enormous. The international protests against the Vietnam War, for example, were instrumental in bringing to an end that horrible conflict.

SHOTS is a record and reminder of those days of rage. David Fenton documented people who in one way or another put themselves on the line for what they believed in, despite enormous odds. The spirit of protest was not the stuff of corporate machinations—it consisted of individuals…flesh and blood, young and old, black and white, rich and poor, together and alone…a true democracy of spirit. Although his work was published at the time in counterculture and underground publications, as well as in the mainstream press, Fenton photographed as a way to document his experiences.

A compelling legacy of photographs documenting protest movements and demonstrations informs David Fenton's work. The massive growth of television internationally and the widespread popularity in America of publications such as *Look* and *LIFE* disseminated visual images to a larger audience than ever before. Photo essays such as David Douglas Duncan's images of GIs desperately fighting in Korea, published on Christmas Day in 1950 by *LIFE*, stunned America. Duncan's photographs had the power not only to inform people but also to move them.

In the 1950s, photographers, viewed as a threat for their controversial subject matter, were often ostracized. The influential Photo League in New York City, dedicated to documentary photography, collapsed in 1951 after many of its members were blacklisted.

In the 1960s, photographs of Civil Rights demonstrations and Vietnam War protests often shocked and startled the world. In 1963, Charles Moore photographed black demonstrators in Birmingham, Alabama, being attacked with high–velocity hoses, the force of the water brutally pushing them up against a wall. This photograph, perhaps more than any other at the time, raised awareness and support for Civil Rights demonstrators.

James Karales documented a non–violent march organized by Martin Luther King, Jr., from Selma to Montgomery, Alabama in March of 1965. Karales' memorable image of a line of marchers carrying an American flag under a foreboding sky seemed to anticipate what ultimately transpired. State troopers attacked the peaceful demonstrators with teargas and brutally beat them. Student photographer, John Filo, won the Pulitzer Prize for his unforgettable image of a young woman kneeling in horror at a dead student just shot by the National Guard at Kent State University in 1970 during a protest against President Nixon's decision to send troops to Cambodia.

David Fenton was only sixteen years old when he started taking photographs of demonstrations and protests. After leaving high school in 1967 and joining Liberation News Service, he became swept up by the ideals and goals of the resistance movements. The access afforded him by working for LNS, part of the alternative press, provided a level of intimacy to his subjects out of reach to most mainstream journalists. He was not an outsider.

Protests and demonstrations at that time were often a strange mix of celebration and tension. The hope and energy of collective protests stood in contrast to the fear of police brutality and the sting of teargas. Fenton's photograph (page 97) of an antiwar protest in Washington, DC, in 1970, shows a rebellious but joyous scene. Set against the formal backdrop of the Lincoln Memorial, demonstrators dance in the Reflecting Pool while waving a flag. However, in another photo (page 37), young men and women arrested in Chicago have mixed expressions of fear and determination on their faces.

One of Fenton's most compelling photographs (page 108) is of a man, seen at many peace demonstrations, crucified on a full–size cross. The crucified protester wears a peace emblem on a chain around his neck while a devout older woman stands in front holding her hands together in prayer. Though acting alone and tied to the cross, this man and his silent act of protest evoked tremendous emotion wherever he appeared.

Fenton's image of poet Allen Ginsberg at a Black Panther Party rally in 1970 (page 27) perfectly captures the calm in the center of the storm. Chanting mantras to dispel "bad vibes" and practicing meditation during demonstrations, Ginsberg was at the forefront of the struggle for peace and justice. His brilliant critical analyses of those troubled times in speeches, essays and poetry gave strength to the movement.

A sense of solidarity and justice is evoked in Fenton's portrait of the Chicago 7 with their attorneys, taken after the group's acquittal on conspiracy charges in the infamous trial that followed the riots at the 1968 Democratic National Convention in Chicago. It was at those demonstrations that protesters spontaneously started chanting, "The whole world is watching," in reaction to the police brutality being broadcast live on television throughout the world.

Fenton's photographs of activists who were popular figures, like Muhammad Ali with the Black Panthers in New York City in 1969, and John Lennon and Yoko Ono at the *"Free John Sinclair"* rally in 1971, documented the contribution of public figures whose support galvanized large numbers of people. Poets historically challenged the status quo. Folk and pop music came together in the mid–1960s and created the genre of the socially conscious 'popular song.' Those artists inspired and influenced millions of people throughout the world.

SHOTS takes us to a time that in many ways was heroic. People were passionate enough to take their beliefs to the streets. It was protest…revolution in fact…that built America. David Fenton's *SHOTS* reminds us of those ideals.

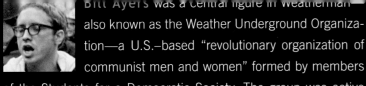

Bill Ayers was a central figure in Weatherman— also known as the Weather Underground Organization—a U.S.–based "revolutionary organization of communist men and women" formed by members of the Students for a Democratic Society. The group was active from 1969 to 1976, and advocated the overthrow of the United States government and capitalism through a campaign of bombings, jailbreaks and riots. Ayers lived underground for ten years, an experience he wrote about in his memoir, *Fugitive Days*. Now married to fellow Weatherman member Bernardine Dohrn, Ayers is currently a school reform activist and a professor of education at the University of Illinois at Chicago.

Marshall Bloom was the co–founder of Liberation News Service (LNS), the "Associated Press" for more than 500 underground newspapers during the 60s. A cultural and political activist in the course of his short life. Bloom transformed from high school conservative into civil rights worker, charismatic student rights activist, proponent of a "new journalism," and antiwar radical. He was the target of government harassment and a leader in the "back–to–the–land" movement. In the fall of 1969, Bloom committed suicide at the age of 25.

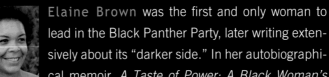

Elaine Brown was the first and only woman to lead in the Black Panther Party, later writing extensively about its "darker side." In her autobiographical memoir, *A Taste of Power: A Black Woman's Story*, Brown recounts the story of her childhood in the ghettoes of north Philadelphia and how she became the leader of one of the most widely publicized militant civil rights groups in U.S. history. Today, as an activist, writer and lecturer, Brown oversees several local civic–minded initiatives, including a Free Breakfast Program and Sickle Cell Anemia Testing. She is the Director of Political Affairs for the National Alliance for Radical Prison Reform, a board member of Mothers Advocating Juvenile Justice, and Vice President of the Dr. Huey P. Newton Foundation.

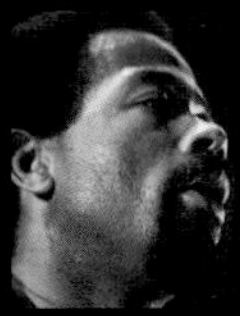

Eldridge Cleaver, an early member of the Black Panther Party (founded in 1966) became famously controversial as the group's outspoken Minister of Information. His 1968 book *Soul On Ice*, based on essays he had written in prison years earlier, cemented Cleaver's reputation as a spokesman for Black Power. That same year he was wounded in a Panther shootout with Oakland police. Cleaver jumped bail to escape, fleeing first to Algeria and eventually landing in Paris. He returned to America in 1975. In later years Cleaver renounced his former radical views, becoming a born–again Christian and embracing conservative political causes, even running for political office as a Republican. He suffered well–publicized struggles with drug addiction in the years before his 1998 death.

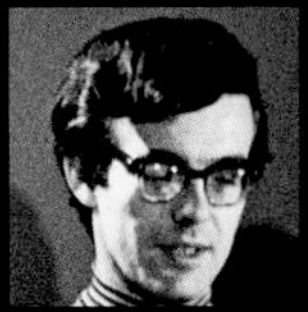

Rennie Davis was the National Director of community organizing programs for the Students for a Democratic Society, the radical 60s student political movement that acted as the umbrella organization of smaller factions, including Weatherman. A movement activist based in Chicago, Davis did most of the organizing for the 1968 Democratic National Convention week demonstrations. He was one of two defendants to testify at the Chicago 7 trial. Later in his life, he became a venture capitalist and lecturer on meditation and self–awareness.

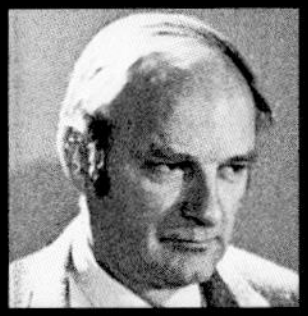

David Dellinger was one of the eight radicals charged with conspiring to incite riots around the Chicago–based Democratic Party Convention in 1968. Dellinger's fellow defendants included Bobby Seale (Black Panthers), Tom Hayden (Students for a Democratic Society), Rennie Davis (National Mobilization Committee), Abbie Hoffman and Jerry Rubin (Youth International Party), John Froines and Lee Weiner. When Seale, the eighth member of the group who repeatedly interrupted court proceedings, was removed from the case, the group became known as the Chicago 7. Described by prosecutors as the "chief architect of the conspiracy," Dellinger held the chair position of the National Mobilization Committee to End the War in Vietnam. The Chicago 7 were eventually acquitted of conspiracy charges in 1970. Dellinger passed away in 2004.

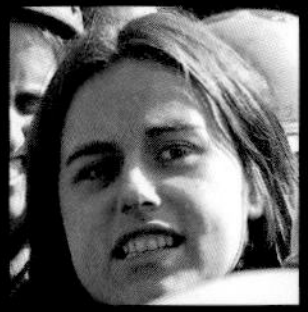

Bernardine Dohrn held a leadership role in the Weatherman and was considered the organization's figurehead. She spent the 1970s living underground and was on the FBI's Ten Most Wanted list. Today, Dohrn serves as an Associate Professor of Northwestern University, and Director of the University's Children and Justice Center.

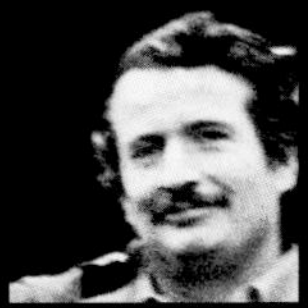

John Froines was one of the forgotten defendants of the Chicago 7 conspiracy trial. Not individually charged with inciting a riot like his fellow activists, but rather with making incendiary devices, Froines and Lee Weiner were acquitted by the jury. His activism dates back to 1964, when he was chair of Students for Johnson at Yale University. He later joined the Students for a Democratic Society and founded the Radical Science Information Service. He joined the UCLA faculty as a professor in its School of Public Health in 1981 after a stint in the Carter Administration as OSHA's Director of Toxic Substances.

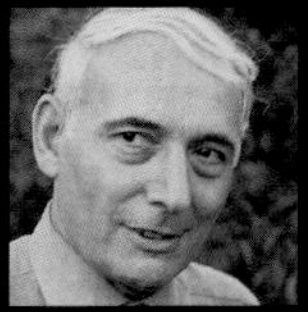

Charles Garry, the official legal representative for the Black Panther Party, was a radical lawyer and public relations counsel who defended Jim Jones and his Guyana settlement a year before the Jonestown massacre. When relatives and defectors said that the People's Temple was a dangerous place and that Jim Jones was a criminal, Garry defended the cult, saying it was a bold socialist experiment under attack by the reactionary, fascist American government. Charles Garry's other clients, Angela Davis and Huey P. Newton, sent messages of revolutionary solidarity to their brothers and sisters in Jonestown. Garry also defended Huey P. Newton from the charge of murdering a policeman named John Frey.

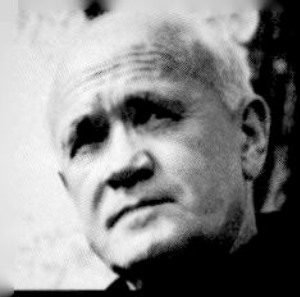

Jean Genet was one of the most controversial and prominent figures to shape modern French literature. A prolific playwright, novelist and poet, Genet supported the Paris student uprising in 1968 and, on assignment with *Esquire*, covered the 1968 Democratic National Convention.

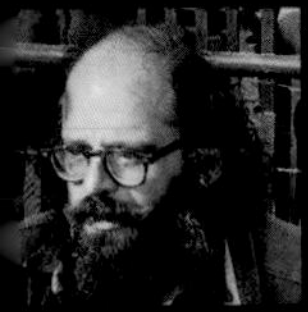

Allen Ginsberg was the central poet and figurehead of the Beat movement. His poem "Howl" became the literary manifesto of his generation, and led to his 1961 work *Kaddish and Other Poems*, a stream–of–consciousness account of his mother's life and death in a mental hospital. Ginsberg was also a ubiquitous presence at many of the political protests and cultural events that marked the 1960s.

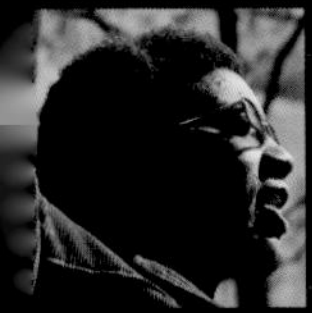

Fred Hampton was a high school student when he joined the Black Panther Party. By the age of 20, he had become the leader of the organization's Chicago chapter. Hampton maintained regular speaking engagements and organized weekly rallies at the Chicago federal building on behalf of the party. During his too–short life, he worked with a Free People's Clinic, taught daily morning political education classes and launched a community control of police project. He was also instrumental in the Black Panthers' Free Breakfast Program. He was shot to death while sleeping by heavily armed Chicago policemen in 1969.

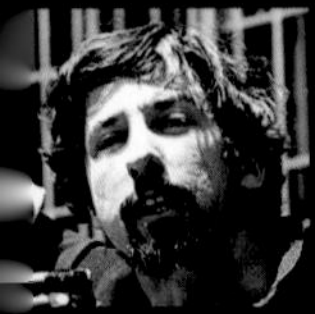

Tom Hayden was largely viewed as the chief ideologue of the New Left. He drafted the famous Port Huron Statement in 1962 expressing the idealism of the New Left and became a co–founder of the Students for a Democratic Society. In the early 60s, Hayden participated in civil rights work in the South and in the black ghettoes of Newark, New Jersey. He later shifted his focus to efforts to end the Vietnam War, twice making trips to North Vietnam. After the Chicago 7 trial, Hayden married (and later divorced) activist actress Jane Fonda. He later served a term as a California State Senator.

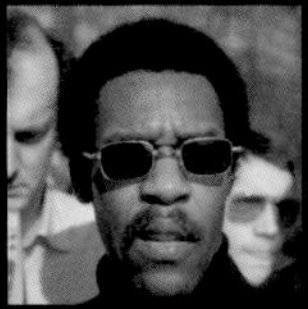

David Hilliard was one of the first members of the Black Panther Party and became Chief of Staff of the organization when Huey P. Newton was arrested in September of 1968. In 1993 Hilliard helped establish the Dr. Huey P. Newton Foundation, a nonprofit educational organization that offers community–based programs to the public, including literacy, voter outreach and health services. Hilliard is author of the memoir *This Side of Glory*, an eyewitness account of the Black Panther movement.

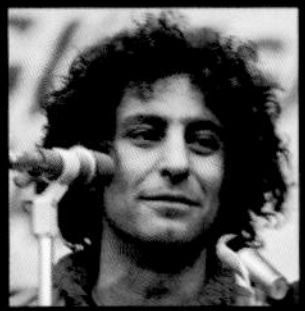

Abbie Hoffman was a leader of the Youth International Party, or Yippies. Hoffman began his career in political activism in the early 60s with the Student Nonviolent Coordinating Committee. In 1968 he began the loosely organized Yippie movement. Hoffman underwent plastic surgery in 1974 and assumed the underground alias "Barry Freed" to avoid trial on charges of possessing cocaine. He stayed underground in upstate New York until 1980, when he surrendered to authorities. He resumed his political activism in 1982 but was arrested for the forty–second time while protesting CIA recruitment at the University of Massachusetts in 1987. In 1989, the self–described "orphan of America" was found dead in his home in New Hope, Pennsylvania.

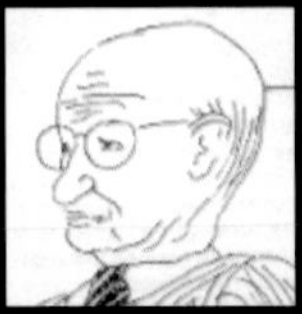

Judge Julius Hoffman presided over the conspiracy trial of the Chicago 7. During the trial, Judge Hoffman was scrutinized by the press for his handling of this case, which included actions such as prohibiting many defense witnesses from taking the stand and insisting on Saturday sessions. Hoffman was later merely scolded by the Seventh Circuit Court of Appeals, which reversed all of the convictions. Hoffman became the favored courtroom target of the

Chicago 7 defendants and was described by Tom Hayden as "a perfect representative of a class of dinosaurs that is vengefully striking out against the future." At the end of the five–month trial, Hoffman issued over 200 citations for contempt of court against the defendants and their attorneys. He died in 1983 at the age of 87.

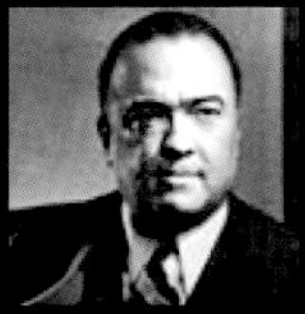

J. Edgar Hoover was appointed Director of the FBI on May 10, 1924 and remained so until his death in 1972. To date, he is the longest–serving leader of an executive branch agency, having served under a record eight presidents, from Calvin Coolidge to Richard Nixon. He is credited with creating an effective law enforcement organization, but has also been accused of flagrantly abusing his authority, blackmailing notable public figures, and unwarrantably engaging in political persecution.

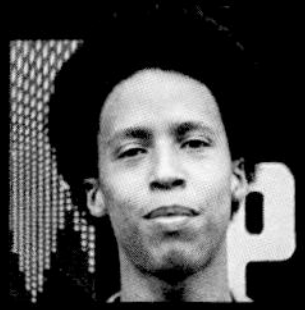

Jamal Joseph is a writer, director, documentary filmmaker and professor at Columbia University Graduate School of the Arts. Joseph, a former Black Panther Party member, and the youngest co-defendant in the Panther 21 case, is the co-founder of *The International Black Panther Film Festival*. He also co-founded IMPACT Repertory Theatre, a multi-disciplinary arts and leadership training program for youth ages 12 to 18, with co-producer Voza Rivers. IMPACT emphasizes creative self-expression as a means for community service. Joseph has directed over 25 feature films and documentaries, including *Heal the Rainbow and What'cha Gonna Do About Hate.*

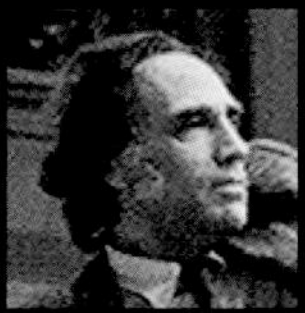

William Kunstler was the flamboyant lead defense attorney in the Chicago 7 conspiracy trial. His performance earned him a sentence of over four years in prison for contempt of court due to his increasingly bitter confrontations with Judge Hoffman. After earning degrees from Yale and Columbia Law Schools, Kunstler turned from a small business and family law practice to civil liberties law. His clients over the years included Lenny Bruce, Stokely Carmichael, American Indian Movement leaders, Jack Ruby, Martin Luther King, Jr., Malcolm X, and Islamic terrorists. He died in 1995 at the age of 76.

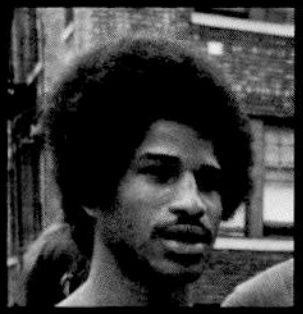

Felipe Luciano was a co–founder of the Young Lords Party. Committed to "the fight for freedom for all who are oppressed," the party focused on the importance of community empowerment, ethnic pride and civil rights as a means to changing the color and complexion of politics, society and culture. Luciano was also one of the original Last Poets, well–known rappers of the civil rights era. Experienced in both media and community activism, Luciano has won acclaim in radio, television, journalism, stage productions, music and poetry. The recipient of two Emmys and an ACE cable TV award, Luciano is the first Puerto Rican to anchor the news for WNBC in New York. A film about the Young Lords is currently in development at HBO.

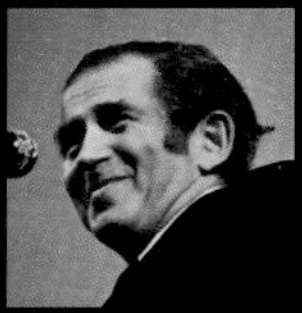

Norman Mailer was born in New Jersey, and grew up in Brooklyn, New York. Mailer graduated from Harvard during World War II and served as a sergeant in the Pacific. After the war he wrote his first novel in 1948, *The Naked and the Dead (now in it's 50th edition)*, which was based on his wartime experiences in the Philippines. This book launched Mailer, at the age of 25, as a national celebrity. In the late 1950s, Mailer wrote several characteristically provocative essays on sex, drugs, race and violence, including the 1957 "The White Negro," which drew comparisons between racial tension in the U.S. and the alienation of the Beat Generation. Around this time, Mailer also co–founded *The Village Voice*, the first of America's alternative weeklies. In the 1960s, Mailer reported on the social upheaval around the civil rights and antiwar movements, as well as the rising counterculture and sexual revolutions. He was arrested at the Pentagon while demonstrating against the Vietnam War in 1967, an experience he recounted in the Pulitzer Prize winning book *The Armies of Night* (1968). Now in his 80s, Mailer has over 40 published works to his credit, including *The Deer Park* (1955), *The White Negro* (1957), *An American Dream*, *The Executioner's Song* (1979), *The Prisoner Of Sex* (1971), *The Fight* (1975), *Ancient Evenings* (1983), *Tough Guys Don't Dance* (1984), *Harlot's Ghost* (1992), *Oswald's Tale* (1995), *The Gospel According To The Son* (1997), *The Time Of Our Time* (1998) and *The Spooky Art* (2003).

 Huey P. Newton, along with Bobby Seale, founded the Black Panther Party for Self–Defense in the 60s to combat the racist oppression of blacks in America. The Panthers monitored police action, and Newton became a magnet for police hostility. In 1967, he was charged with the murder of a police officer, inspiring an intensive "Free Huey" campaign by his supporters. His 1968 conviction was overturned in 1970. In 1989, Newton was killed in a drug–related incident.

Richard M. Nixon, former Congressman, Senator, and Vice–President to Dwight D. Eisenhower, was the 37th President of the United States (1969–1974). He led the United States' withdrawal from Vietnam and informally recognized the People's Republic of China. The Watergate scandal at the beginning of his second term led to his resignation.

James Rector was killed on May 15, 1969 (a day that later became known as Bloody Thursday), when demonstrators in People's Park, Berkeley, were attacked by heavily armed police-men. Rector was shot on a rooftop while he watched the action below on Telegraph Avenue, having scrambled up there to get out of the line of fire and tear gas. A shot the size of three marbles ripped through his chest cavity, killing him.

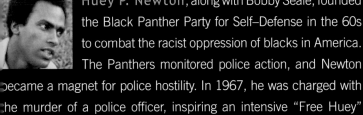 **Terry Robbins** was a member of the Weather Underground, who along with fellow founding members Diana Oughton and Ted Gold, was accidentally killed by a nail–studded bomb that prematurely exploded in the basement of a Greenwich Village townhouse on March 6, 1970. Robbins initiated the later famous name for this well–known antiwar group when he suggested the use of a line from the Bob Dylan song *"You Don't Need a Weatherman to Tell Which Way the Wind Blows."*

Jerry Rubin was the radical co–founder of the Youth International Party, or Yippies. He was most famous for coining the catchphrase "Never trust anyone over thirty." Prior to his attempt to merge political and lifestyle liberation beneath the Yippie banner, Rubin edited a youth page for the *Cincinnati Post*, studied sociology in Israel, joined the Free Speech Movement, ran for mayor in Berkeley, California, and led a march on the Pentagon. In the 1980s, Rubin became a business entrepreneur on Wall Street. He died in a fatal car accident in 1994.

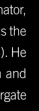 **Ed Sanders** was a prominent member of the Youth International Party (Yippies), a highly theatrical political party founded in 1967. The Yippies were an offshoot of the free speech and antiwar movements, and Sanders (founder and lead singer of The Fugs) was often cited as a link between the Beat and hippie generations within the movement. Sanders was a poet, singer and social activist who wrote his first major poem, *Poem from Jail*, on toilet paper in his cell after being jailed for protesting against nuclear proliferation in 1961. In 1971, Sanders wrote *The Family*, a profile of the events leading up to the Tate/LaBianca murders. He currently lives in Woodstock and publishes the *Woodstock Journal*.

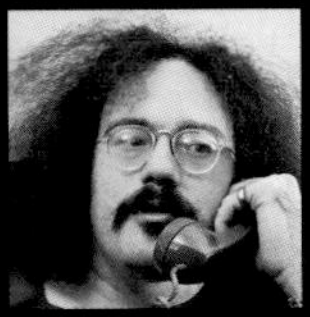

John Sinclair has been called "*The Last of the Beatnik Warrior Poets,*" "*The Hardest Working Poet in Show Business,*" an American cultural icon, and a founding father of the international counterculture. For the "Free John Sinclair" rally, John Lennon was inspired to compose a song in his name. Sinclair's sentence—for possession of two marijuana cigarettes—assisted in the reversal of Michigan's marijuana laws and aided in the enactment of Ann Arbor's epochal five dollar fine for the possession of weed.

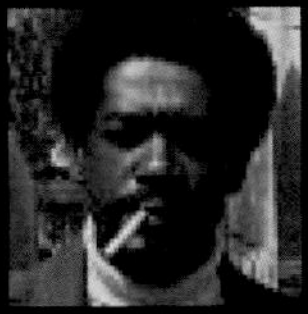

Bobby Seale co–founded the Black Panther party for Self–Defense with fellow activist Huey P. Newton in 1966 after the assassination of Malcolm X. Seale was also one of the Chicago 8 (later the Chicago 7) defendants, but Seale hurled frequent and bitter attacks at Judge Hoffman, calling him a "fascist dog," a "pig" and a "racist," among other things. On October 29, 1969 the outraged judge ordered Seale bound and gagged. Finally, on November 5, Hoffman removed Seale from the case and sentenced him to four years in prison for contempt. The sentence was later reversed.

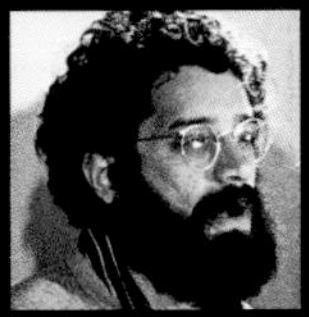

Lee Weiner faced two charges of conspiracy and the making of incendiary devices, along with John Froines, in the Chicago 7 conspiracy trial. At the time of the trail, he was a teaching assistant in sociology at Northwestern University. After being acquitted of both charges, Weiner continued to protest for various causes. He has worked for the Anti–Defamation League of B'Nai B'rith in New York and participated in protests for Russian Jews and more funding for AIDS research.

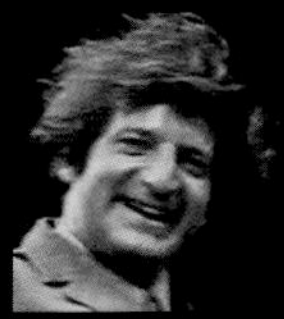

Leonard Weinglass was a defense attorney in the Chicago 7 conspiracy trial. Though he generally avoided the highly charged rhetoric of his co–counsel, William Kunstler, he was nonetheless sentenced to twenty months in prison for contempt. After graduating from Yale Law School, he was co–chair of the left–leaning National Lawyer's Guild. He has represented Pentagon Papers defendant Anthony Russo, Angela Davis, Jane Fonda, Bill and Emily Harris of the Symbionese Liberation Army, and Amy Carter, daughter of President Jimmy Carter, who was charged with seizing a University of Massachusetts building in 1987 in protest of on–campus recruitment by the CIA.

Following Page: Antiwar rally, Washington, D.C., May 9, 1970

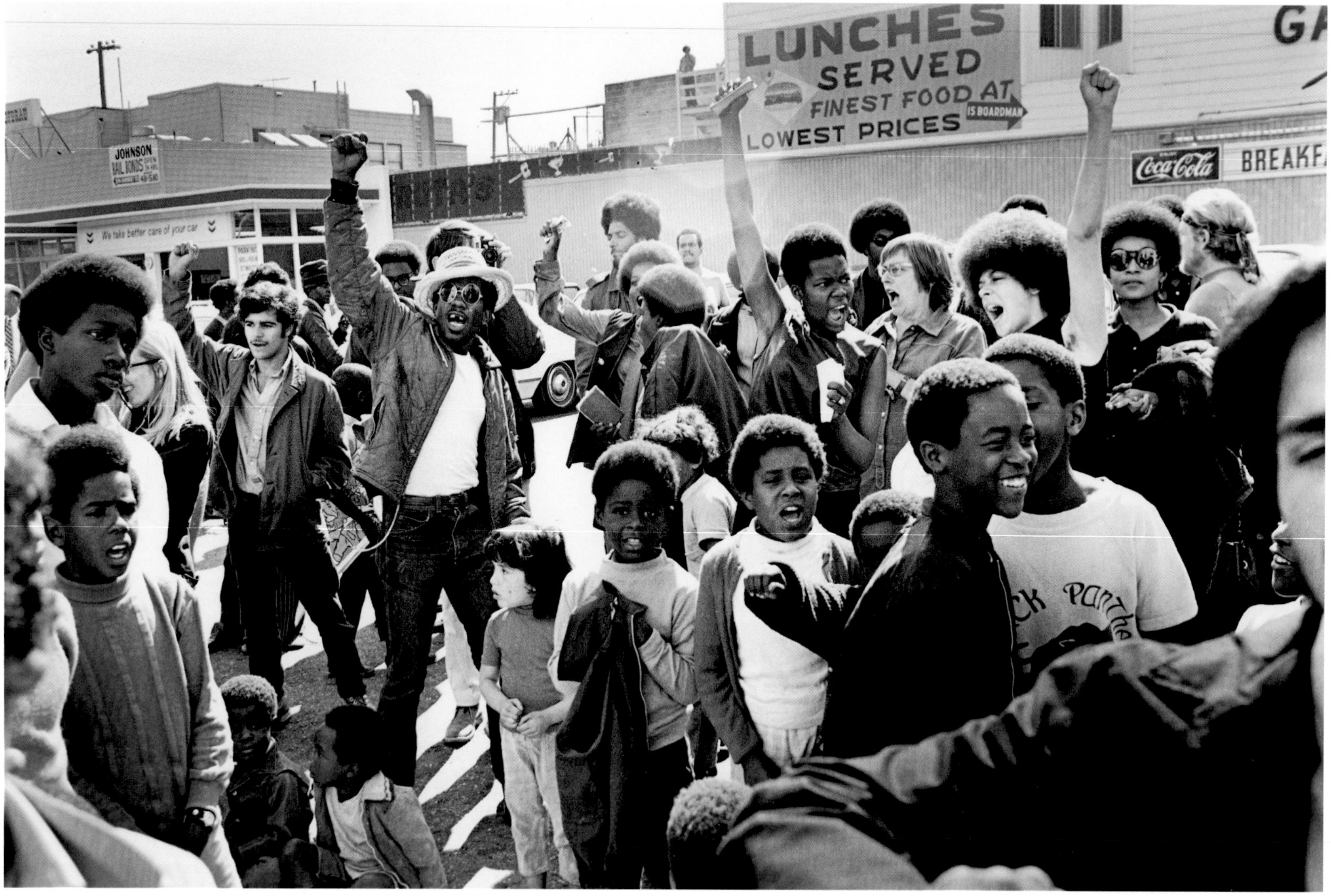
LUNCHES
SERVED
FINEST FOOD AT
LOWEST PRICES
15 BOARDMAN
JOHNSON
BAIL BONDS
Coca-Cola
BREAKF
We take better care of your car

Crowd near Black Panther Party headquarters, Oakland, CA, August 1969